A BRIEF HISTORY OF JAPAN

A BRIEF HISTORY OF JAPAN

**SAMURAI, SHŌGUN AND ZEN:
THE EXTRAORDINARY STORY OF THE LAND OF THE RISING SUN**

JONATHAN CLEMENTS

TUTTLE Publishing

Tokyo | Rutland, Vermont | Singapore

"Books to Span the East and West"

Tuttle Publishing was founded in 1832 in the small New England town of Rutland, Vermont [USA]. Our core values remain as strong today as they were then—to publish best-in-class books which bring people together one page at a time. In 1948, we established a publishing outpost in Japan—and Tuttle is now a leader in publishing English-language books about the arts, languages and cultures of Asia. The world has become a much smaller place today and Asia's economic and cultural influence has grown. Yet the need for meaningful dialogue and information about this diverse region has never been greater. Over the past seven decades, Tuttle has published thousands of books on subjects ranging from martial arts and paper crafts to language learning and literature—and our talented authors, illustrators, designers and photographers have won many prestigious awards. We welcome you to explore the wealth of information available on Asia at **www.tuttlepublishing.com**.

Published by Tuttle Publishing, an imprint of Periplus Editions (HK) Ltd.

www.tuttlepublishing.com

Library of Congress Cataloging in Publication Data
Names: Clements, Jonathan, 1971- author.
Title: A brief history of Japan : samurai, shogun and zen : the extraordinary story of the land of the rising sun / Jonathan Clements.
Description: First edition. | Tokyo ; North Clarendon, VT : Tuttle Publishing, 2017. | Includes bibliographical references and index.
Identifiers: LCCN 2016055712 | ISBN 9784805313893 (pbk.)
Subjects: LCSH: Japan--History.
Classification: LCC DS835 .C55 2017 | DDC 952--dc23 LC record available at https://lccn.loc.gov/2016055712

ISBN 978-4-8053-1389-3
ISBN 978-4-8053-1844-7 (sale in Japan only)

Distributed by:

North America, Latin America & Europe
Tuttle Publishing
364 Innovation Drive, North Clarendon VT 05759 9436, USA
Tel: 1(802) 773 8930; Fax: 1(802) 773 6993
info@tuttlepublishing.com
www.tuttlepublishing.com

Asia Pacific
Berkeley Books Pte Ltd
3 Kallang Sector #04-01
Singapore 349278
Tel: (65) 6741 2178; Fax: (65) 6741 2179
inquiries@periplus.com.sg
www.tuttlepublishing.com

Japan
Tuttle Publishing
Yaekari Building 3rd Floor
5-4-12 Osaki Shinagawa-ku
Tokyo 141 0032 Japan
Tel: 81 (3) 5437 0171; Fax: 81 (3) 5437 0755
sales@tuttle.co.jp
www.tuttle.co.jp

27 26 25 24
14 13 12 11 10 2407VP
Printed in Malaysia

CONTENTS

CHINA
RUSSIA
NORTH
KOREA
SOUTH
KOREA
Sea of Japan
Hons
Kanaza
Fukui
Matsue
Tottori
Kyoto
Ots
Himeji
Kobe
Nara
Okayama
Hiroshima
Osaka
Sakai
Tsushima I.
Yamaguchi
Takamatsu
Wakayama
Kitakyushu
Matsuyama
Tokushima
Shikoku
Fukuoka
Kochi
Saga
Oita
Kumamoto
Nagasaki
Kyushu
Miyasaki
Philip
Kagoshima
Se

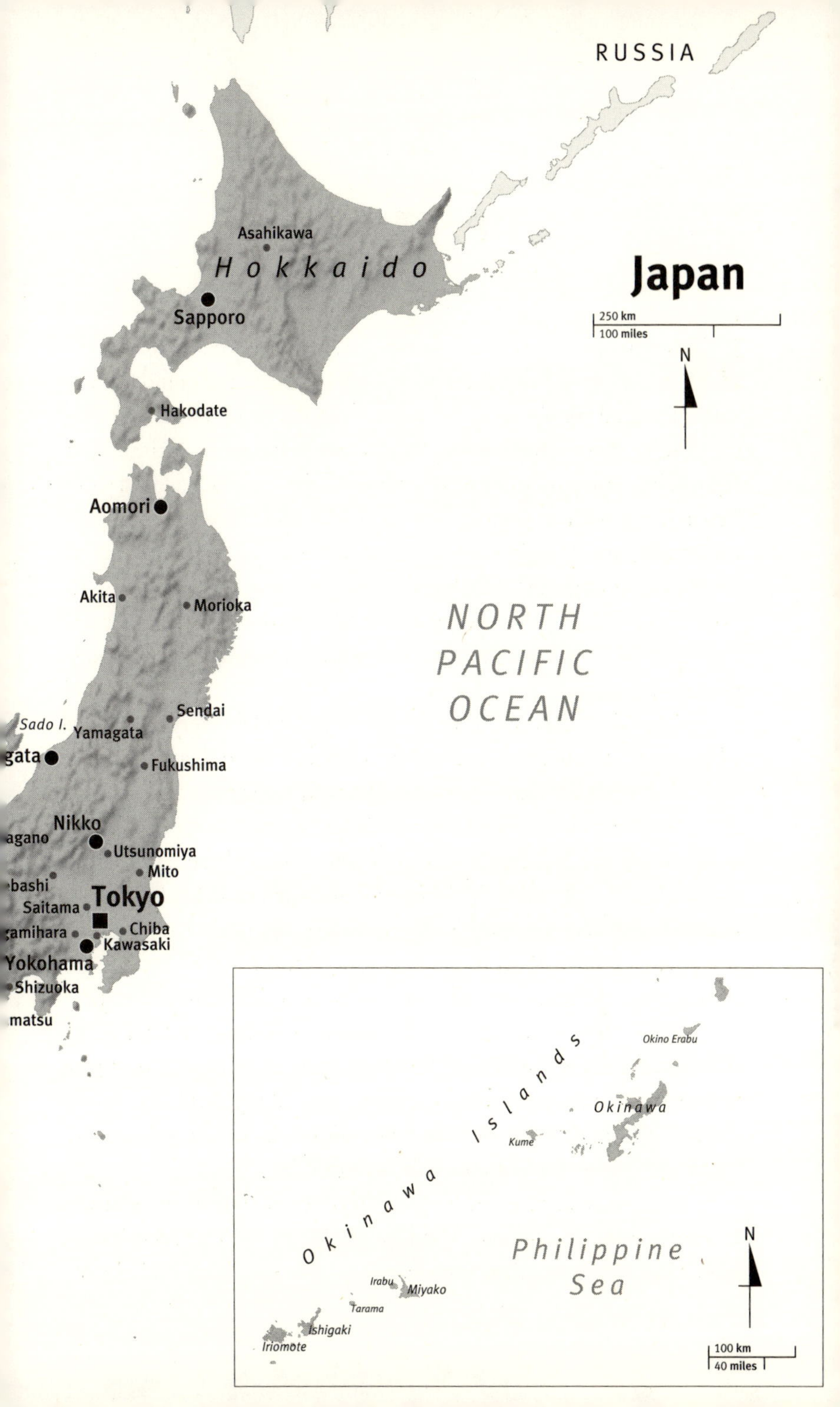

Japan
250 km
100 miles
N
RUSSIA
Hokkaido
Asahikawa
Sapporo
Hakodate
Aomori
Akita
Morioka
NORTH PACIFIC OCEAN
Sendai
Sado I.
Yamagata
gata
Fukushima
Nikko
agano
Utsunomiya
Mito
bashi
Tokyo
Saitama
Chiba
amihara
Kawasaki
Yokohama
Shizuoka
matsu
Okino Erabu
Okinawa Islands
Okinawa
Kume
Philippine Sea
N
Irabu
Miyako
Tarama
Ishigaki
Iriomote
100 km
40 miles

Preface

The first time I arrived in Japan, I was more prepared than most newcomers. I had been studying in Taiwan, and could already understand all the signs on the street, even if I could not necessarily pronounce them. Quite by accident, I was arriving not in the Tōkyō region, but in Japan's ancient heartland of Kyōto, which would soon bewitch me with its history and culture. I was there to study pre-modern Japanese foreign relations and Japanese literature. I shopped like it was going out of fashion, shipping home box after box of books and CDs, VHS cassettes and shōgi boards. I had been studying Japanese for several months, and was sure that one day it would all fall into place.

Twenty-five years and three degrees later, I still felt very much like a beginner. On my most recent trip to Japan, I was old enough to be the father of the student I once was. I hardly bought a thing, knowing that online stores would ship anything I wanted to my homeland at the touch of a button. Instead, I poked around obscure museums in search of locally published histories and unchronicled folklore. I trudged across ancient battlefields to understand the meaning of old war poems. I watched my son as he played, alone, in a well-appointed, impeccably clean playground. I counted the secondhand stores that had sprung up in Kyōto's Teramachi shopping district, and marveled that it was easier to buy diapers for adults than for children. I dropped in on friends in Nagoya whose young son was taking part in a dragon-dance—although there were so few children in the neighborhood that their dragon looked more like a crocodile.

I was now an author, the biographer of several figures in Japanese history—Prince Saionji and Admiral Tōgō, the teenage rebel Amakusa Shirō and the pirate king Coxinga. My speciality had always been the snatching of weird and wonderful stories, and their popularization for a general audience. What could be more weird and wonderful than the story of an entire nation, from its mythical beginnings to its near future?

The toughest decision facing the author of a book like this is what to leave out. Tim Hannigan's trail-blazing *A Brief History of Indonesia* has set the tone and attitude for this series, and I have followed his template as closely as possible. Like him, I must face the impossibility of a story that spans millions of years, with a cast of thousands, somehow hitting the high points without dumbing down or talking up. Many before me have tried to tell the story of Japan in such a manner. Many have been defeated by the discipline of history itself—the ready temptation to cavil and kvetch about any definitive statement. How feudal was the feudal period? How closed was the Sakoku era?

Whom to mention? Whom to discard? Which of the 125 emperors is worth including? Which of the dozens of shōguns? And should I put an "s" on the end of shōgun? Who will make the cut from Japan's writers and artists, philosophers and samurai? When others have written entire books about the subjects of single pages—even single lines—the task is daunting.

I thought back to the person I was before I arrived in Japan, before I even started learning Japanese; what would he want to know? What stories would he have first wanted to hear; what would have first fired him up to learn more about this incredible, endlessly surprising country? And should things be set out so that it isn't a confusing jumble of multisyllabic names?

Unlike, say, China, where history can be broken up into discrete dynasties, there is only one dynasty in Japan, and it claims to have ruled the nation since the dawn of history. Some quibble with this, and it is likely that scholars in the near future may start to reimagine the single imperial line as several linked pockets of relation and influence, such as Herman Ooms's recent suggestion that eighth-century Japan was ruled by a "Tenmu dynasty." In the meantime, historians and educators are obliged to find another way of breaking up Japanese history; they usually plump for some sort of system that notes who was really in charge. You won't be far into this book before you realize what a wild-goose chase this is, since power in Japan is all too often a matter of shifting consensus and implied needs. Samurai would go to war over what the wishes of their chosen candidate for emperor *would be* if they were successful in putting him on the throne; shōgunal regents agreed what their infant charge *would probably want*, if only he could speak.

In this book, I have concentrated on specific moments of transformation—the settlement of Japan itself and the arrival of a new wave of emigrants from the Asian continent. Later chapters deal with several crucial periods of foreign contact and the aftermath of each: the arrival of Chinese culture and Buddhism, and then the period in which Japan forged on without such foreign contacts; the arrival of early Christian missionaries, and the brutal 200-year seclusion that followed their expulsion; the arrival of colonial powers in the nineteenth century, with the revolutionary changes they introduced to Japanese society, followed by Japan's troubled, martial entry into the modern world; and finally, the immense and far-reaching impact of the US Occupation from 1945 to 1952, which left Japan changed once more. On each occasion, Japan is flooded by foreign culture and ideas, seems at first to ape them, but then adapts and transforms them into something original. (I almost used the word "unique" there, but the "myth of Japanese uniqueness," *nihonjinron*, is itself a controversial topic.)

Meanwhile, the historian of Japan has to contend with a counterintuitive and unexpected development in recent years. The older Japanese history is, the more new discoveries there seem to have been. The general reader might be forgiven for thinking that Japan's ancient history is fixed and immobile, but so much has happened in the field in the last generation that the distant past often seems vibrant and alive. In part, this is because of the incredible effect that late twentieth-century Japan's surging economy had on the building trade. New towns sprang up in places like Tōkyō's Tama Hills suburb, leading to a number of accidental archaeological finds, as well as races against time to gather information before it was smothered by a car park or shopping mall. The expense of such rescue archaeology in Japan multiplied tenfold between 1970 and 1977, and tenfold again by 1992. It reached a plateau thereafter as Japan's ballooning economy deflated once more, but the effects on archaeology reverberated for another decade as scholars pored over their new data. For years afterward, Japanese archaeology saw incredible finds and game-changing new theories, challenging much of the previous wisdom and leaving many earlier history books outdated and irrelevant.

Politics remains a powerful influence on Japanese history. When it comes to ancient times, the big problem comes from the reality gap between a national mythology that claims the emperors are all descended from the Sun Goddess and archaeology that suggests that they are descended from Korean aristocrats. Although the prominent nobleman Tokugawa Mitsukuni did dig up an old tomb in 1692, he swiftly put back whatever it was he found. All deliberate excavation of tombs was declared illegal in Japan in 1874, and although conditions thawed in the twentieth century, the Imperial Household has long been obstructive regarding the excavation of grave mounds that are likely to contain the ancestors of the current emperor.

In 1976, amid a popular publishing boom obsessed with Japan's prehistoric past, archaeologists were forbidden once more from opening imperial graves. Some of these sites undoubtedly were robbed long ago, but there is no telling what historical riches await in some of the great tombs that lie unexamined in Japan. The first chapter of this book, "Prehistoric and Mythical Japan," is hence separated from the second by a wall of legends, because there is still no means of accurately examining the period before 700 CE. Imagine, for a moment, how different our understanding of China would be without the materials unearthed since 1970 in Chinese grave sites: we would know nothing of the First Emperor's Terracotta Army, nothing of the legal statues of the Qin, or the unexpurgated *Daode Jing*, nothing of the military textbooks of Sun Bin. Apologists might just as readily praise the Japanese for remaining so in touch with their roots, and so respectful of their traditions, that they do not authorize the ransacking of old tombs. But at the moment, Japan's imperial graves remain closed to archaeology, and that drastically reduces the chances of ever uncovering a Japanese manuscript that predates the 700s.

I find it particularly frustrating because, for me, the most interesting element of early Japanese history lies in its early connections with Korean states such as Kara and Baekje. Korean exiles provided entire branches and houses of what would become the Japanese nobility, regarded as close enough relatives that their native ranks would transfer across to Japan. Contacts with Japan are frequently mentioned in the Korean *Baekje Annals*, until 428 CE, when all mention of the country is dropped for the next two centuries—an omission that has yet to be satisfactorily explained. But more recent history, particularly the early twentieth century, has so politicized the discussion of Korean–Japanese contacts that academics are put off by its toxicity.

In 2008, a handpicked group of scholars was allowed to enter the giant Gosashi grave mound, rumored to be the resting place of the legendary empress Jingū, for a grand total of 150 minutes. The investigators were not allowed to touch anything, and were swiftly shooed out again. A stiffly worded fax to *National Geographic* reminded the scientific community that in Japan, such sites were not part of a forgotten ancient culture, but directly linked to the incumbent head of state. It read, "Imperial Household religious ceremonies continue to take place at tombs and mausolea. As they are objects of remembrance and veneration for the public and imperial family, preserving their peace and dignity is of paramount importance."

The current emperor, known abroad as Akihito, more properly as Emperor Heisei by the policy I use in this book (see "Notes on Names"), has muddied the waters a bit by acknowledging *some* of his Korean ancestors, but only several dozen generations down the family tree, allowing for the possibility that his other forefathers were still super-powered beings who descended from space. Meanwhile, the Koreans can be defensively nationalist about their relationship with Japan. Kara (or Kaya, or Gaya, or Imna…) was a Dark Age state in the southern Korean peninsula that probably provided ancient Japan with many of its introductions to mainland culture. The word *kara* endured in Japanese as a term for the mainland (as in the word *karate*, which originally meant "Chinese hand"), but the state was referred to in Japanese as Mimana. However, since that name only turns up amid ancient Japanese claims of having conquered it, one uses that proper noun in the presence of Korean historians at one's peril. Early in the twenty-first century, a Korean academy tried to establish some sort of common ground on cross-straits archaeology from the contentious fourth century CE, but their Japanese counterparts refused to cooperate on a joint statement. Japan's ancient history remains, at least in part, a matter of religious belief that brooks no tampering.

Although this is not intended as an academic book, I have done my best to reflect trends in modern scholarship, which include history as viewed through changes to the climate and environment. There have been impressive developments in the last generation in such concepts as the "invention of tradition," the eco-history of Japan, and some remarkably original uses of what we now call "big data." My favorite remains the group of boffins who extrapolated medieval climate conditions by tabulating the varying dates of annual cherry-blossom parties. Scholars have also learned much in recent years by investigating previously marginalized groups such as women and the underclass, as well as groups on the Japanese periphery. I note here, for example, that the oldest human remains anywhere in the Japanese archipelago, from circa 30,000 BCE, were found in the Ryūkyū Islands, while the culture of the Ainu in Hokkaidō may offer us the merest glimpse of the way of life of Japan's indigenous inhabitants.

Point of Departure: Cipangu

China, 1280 CE—Marco Polo saw it with his own eyes. The river Yangtze was thick with ships great and small: ocean-going traders, robust war junks, and huge numbers of shakily repurposed river boats. All were being readied for the latest great enterprise of the new emperor, the Mongol Kublai Khan: a massive armada that would cross the sea to annihilate the defiant island kingdom of Cipangu.

Nobody in the West had ever heard of this Cipangu before. Marco Polo's account was the first to even mention it in a European language. When he did, he drew on years of propaganda designed to fire up the conscripts of Kublai's navy, as well as lies and spin concocted by reluctant Korean allies.

In his intimidating correspondence with the rulers of Cipangu, Kublai had belittled the nation as a jumped-up barbaric kingdom, uncomprehending of courtly etiquette and ignorant of the trouble it would be in if it did not submit to him. However, in his exhortations to his armies, he made sure that everybody knew how incredibly rich Cipangu was.

"They have," enthused Marco Polo on the basis of no evidence whatsoever, "gold in abundance, because it is found there in measureless quantities."

Kublai Khan had already made one attempt to invade the island kingdom after a decade of increasingly antagonistic diplomatic exchanges. Not only the people of Cipangu, but also their Korean counterparts, had literally spent years lying about the distance to the islands and the likelihood of strong resistance. Embassies had been fobbed off with numerous wily excuses, and often failed to work out whom they were supposed to be addressing. The natives infamously claimed to have an emperor of equal standing to the ruler of China, but the man who sat on their throne in 1274 was only a figurehead. His father, the former emperor, had abdicated, allowing him to meddle in politics from behind the scenes. His mother supposedly had no power of her own, but was a member of the powerful Fujiwara family, obliging the new emperor to listen to the wishes of his grandfather and uncles. His wife, meanwhile, was a scion of the Minamoto family, another powerful clan with vested interests.

And yet none of this really mattered, because foreign policy and many local issues were in the hands of the emperor's barbarian-suppressing supreme general, the shōgun, in the town of Kamakura. But the shōgun was himself a puppet of yet another group, the Hōjō clan that had secretly run the islands for many decades. His own job was delegated to a regent, the *shikken*, who at the time was a callow youth of twenty-three, leaning on a shadowy council of advisers. Your guess is as good as mine, and certainly as good as Kublai's, as to who was really in charge.

Such obfuscations were not unique to Cipangu. The Mongols were getting a similar runaround far to the south in what is now Vietnam, where any request for a direct answer would be passed around a series of grandly titled bigwigs, any one of whom might waste another couple of months by sending back a request for clarification. The land that Marco Polo knew as Cipangu was impossible to understand, beyond a distant horizon, itself at the very edge of the known Asian world, and apparently controlled by a nebulous, invisible hegemony of power brokers and alliances. This would not be the last time it was described in such terms.

Still, at least Kublai could mention all that imaginary gold. His troops were drunk on stories of it. The armies that had pushed Mongol rule all over Asia were ready to advance on these unknown islands, hoping thereby to shut down so-called pirate bases. What happened next is one of the greatest war stories of human history.

Kublai's first armada, in 1274, swiftly snatched the islands of

Tsushima and Iki in the 200-kilometer (124 miles) strait. The huge fleet packed into the wide sweep of Hakata Bay, which had been for centuries the gateway to the islands for any foreign shipping.

The natives were waiting for them.

The country had not seen a meaningful battle for two generations, and the members of its warrior class, the samurai, were spoiling for a fight. They had, however, distinctly odd ideas about how a battle should proceed. The Mongols and their Korean and Chinese allies watched in bafflement as a soldier clad in strange armor tied with brightly colored silks shot a noise-making "humming-bulb" arrow over their heads. It screamed in the air on the blustery November day, intended by the defenders to signal a parley and a series of small bouts between champions.

The Mongols retaliated with a volley of deadly poison arrows. They were not there to take part in some local battle ceremony. They were there to invade.

The fighting that broke out was so fierce that it cost the defenders a third of their military manpower by the end of the first day. The Mongols, however, had no way of seeing over the wall. Unsure of their ability to hold a beachhead that was all but encircled by enemy fortifications, they retreated back to their ships to await the dawn.

The natives had other plans, taking to the waters in a swarm of little boats piled high with kindling. They crept aboard the enemy ships, starting fires and knifing sailors, although many of the flames were soon put out by heavy rain.

Soon the wind whipped up even further; the natives pulled back, looking on as the elements carried on the fight for them. The mother of all storms pounded down on the armada, overturning smaller boats and threatening to bash the close-packed ships into each other. Captains ordered their crews to push their vessels into deeper waters where the swell would not be so dangerous.

But it was too late. The storm had escalated into a monstrous typhoon that dashed the invaders against the coastline and into each other, swamping them and overturning them, crushing troop transports and supply vessels. It was soon too dark to see, but the defenders on land heard the powerful crack of timbers and the screams of men and horses.

The following morning as the sun parted the clouds, Hakata Bay was carpeted in driftwood. A handful of soaked survivors washed ashore at several points along the coastline, where they were swiftly put to death. A few of the larger Chinese ships made it out and ran straight for home.

A year later, a new embassy arrived from Kublai, presenting the *shikken* regent with a golden scroll that offered to make him the "king of Cipangu." It was a gesture of reconciliation, suggesting that everybody could spare themselves further trouble if the natives just bowed to the khan and admitted that he was their overlord. The regent made his feelings plain by having all the ambassadors executed.

It was Kublai's retaliation—an even larger fleet—that Marco Polo saw being assembled. Thanks to modern marine archaeology, we now understand the significance of his report of 15,000 ships on the river Yangtze—a great distance from the Korea Strait, and a reflection of numerous botched and poorly organized planning decisions. Kublai's second fleet was packed with everything the Mongol warlords could scrape up, including condemned barges and creaking riverboats. The timbers were warped; even the nails have been shown to have a high sulfur content, suggesting that corners were cut in every possible stage of sourcing and construction. Overloaded with horses and supplies for a long campaign, packed so closely with men that three thousand troops were dead from disease before land was even sighted, the armada set sail in two task forces, one from Korea and the other up the coast from the mouth of the Yangtze.

Fearful of being boxed in again at Hakata Bay, the Mongols dithered offshore, many of their unseaworthy vessels lashed together in a vast floating fortress. They were particularly wary of a seaborne attack, since many of their troops were timid Chinese and Korean conscripts, worried about reports of "dragons in the water" and all too ready to surrender. They had started out with three months' supplies, two-thirds of which they had already consumed, and they had still not made permanent landfall.

Samurai boats came out to the armada in ones and twos—numbers so small that the Mongols assumed they were there to offer terms. But the boats contained suicidal platoons on one-way missions; they cut down their own masts to make boarding ramps and stormed the larger warships.

And then the *real* storm came: a second typhoon, even more powerful than the earlier one. Modern marine archaeologists, examining the smithereens on the sea bed, estimate it to have been a Category 3 storm—a "major hurricane" with gusts of 199 kph (123.5 mph) that whipped up waves into storm surges of up to 4 meters (13 feet). Equivalent modern storms have been seen to strip the roofs off buildings, blow away mobile homes, and uproot trees. For the close-packed boats of the Mongol armada, it was a veritable apocalypse. Some 30,000 men managed to make it ashore from the sinking boats—bedraggled, starving, and without fresh water. They were easy pickings for the samurai defenders.

The Mongols had every intention of coming back for a rematch, but they never did. An office within Kublai's administration was supposedly tasked with putting together a third armada, but it was underfunded and overlooked, and largely powerless after 1286. Kublai died in 1294, and his descendants more or less ignored the indomitable islands in the east.

The great storms gained their own legendary status among the natives. Before long, certain religious cults were claiming that the no-show by a third armada was the result of their intensive prayers. The Mongols, it was now claimed, had been fought off not merely by the warrior elite, but by the combined efforts of the entire nation, and even by the very elements themselves. In sending the weather to deliver the death blow, the gods had sent a Divine Wind, or Kamikaze. Their country, the locals believed, was special; it was unique; it was blessed by its particular gods and would never know defeat.

For decades afterwards, guards on the shores watched the seas for a new attack, but none came. Meanwhile, the defense took its toll in a different, mundane way. It was not merely the loss of life; it was the colossal expense of the project, which bankrupted many local lords. When, in earlier times, the samurai had been fighting one another, there was always a loser whose lands could be confiscated as the spoils of victory. But when the enemy came from another country, they left nothing behind but their dead; there was no reward that could be bestowed. Within a generation, the Kamakura shōgunate's hold on power had collapsed, and the samurai had turned upon each other in another civil war, this time in the name of *two* rival emperors.

As for Marco Polo's Cipangu, word of it was carried back to Europe. His tall tales of great riches and fierce knights would enter popular parlance. Two centuries later, Christopher Columbus would set out in search of the Spice Islands and this legendary Cipangu, sailing west in the hope of reaching the East, and finding something entirely unexpected.

Today, we know more about the land that would be called Cipangu, Xipangu, Xipang, Japón and then Japan in the languages of the West. But even in a modern, interconnected world, this name often seems at one remove. "Nippon" was the local people's own word for their archipelago, deliberately coined to imply that Japan was the land "of the rising sun." Today, with the additional allusions offered by modern time zones, it is often regarded as a land a few steps into our own future, or a grim vestige of a warlike past. This is its story.

CHAPTER 1

THE WAY OF THE GODS: PREHISTORIC AND MYTHICAL JAPAN

The old women said the sea used to be lower. There were bays and inlets that had once been flat ground but were now steeped in saltwater. It was getting harder to find deer. There used to be all sorts on the wide plains. The old women said that they were good meat. The old women had plenty of stories like this, but the young only knew what they could see themselves.

The men hadn't caught a deer for months. But there was always food. Down by the shore, you could pull shellfish from the shallows. One day, one of the girls pulled up something else—a bone knife.

The old women said that we, or people like us, had once lived there, but now the land was returned to the sea.

The old women said that if the deer were gone, then we would soon follow. We should leave these long, thin islands and head north, to the greater lands beyond the rising sun.

Everybody knew they were there. You could see the clouds that formed above them. You could see the birds that returned there. Some of the fishermen, straying too far in their canoes, even claimed to have seen the lands themselves: lush and green, with smoking mountains.

Not all the old ones agreed. Most of the womenfolk did not mind the dwindling deer. Stick to the fish from the reef, they said. Save nuts and berries in jars against lean times. There were always shellfish to be pulled from the mud, and mud to make pots.

Then there were Ship People. They came from the direction of the setting sun. If we moved, they might not find us again. The Ship People came to take our cowrie shells, and traded them for magical wonders: hard tools that did not break; the pig creatures that ate anything and yielded succulent meat; the wondrous disc that reflected everything it saw, shining with the sun's light when turned upon it, revealing your true self when you stared into it.

The old people argued about the future, and their children were dragged in like canoes at the edge of a whirlpool. All were agreed there were too many of us. The shoreline was getting crowded. You had to walk further into the shallows to find enough shellfish for dinner. It took longer and longer to find fruits from the forest. We should move on, onward toward the rising sun, to the new lands that looked so green.

No, some said, we should stay. Save more shells for the Ship People, to trade for more of their pigs and their strange seeds.

The arguments had been boiling for months, even years, but people were hungrier than they admitted, and that made them easier to anger. The wiser old women feared encounters with other tribes.

What if there are already people in the green lands, they wondered. What then?

But the menfolk were sure of themselves. We shall wield our mallet heads, they said. Wielding our stone mallets, we will crush them.

Both sides thought they had won. The fishermen and their families got into their boats and headed to the north and east. They took any of the forest folk who wanted to go. But simply by leaving, they were making it possible for others to stay. Tell the Ship People—they said—tell them that we have gone toward the rising sun, where the lands are so plentiful that we will live forever. Tell them that, if any of you survive the next winter.

Japan was born fifteen million years ago, pushed away from the edge of Eurasia by the formation of the Japan Sea. At the time it was quite flat, but it sits at the confluence of three massive tectonic plates—the Eurasian, the Pacific, and the Philippine—which mashed together to buckle and warp the land into towering mountains. These heights, young in geological terms, created steep watercourses and fast rivers that rushed down toward the sea, dragging sediment with them.

Elsewhere, the tectonic plates were forced downward. Only a million years after Japan was first formed, its first volcanoes burst into life, peppering the landscape with its oldest craters. Two million years ago, the northern part of the island of Honshū was ripped apart by huge eruptions, the scars of which still form circular lakes and ridges, some miles wide. The map of Japan remains dotted with suspiciously round lakes and islands, or curved bays that indicate the forgotten edge of ancient craters. Even in the era of human settlements, occasional disasters have depopulated entire regions. Parts of Japan have been settled "for the first time" on multiple occasions, the newcomers being unaware that the bones of earlier inhabitants lay beneath their feet, under layers of ash and mud.

Even today, a tenth of the world's active volcanoes can be found in Japan. Throughout its history, the nation's geographical situation has led to periodic disaster—not merely volcanic eruptions, but landslides caused by the precarious purchase of soil on its steep mountains, and earthquakes from the continued push and shove of underground forces. From Japan's times of legend through to the modern era, there are tales of entire mountains falling into the sea; of new islands born from a flaming abyss; of the ground tearing itself apart only to invite great, overwhelming inrushes of the sea. It is no coincidence that *tsunami* is a Japanese word. Once every 800 to 1,100 years, for example, the sediments of north Japan show the evidence of a "tsunamigenic" deposit—a thick layer of mud left behind by an immense flood from the sea, caused by an offshore earthquake in a fault line to be found 70 kilometers (43.5 miles) away on the sea bed. Court chronicles in 869 CE reported an earthquake and an onrushing tidal wave that killed a thousand people and wiped out the garrison town of Tagajō. It would be 1,142 years before the process repeated itself in 2011.

Japan confounds all expectations. It never fails to surprise. Modern visitors can still be shocked by how green it is—even now, one of the local names for the land is the Green Archipelago (*midori no rettō*). True enough, contemporary cities are all too often a charmless jumble of skyscrapers and storm drains, their landscapes ruined by big-box supermarkets. But Japan's cities huddle on a remarkably small area of land, much of it only reclaimed from the sea in the last century. Tōkyō, Nagoya, and Ōsaka occupy the only large areas of flat terrain in the whole country south of Hokkaidō: the plains of Kantō, Nōbi, and Kansai. Even these, however, are relatively small by global standards.

Inland, more than two-thirds of Japan's area comprises uninhabitable mountains, thickly forested today with non-native trees. In prehistoric times, the land was covered in woods of evergreen oak, *hinoki* cypress, and camphorwood. It was these native trees that supplied the lumber for the earliest Japanese buildings, although today they are so rare that they are usually only found on holy ground, preserved within the precincts of temples and shrines. These forests were rapaciously destroyed by the middle of the Dark Ages, cleared to meet a rising need for farmland and for firewood as fuel in a land with poor-quality coal, but also felled for building material. Eschewing stone for most construction, the Japanese preferred to work with wood. The largest wooden building ever built, the great Buddhist temple of Tōdaiji in Nara, required 900 hectares of forest—about nine square kilometers. And wooden materials need regular replacing, which ensures not only continued drains on resources, but also means that much of "old" Japan is actually more recent.

By the time the Japanese first began to write down their own history, those ancient forests were disappearing, replaced by red pines, deciduous oaks, and greater concentrations of chestnut and walnut. This modern appearance is also the result of a bold, concerted effort at reforestation dating from the sixteenth century, when Japan's overlords realized that the continued plundering of the hillsides would have a disastrous effect on farming. Just over half of Japan's land area is forested today.

Japan is also a *long* country: its southernmost reaches in the Ryūkyū Islands share the latitude of the Bahamas; its northernmost point in Hokkaidō matches that of Quebec. Although recent centuries and the draconian codes of the samurai have forced a certain homogeneity of culture on the Japanese, with regional differences often confined to genteel subtleties of clothing or refined differences in cuisine, ancient Japan was much more diverse, spanning everything from subtropical islanders to snowbound bear hunters.

Japan's latitude places much of its land mass closer to the south than much of Europe, making it substantially warmer than those countries that decided the norms of a temperate climate. It is also wetter—even in the middle of Japan's Alps, you are never more than 100 kilometers (62 miles) from the sea; humidity is high and summer rains help a strong growing season. This, in turn, means that swings in global climate can often have the opposite effect in Japan than in those latitudes where most English-language historians live. When global temperatures took a turn for the warmer, European historians celebrated Roman vineyards in England and Viking colonies in Greenland, but Japan suffered droughts and disease. When global temperatures dropped and Elizabethan Londoners looked out glumly on a frozen Thames, a cooler, more temperate Japan experienced a boom in agriculture and population.

One of the most crucial elements of Japanese geography has been the size of the Korea Strait (known in Japan as the Tsushima Strait, so named for the island in its middle) that separates it from mainland Asia. With a width of 200 kilometers (124.5 miles) at its narrowest point, this body of water arguably keeps Japan at a perfect "Goldilocks" distance—not so far as to make it impossible to trade and communicate, but far enough to prevent most large-scale military operations. The crossing was safe enough for a premodern ship that could afford to wait out storms in a safe harbor, but famously deadly to an armada of hostile enemies with no safe port.

Humans first arrived before the strait was formed. At the end of the last Ice Age, southern Japan was linked to Korea first by a land bridge and then, for some time, by a strait narrow enough to make the opposite shore tantalizingly visible. In the far north, Japan was linked to Siberia by a similar land bridge that connected Hokkaidō to Sakhalin and the Russian coast. To the south, the Ryūkyū Islands were larger, and mostly within sight of each other, all the way from proto-Taiwan to the edges of the Japanese mainland. Settlers hence approached the region from both north and south.

Somewhere off the Japanese coast, no doubt, there are multiple archaeological sites that were once home to these forgotten peoples, now drowned beneath the waters that rose at the end of the Ice Age. Unfortunately, these areas also formed much of the flat plains that afforded hunting opportunities for big game: the grasslands where the ancient Jōmon people once hunted bison, for example, are now beneath the sea.

Their descendants wandered inland, into the river valleys and the coasts. In the far north of Honshū, Aomori Bay offered a vast foraging area for crustaceans, fish, and seaweed. In the south, the straits between the islands of Honshū, Shikoku, and Kyūshū formed an idyllic Inland Sea, protected from storms but rich in marine life. The currents forced through these passages sometimes created treacherous whirlpools—in Japanese, *naruto*—but otherwise the Inland Sea was, and still remains, a beautiful patch of gentle water, scattered with green islands.

This protected waterway has had a powerful influence on the development of the Japanese state, encouraging marine commerce and transport links. Where there are fishermen there are fishing boats, and where there are boats there are easy links to transport produce and goods to the next island and across the horizon.

Excavations of ancient graves find bodies dusted with red ochre (an adornment mentioned in some Chinese sources), and an aristocratic class of women wearing single-piece shell bracelets too tight to be removed and too delicate to allow for the possibility of manual labor. Whoever these women were, they presumably donned their bracelets in childhood and left them on permanently thereafter, suggesting a class of priestesses or shamans who were not expected to hunt or gather.

Many of the adult bodies seem to have had certain teeth removed—four lower incisors and two lower canines, possibly at the time of marriage or at several ritual occasions in maturity. Others had forked incisions in their teeth, seemingly filed in particular patterns to denote a tribal association or relationship.

Ceramics remain one of the main means of examining a prehistoric society; although complete artifacts rarely survive, their shards are remarkably hard-wearing. The early Japanese left astonishingly beautiful pots and figurines marked with rope-like patterns or multiple string-like rows of rolled clay. In 1877, the archaeologist Edward Morse described his findings of such prehistoric Japanese pottery as "cord-marked"—translated into Japanese as "Jōmon," this became the standard term use for the dominant culture of the Japanese islands from the end of the last Ice Age until around 300 BCE.

These pots may have flourished among the Jōmon people *because* of the climate, as the cooler conditions of the Younger Dryas of around 10,000 BCE forced them to store large quantities of acorns, nuts, and berries for winter food. By the later Jōmon period, there is evidence of trade between isolated communities. Commodities traveled far from their place of origin, at first in long, thin dugout canoes—examples have been found that were three meters (10 feet) long and barely half a meter (1.5 feet) wide. A fashion for chunky jade beads spread across the north, while multiple tribes began using obsidian arrowheads and scrapers, gaining the sharp volcanic glass from three main sites in the south, central, and northern regions. Tribes far inland were found to have dined occasionally on swordfish. The remains of bears have also been found in Jōmon sites—Jōmon archers are believed to have used arrows poisoned with aconite to bring down larger prey.

Today's Japanese archaeologists twitch at the term "hunter-gatherer." They don't like the implication of rootless foraging that the phrase inevitably evokes, arguing instead that even the early Jōmon appear to have been far more organized. Living in a realm of relative abundance, they enjoyed a semi-sedentary existence in villages, but headed outward on "collecting" expeditions in multiple directions, depending on the time of year and the food that was in season. These goods were then stored in their distinctive pots. The Jōmon people appear to have undertaken limited horticulture, but nothing so serious or widespread as to be called farming.

It is said that the First Emperor of China had heard stories of legendary isles of the immortals found somewhere to the east of his realm. According to several courtiers and self-appointed experts, the secret of eternal life was waiting somewhere in that direction. However, only qualified wizards, pure youths, and maidens could approach these hallowed lands.

Determined to grab the elixir of eternal life for himself, the First Emperor ordered the oddest of colonial enterprises—a flotilla crewed by a thousand virgins, which sailed away from the Chinese coast sometime around 212 BCE. They were turned back by sea monsters—or so claimed their untrustworthy leader, Xufu. When the First Emperor eventually heard this excuse, he sailed for a while along the Chinese coast, standing at the prow of his ship with a crossbow, presumably hoping to harpoon any unlucky whales. Xufu's virgin fleet set off again two years later, sailing into the sunrise, never to be seen again.

There is no direct evidence that the sailors of the virgin fleet—if it even ever existed—reached Japan. If they did, they would have cut a strange dash amid the tribes of the later Jōmon period. But the story of the First Emperor's venture has often excited Asian novelists and poets, who have wondered if one of the many tribes that made up ancient Japan was really a Chinese colony.

Sometime after the era of the First Emperor, the gazetteer known as *The Classic of Mountains and Seas (Shanhai Jing)* made what may have been the first written reference to the land of Wa, somewhere out in the northeastern sea beyond what is now known as Korea. This claim sits amid a bunch of "here-be-dragons"-type suppositions, including giant crabs, a salamander with a human face, and a tribe of mer-people that apparently lived in the ocean nearby. However, the term Wa would come to be used to refer to the Japanese islands for the next few centuries.

There has been much speculation about the origins of this name, including some fanciful ideas: that it was a mistranslation of Japanese attempts to say "our country" *(wa ga kuni)*; that it is a mangling of the name of Duke Ngwa, a legendary chieftain sent from what is now the Shanghai region to colonize the seas; or that it is perhaps intended to mean "vassal." However, the most likely interpretation is that the Chinese intended "Wa" to mean the land of "dwarves"—a reference to the small stature of the indigenous people, particularly from the lofty perspective of their newly arrived rulers.

Beyond the archaeological record, our understanding of the Japanese past largely drops out of the sky in the early 700s CE, when courtiers collaborated on two documents designed to replace lost archives—the *Kojiki (Account of Ancient Matters)*, and the *Nihongi* or *Nihon-shoki (Chronicles of Japan)*. There were earlier histories, but they were burned during a palace coup, and these more recent books were attempts to both reconstruct the lost information and redact the parts of it that did not serve the rulers' agenda. We deal with their annalistic materials—lists of rulers, wars, and real-world events—in the next chapter, but their accounts of Japan's mythical past most likely reflect distant and garbled retellings of the beliefs of the earliest inhabitants.

"Thus," wrote the compilers of the *Kojiki*, "though the world's beginnings are far-off and distant, early sages speak of an age where spirits were born and people first established."

In the beginning, they say, there was formless chaos, from which the two opposing principles, Heaven and Earth, separated. Some unexplained interaction of these primordial forces created the first gods. There is a reed-like line between them, implied by the rotation of the Pole Star about its axis, and from this line came shadowy early super-beings. From them, somehow, comes a brother-sister pairing of the gods Izanagi (the Beckoner) and Izanami (the Beckoness). Standing on the bridge between Heaven and Earth, they churn the waters of the sea with the tip of their jewelled spear. The first islands form from the sacred waters that drop from the tip, and the couple descends to live there.

Very quickly, they realize that their bodies are different, and seek to cancel out these differences by sleeping together. They arrange a marriage ceremony in which they approach each other in a circle around the pillar of heaven (central roof-posts being a feature of Yayoi-period architecture) and greet each other.

Their first two children are deformed and disowned. They burn bones to attract the advice of their divine ancestors, and are told that Izanami has botched the ceremony by speaking first—something a woman should never do. They restage the ritual, this time with Izanagi speaking first, and the happy couple's union produces a set of islands, seemingly a prehistoric rundown of Kyūshū and its environs, the Inland Sea and the lower part of Honshū. In addition to their brood of geographical features, they also spawn a number of gods (*kami*). The last is the personification of fire, which kills Izanami in childbirth.

Death in the time of the gods is not necessarily a permanent condition, however. Even Chinese chroniclers in the Dark Ages noticed the odd Japanese custom of leaving a body in state for ten days on the off chance that it might spring back to life. Resolving to retrieve his wife from Yomi, the land of the dead, Izanagi travels there, only for her to tell him that he is too late. (The name Yomi, meaning "Yellow Springs," suggests perhaps a volcanic region of sulfurous pools, but is also a cognate with a similar Chinese name for the underworld, and so may be a mainland import.) The dead may only be retrieved from Yomi if they have never eaten its food, but Izanami has already dined. Refusing to take her word for it, Izanagi lights a magical torch, which reveals his wife's body already crawling with maggots, and her flesh peeling off to create the eight deities of thunder.

Izanagi flees, pursued first by hags sent by his wife, then by warriors of the undead, then by the eight gods of thunder, and finally by Izanami herself. He flings away his clothes and possessions, creating many new landmarks in what are now forgotten or disappeared places. At the gateway to the underworld, he rolls a boulder in front of the entrance, shutting his wife within and leading to an unholy spousal row.

She threatens that if he blocks her path, she will curse a thousand mortals to die every day. He counters that he will arrange fifteen hundred births a day to hold her off, thereby establishing the cycle of human life and the growth of human society.

And so Izanagi is a bachelor once more, still shedding gods like dandruff, particularly when he bathes to wash away the taint of the underworld. He washes his eyes in a stream, for example, creating the sun goddess Amaterasu (Heaven Shines) and the moon god Tsukiyomi (Moon Counting). And he blows his nose, creating a whole host of new troubles by making the storm god, Susano'o (Rushing Raging Man).

A possible confusion over the nature of such gods survives today as a pun in Japanese, where *kami* means both "god" (written with a word imported from China) and "above." But in the Ainu language—which is spoken today only among the people of Hokkaidō, but was once possibly spoken substantially further to the south—the very similar word *kamuy* also means "above," and is used to describe tribal totems. It seems that the confused tale of Japan's time of gods may indeed represent a hodgepodge of origin myths from assimilated local tribes, whose odd geographic features, totems, and guardian deities have been coopted into a sprawling, ever-growing narrative. Some of the names may even refer to places in what is now Korea, thereby making them impossible to find on a map of Japan.

In any case, the tale goes on: the sun and moon fall out when the latter murders a minor goddess of food, separating day and night thereafter. Izanagi himself fades from the story after he is last seen arguing with Susano'o, the Rushing Raging Man, over his responsibilities. Susano'o, like Izanagi's other children, has been given a realm to rule over, but instead sits weeping because he wishes to meet his mother. Banished by Izanagi, Susano'o stops off to see his sister on his way out, leading to a contest with the sun goddess over who can create the most divinities. Although this appears at first to be good-natured and cordial, before long Susano'o is acting like the very worst of divine siblings—letting horses run wild on his sister's rice paddies, shitting under the throne in her palace just before the sacred time of harvesting first fruits, and in a final indignity, ripping a hole in the roof of her weaving hall and throwing in the flayed corpse of a pony.

As one well might, the sun goddess Amaterasu flees into seclusion, shutting herself away in a cave and plunging the world into darkness. The various thousands of deities assemble in panic and try to lure her out of the cave, hanging a sacred mirror on a nearby tree along with a comma-shaped jewel, and performing several rituals that mean nothing to today's readers but may evoke some half-remembered ceremony of olden times. Considering that this mirror and jewel (or their more modern facsimiles) are two of Japan's three sacred treasures, it is likely that the tale of the disappearing sun goddess reflects a disaster in ancient Japan—an eruption, an eclipse, or perhaps even 536 CE, the year without a summer—which obliged the various contending tribes of indigenous and newcomer peoples to collaborate. Notably, the several contradictory accounts contained in the *Nihongi* do not merely name the gods and their various methods, but annotate them with the family names of their descendants at the Japanese court in the 700s, when the tale was written down.

Eventually, Amaterasu is lured out by the raucous shouts that greet a lascivious dance performed by the Terrible Female of Heaven. Wondering what could possibly be so interesting in the world, since she is no longer in it, Amaterasu pokes her head out of the cave and is swiftly dragged into the open. The gods tie a sacred cord to her that will prevent her from going back into the cave, and the sun is no longer able to disappear.

Susano'o is censured and banished for his acts—hardly much of a punishment, as he was already leaving when he stopped in to see Amaterasu in the first place. Not to be outdone, he kills a fertility goddess as he sets off, scattering the ground with grains, which suggests at least part of the story had its origin in the cycle of the seasons. He then descends to earth, where he runs into an old couple who offer him the last surviving one of their eight daughters if he will slay the eight-headed, eight-tailed dragon that has killed all the others. Susano'o sets a trap by leaving out strong rice wine that has been brewed eight times, which gets the dragon so drunk that the god is able to defeat it. While ripping open its corpse, he finds a sword embedded in its tail—the Sword of the Gathering of Clouds of Heaven—which he presents to his sister Amaterasu by some way of apology.

And so the stories go on, in the *Kojiki* and the *Nihongi*, with multiple generations of begettings and begats as the descendants of these early gods feud and forage, make love and make babies. It does not take much healthy cynicism to see in the stories a recurring and universal motif of tribes jostling for resources and supremacy, and legitimizing their victories in retrospect by claiming to enjoy the favor of the gods.

Amaterasu's grandson Ninigi, whose full name translates as "Truly Winning Have I Won with Rushing Might Ruling Grand Rice Ears of Heaven," is sent down to rule the entire land, bearing sacred treasures to prove he is divine—the Sword of the Gathering of Heaven, the mirror that once captured the light of Amaterasu herself, and a comma-shaped jewel—the significance of which remains unclear. There are some more couplings and plighting of troths, and three generations later, it is Ninigi's descendant, Jinmu, who is recorded in the annals as the first emperor of Japan.

Jinmu, it was said, was born on the southwestern isle of Kyūshū, and began a long march eastward along the coast of the Inland Sea in search of a place that would be more suitable for ruling the whole archipelago. With the aid of a three-legged crow sent down by Amaterasu to guide him, he finds a wondrous paradise—a verdant plain backed by marvelous hills, rich in fruits and games, and with ample room for expansion. This is Yamato, the "Gateway to the Mountains" and the heartland of the emperors.

The stories of Jinmu, as recorded in the *Nihongi*, are themselves echoes of Stone Age folktales, complete with tribal chants celebrating the crushing of enemy skulls with rocks and the subhuman status of the hero's "Shrimp Barbarian" foes. Jinmu himself springs into song to inspire his men, but it is not clear if he is composing new war chants or is simply the first to be recorded performing verses that date even further back into ancient times.

In a sense, only the religious elements of prehistoric Japan endure in some form today. Many grave mounds still exist, often in incongruous locations—little green hillocks of woodland shoved in the middle of a shopping district or housing estate. Certain beliefs also appear to have survived in some form down through the centuries, in the form of Japan's indigenous religion of Shintō, "the Way of the Gods."

We should be careful not to see prehistorical parallels when they are not necessarily there—many elements of modern Shintō, including the very idea that it is an organized "religion," are relatively recent innovations. Still alive in modern Shintō is the sense that human beings are closely connected to the sacred: daily life is steeped in portents and intimations of the divine; shrines persist in the middle of bustling shopping districts; one rarely has to wander far from the roadside before bumping into a rock tied with sacred rope or some similar such indicator of reverence for nature spirits. Shintō is often confused, even by the Japanese themselves, with folk traditions specific to particular locales, associated with local landmarks or the marking of the seasons of the agricultural year. Other superstitions and events lift—inadvertently or otherwise—elements of Buddhist belief.

Shintō—at least the uses to which it was put by the editors of the *Kojiki* and *Nihongi*—is more than a mythology. Its beliefs remained a central underpinning of the Japanese nation until 1945, and are still implicit in many rituals performed by Japan's ceremonial head of state, the emperor. New emperors still offer a sheaf of rice to Amaterasu, and incumbent emperors annually offer harvest donations to the gods in general.

Many of Shintō's nature gods were reinterpreted with the advent of Buddhism in the medieval period, reimagined as Japanese incarnations of Buddhist saints. There has certainly been a degree of admixture at a folk level, and many Shintō shrines offer protective amulets or wooden prayer boards (*ema*) in return for "donations" by visitors who were once called pilgrims but who are increasingly regarded and treated as mere tourists. Visit a Shintō shrine today and you will see visitors washing their hands at an entrance spring, clapping their hands together to startle away evil spirits, and offering prayers for a variety of ancient and modern concerns: lost objects, safe childbirth, cures for disease and infertility, success in education or a career. They might even offer a donation for the chance to draw a prophetic message or omen written on a ticket or a slip of wood.

At certain crucial moments in Japanese history, Shintō has been invoked as an element of Japanese culture that is inarguably homegrown. Whenever foreign influences loom, be they Buddhist scriptures or Christian preachers, or even the onset of the modern world itself, Shintō is a fallback position. It arose in Japan; its stories relate to Japanese folk beliefs and geography. It is manifest in weathered ropes binding rocks; wooden wands decorated with paper leaves; ancient trees and sacred gardens; and in the great mountains that loom in the hinterland. A poem from the time of the composition of the *Kojiki* and *Nihongi* offered praise to an unidentified sovereign, expressing a wish for eternal peace with an unscientific, deeply devout Shintō sensibility of the natural world growing in stature with age:

May your reign
Last for a thousand upon eight thousand years
Until mere pebbles
Grow into mighty rocks
Thick with moss.

A thousand years later, it was adopted as the lyrics to the Japanese national anthem, which takes its name from the opening line: *Kimigayo*. Every day, Japanese schoolchildren, sportsmen, and politicians rise to their feet and sing lyrics invested with an ancient, atavistic power. Emperor Jinmu's three-legged crow still flutters on the flag of the Japanese Football Association—an extra limb presumably being a great advantage in soccer.

CHAPTER 2

THROUGH THE KEYHOLE: THE PEOPLE OF WA

Not even Japan's two most ancient chronicles can agree what happened to the fourteenth emperor, Chūai. The simplest account, in the *Nihongi*, is that he was overseeing a war against a rebellious tribe, the Bear People in Kyūshū, when he was struck by an arrow and died. The *Kojiki*, however, has a far more supernatural tale to tell.

Near the edge of his island domain, it said, Chūai was partway through his campaign against the Bear People, resting in one of his subsidiary palaces, plucking idly at a musical instrument, when one of his wives—known to posterity as Jingū—began speaking with a voice that was not her own. She spoke of a land to the west, rich in gold and silver, and told him that it belonged to him.

Chūai was plainly irritated by her comments, and stopped playing. He had stood on the cliffs and faced the west, he told her, and there was nothing there. But instead of taking the hint and staying silent, Jingū uttered a deathly curse.

"You will no longer rule All Under Heaven," she spat. "Now, turn in your final direction."

His chief minister blanched visibly, and stammered that the emperor should continue to play his instrument. Angrily, Chūai went back to his music, but only plucked at the strings occasionally. The notes grew further apart…then discordant…then suddenly ceased.

Courtiers took up lamps and approached him only to find that he was dead.

The chief minister asked for divine inspiration, but the answers he received the following day from his oracles matched Jingū's odd words. The next emperor, he was told, was still in Jingū's womb—this was the will of the Sun Goddess, and of three other previously unheard-of deities.

It is not all that clear from the *Kojiki* where these words came from. Possibly they came from Jingū herself, who continued to utter strange phrases, calling on her people to assemble a fleet and to calm the waters by scattering chopsticks and toy boats on the sea. She led her fleet away and returned some time later, proclaiming that she had subdued the lands across the sea. Some stories said that the King of Silla had joyfully proclaimed her as his ruler. Others claimed that she had dragged him to the seashore and hacked off his kneecaps to make him fall before her, spearing him in the sand and burying his corpse in an unmarked grave.

She returned to her homeland to give birth.

Then, and only then, she put Chūai's body on a funeral barge and sailed back up the Inland Sea to the Yamato heartland. News of Chūai's demise had been suppressed until that moment.

Her stepsons plotted to overthrow her. One climbed a tree to scout the distance, but his perch was uprooted by a giant boar, which ate him.

His younger brother laid in wait for the funeral barge, but as he prepared to attack, the boat disgorged a company of armed soldiers. The two forces fought to a standstill, at which point the leader of Jingū's forces told his enemies that there was no point in fighting, for Jingū was already dead.

To show his sincerity, he took his knife and cut his bowstring.

The stepson's forces responded in kind only to discover that the man's act had been a ruse. Jingū was still alive; her men had hidden spare strings in their topknots, which they swiftly used to turn their bows back into deadly weapons.

Something fishy was certainly going on. Chūai had left for Kyūshū alive, but had come back dead. Jingū had returned from an unknown land, claiming to have carried Chūai's heir in her womb for three years, still communing with the voices in her head. She had turned on her stepsons, and now proclaimed that her supernaturally conceived son was the new emperor.

"The days," said the *Nihongi*, "were dark like night." The bad omen terrified the people, but was eventually dispelled when it was discovered that two priests had been buried in the same grave. When their bodies were separated, the sun reappeared.

Down at the water's edge, the bay was full of beached dolphins.

Some called it a feast sent from the gods, but the dolphins' bodies were already rotting, and their blood stank.

The prince was still a child, but Jingū agreed to serve as his regent until he was of sufficient age. She ruled for sixty-nine years before dying, at which point the aged Emperor Ōjin finally succeeded his odd mother. He died when he was 110 years old.

The era from around 300 BCE to 250 CE, Japan's "iron age," is known to modern archaeologists as the Yayoi period, named for the Tōkyō district where its most famous remains were uncovered in 1884. Its origins, however, lie across the sea in Korea, from which several hundred thousand new migrants would cross the straits in search of a safe home. Asides in the earliest surviving chronicles of the Japanese suggest that these travelers first made their home in Kyūshū, but advanced over several generations along the Inland Sea until they found the best of possible locations, at the "Gateway to the Mountains" (Yamato) near what is now Nara.

These new arrivals hailed from a world that, if it was not openly Chinese, at least aspired to emulate Chinese civilization. They brought with them knowledge of the Chinese writing system, which was used inexpertly and inaccurately in early attempts to transcribe the words and concepts of the Japanese islands. They also brought new technology and materials—most notably metals and the potter's wheel—as well as a culture steeped in patriarchal Confucianism.

Whereas the archaeological record and ancient legends speak of chieftesses and warrior-women, in what may have even been a society where women either held the reins of power or shared it with the men in complementary roles, the newcomers swiftly marginalized the womenfolk. Denied many of their former occupations, women in powerful positions were soon found only in relation to shrines and ceremonies, a position which would be further undermined in subsequent centuries by the advent of Buddhism. In the world of the newcomers, dominated by a Confucian tradition wary of female influence, women were usually seen merely as wives, mothers, and daughters to be wed, appeased, or traded. There were occasional throwbacks, like the ax-wielding Empress Jingū, but even her power base seemed shakily founded on her husband's importance, or perhaps her family's desire to keep hold on power until her son was old enough to wield it. It is in her time that we last hear of female shamans that, in the words of J. Edward Kidder, are "oracular and battle-tested."

The earliest written record of Japan's ancient myths dates from the *Kojiki*, completed in 712 CE, by which time they had plenty of chances to be half-forgotten, re-interpreted and embellished. Although certain elements are liable to form a relatively accurate list of kings and queens or a gazetteer of notable events, others may have been added simply to serve the interests of later figures. Others may simply relate half-remembered accounts of ancient enmities, but are worth repeating for a glimpse of the stories the Japanese tell themselves about themselves.

Although the later *Nihongi* is presented as a straight chronology of a thousand years of wars and deeds, it is far more likely to offer a cluster of separate family lineages that originally happened concurrently: the king-lists of old Yamato; the sagas of the ancestors of the Kyūshū nobility; the last legends of once-proud clans, now invisible beneath new names and alliances. At some point, many may have once regarded themselves as "kings" of one part of Japan or another—Kyūshū, perhaps; the coasts of the Inland Sea; and the Yamato foothills. The line from the Sun Goddess did not merely descend through the emperors, but through some nineteen other clans that claimed descent from her children. It may even conceal subtle differences between different kinds of newcomers—we can place no single great cataclysm that may have led to the largest influxes of migrants, but if there were several waves, it is very likely that they came from different Korean kingdoms—particularly Baekje and Silla, depending on which one had the upper hand. There are numerable dynastic spats, usually justifying the accession of a younger heir above his brothers (or, more usually, *half*-brothers). We might read these incidents as indicators of the tussles behind the scenes between powerful families seeking to influence the next emperor by trying to ensure that his mother comes from their bloodline. If the right fair maiden from the right clan attracted the emperor's eye at the right time, his eldest son might be easily ousted in favor of the infant child of a new favorite, suitably steerable to ensure further influence at court.

Certainly, in the ancient tales of sophisticated gods from Heaven locked in battle with snarling, belligerent gods of Earth, we have all the indicators of a story told by the winners in war for control of Japan. But we also have many signs of a story that has been mangled in transmission. With the benefit of digital archives and internet searches, I can tell you the details of my own ancestors stretching back just over a hundred years, but I can tell you of nothing before then save a few misty allusions and rumors. How much harder was it for the chroniclers of the eighth century, describing events up to a millennium in the past, with nothing to go on but hazy memories of lost scrolls?

For generations to come, lineages of the Japanese nobility were divided into three categories: immigrants, the descendants of emperors, and the descendants of the "gods of heaven and earth." Perhaps the three sacred treasures of Japan are intended to reflect this tripartite-structured Japan as mirror, sword, and jewel—the later arrivals of the mainland with their fancy Chinese mirror, the earlier invaders with their sword of conquest, and the indigenous people with their sacred comma-shaped jewel, regarded as a symbol of wisdom.

Tales related to Jinmu may have been the ancient legends and tales associated with the Ōtomo clan, whose ancestral turf was close to the mainland in Kyūshū, and who were therefore liable to have been involved with the first of the conquering newcomers. But the tales of the tenth emperor, Sujin, seem to draw on the lore of the Mononobe clan, a powerful family that was largely outmaneuvered in the politicking of the early Japanese state, and which appeared to have strong connections to assimilated indigenous peoples. It's not for nothing that Sujin is described as having a council of female shamans, setting a very different policy from the conservative Confucian-influenced newcomers. Sujin's reign is a time of localizing and confining local *kami*, suggesting a poetic allusion to the incorporation and pacification of multiple neighboring clans, from whom he collects tribute in meat and textiles.

Meanwhile, the tales of the fifteenth emperor, Ōjin, seem to cleave closely to the family traditions of the Soga clan, whose strong ties to mainland Asia are reflected in long tangents about diplomacy and cultural exchange.

One day, someone may finally be able to reconfigure the *Nihongi* from its current single-strand thousand-year epic form into three or more interlocking sagas, each spanning the same period of two or three centuries, leading up to the historically verifiable moment in 552 CE when Emperor Kinmei (509–71) received a fateful gift of Buddhist treasures from Baekje. In its earlier pages, we see a muddled narrative of acculturation and conquest, as mountain fortresses riddled with *kami* and demons yield to the march of progress or flee before it. We also hear of the indigenous people, first mentioned as far south as Kyūshū, when Emperor Jinmu declares he has scared away the "Aimishi." The word is a coinage, bits of classical Chinese stuck together in an attempt to make a sound that did not exist in that language.

Eleven emperors later, the *Nihongi* reports on several campaigns of conquest and subjugation by Emperor Keikō, in which he sometimes runs into local barbarians whom he captures and sacrifices, and sometimes runs into locals who welcome him with open arms. The princess Kamu-nashi, for example, "chieftain of that whole country," comes out to meet him waving a tree branch in truce on which were hung a sword, a mirror, and a jewel. Was the tree branch an actual banner-substitute for the barbarians, or was it a facsimile of the multi-branched ceremonial swords wielded by the Korean newcomers? Regardless, the princess enlists the help of Keikō in putting down "rebels" in her own domain—which, it is implied, is henceforth incorporated into his. Meanwhile, his soldiers embark upon pacification not only of the princess's enemies, but of some new ones encountered on the way, such as the ominous, cave-dwelling Earth Spiders, who are clubbed with stone maces until the blood runs ankle-deep. His lieutenants report another land apparently in need of some civilizing:

> In the eastern wilds, there is a country called Hitakami [Sun Height]. The people of this country, both men and women, tie up their hair in the form of a mallet, and tattoo their bodies. They are of a fierce temper, and their general name is Emishi [Shrimp Barbarians]. Moreover, their land is wide and fertile. We should attack them and take it.

Like the Earth Spiders, the Shrimp Barbarians have a name bestowed upon them by their enemies. Possibly it is a reference to their staple food; more likely it is some sort of reference to long whiskers on their menfolk. It could even derive from *emushi*, which may have been the natives' word for a sword. The description of them in the *Nihongi* has enough parallels with accounts in Chinese annals, and with the archaeological record, to confirm what everyone has suspected all along: that the newcomers swiftly assimilated the Jōmon, killing them off or scaring them off their lands to trouble the next generation of conquerors.

Generations later, Yūryaku (r. 456–79), the twenty-first emperor, would boast in a letter to the Chinese that he and his ancestors had conquered 115 barbarian "nations" of these "Hairy People." The Japanese would still be discussing their Emishi neighbors in the time of the 38th emperor, Tenji (626–72), whose emissaries to China were recorded in the *New History of Tang*, and referred to "Shrimp Barbarians" (in Chinese, *xiayi*). On the borders of the land of Wa, say the Tang annals, there are great mountains (the Japanese Alps?), beyond which are the Hairy People.

> The land of the Shrimp Barbarians is a small country in the island of the sea. Its ambassadors have beards that are four feet long. They draw arrows back to their neck, and placing a gourd on the head of a person dozens of paces away, they hit it without fail.

Talk of these Emishi disappears almost entirely from the historical record by the time Japan becomes more recognizable to the reader, even though they are integral to the country's formation. Much of their culture was impermanent; they built in wood and adorned themselves with shells. They did, apparently, raise some impressive stone monuments, accounts of which occasionally crop up in later Japanese annals, but only as they are repurposed. Emishi henges and stone circles, menhirs and stone altars were once found all over Japan, although most of them were ripped up to form the foundations and battlements of medieval castles. The creation of one iconic image of Japan is likely to have involved the destruction of another.

As collaborators, slaves, and mothers, the Emishi formed a substantial part of the Yamato population, while their ancient traditions, distorted and forgotten, surely formed the building blocks of what is still Japan's official religion, Shintō, the Way of the Gods. Emishi folktales, and the ghosts of departed tribes, can be heard echoing in Japan's place-names. Even the modern name of the island of Hokkaidō, the "north-sea-way," may originate in a mishearing of a more specific term *hoku-Ka'i-dō*, "the north road to the Shrimp Barbarians." In centuries to come, whenever the Japanese tried to assert a unique sense of Japaneseness, a declaration that they were somehow different or superior to the cultures of the mainland, they would cast aside the inheritances of Chinese bronze and Korean steel, silk brocades, Buddhism and Tang architecture, Chinese literature and poetry...and what would they be left with? Strip away China and Korea, and you also strip away many of the ancestors of the Japanese themselves. The very core of the Japanese spirit, its very essence even today, is the ghost of the Emishi.

Yamato Takeru, said to have flourished in the first century CE, was a prince of the proto-Japanese who killed his own brother and was banished by his father to the borderlands, where he vanquished various enemies. His aunt, the chief priestess at Ise Shrine, gave him the Sword of the Gathering Clouds of Heaven that was once ripped from the tail of a dead serpent by the god Susano'o. Trapped in burning grassland by a treacherous local warlord, Yamato Takeru used the sword to slash his way out of the fire, thereby giving it the name by which it would be known thereafter: Grass Cutter (Kusanagi).

But while Yamato Takeru was legendary, his time saw communications from real residents of Japan with the elites that then claimed to rule China. In 238 CE, emissaries arrived in China from Himiko ("Princess of the Sun"), the queen of Yamatai, a kingdom likely to have been on the Kansai plain west of Japan's Central Alps. They are probably responsible for much of what ancient chroniclers have to say about their homeland, which is described as a mountainous territory to the "southeast of Korea"—the Korea Strait being the shortest and most obvious means of reaching it.

Much ink has been spilled over Himiko, who may have been a witch-queen "deft in the way of the gods," or possibly a sun-priestess and figurehead. Himiko may not even have been a name, but a title, a contraction of the Japanese for "majestic woman," *himemikoto*. It may even have been a corruption of a term in Japanese that refers to a sister–brother pair ruling as a princess and prince: *hime-hiko*. Whoever she was, her interest in communicating with an unseen Son of Heaven more than a thousand miles away betrays a respect for and awareness of China that may have derived from contacts with the edges of the Chinese realm.

Despite all the descriptions of Queen Himiko in Chinese accounts, there is no mention of her in the chronicles commissioned by the rulers of Japan in the early eighth century. Had she already been forgotten, or was she hidden in the ancient accounts under another name? Perhaps she was Heaven Shining (Amaterasu), the capricious Sun Goddess who dominates early Japanese legend. Perhaps she was Divine Merit (Jingū), the ancient warrior-queen who was said to have been possessed by the Sun Goddess, and who supposedly led a successful war against Korea. Perhaps she was one of several shamanic seers mentioned in the kingly list as helpmeets to male rulers.

To the authors of the *Chronicle of Wei*, a third-century Chinese annal, Himiko was the queen of what was probably the largest of some thirty kingdoms in the archipelago, with a population of 70,000 families. Although there has long been disagreement about the precise location of her domain, the fact that the vast bulk of the Kofun-era tomb mounds are in the Ōsaka–Nara area suggests that she lived there, somewhere in the watershed of the Yamato river. The ancient place-names of the area evoke a Tolkienesque time of simplicity: the Gateway to the Mountains (Yamato) river pierces the hills that divide the plain from north to south at a place called the Great Pass (Ōsaka). To the north is the Good Flat Ground (Nara). At the edges: Mountain Back (Yamashiro), the Splendid Land (Iga) and the Sacred Streams (Ise). The many rivers of the area flow down toward the Riversides (Kawachi), where they meet the sea at the Wavecrest (Naniwa) and the Clear Coves (Suminoe).

The Chinese chroniclers mention a veritable Scrabble-bag of twenty other forgotten kingdoms in Japan, with names like Shima and Ihaki, Kokata and Kanasana. These names seem to have been meaningless to the Chinese, assembled from characters that approximated the sounds in a language that was foreign to them—unless, that is, their informants really were referring to kingdoms with names such as Devil-Slave (Kina), Naked (Luo), and Black Teeth

(Heichi). Nor is there anything but the vaguest of schematics suggesting where these countries were. The discrepancy between the Chinese league (*li*) and a far shorter Korean variant has left all distances impossibly confused, but a little triangulation of distances, geography and archaeology suggests that Himiko's realm was somewhere near the Kansai plain, the site of today's Ōsaka and Kyōto. Her biggest rivals in the kingdom of Kuna to her south, in what is now Wakayama, are described as fine swimmers and divers, habitually barefoot, with bodies and faces heavily tattooed to ward off sharks and dragons.

Her envoys reached China confident that sorcery would keep them safe. They would travel with a "bearer of mourning," a designated guardian tasked with remaining chaste, unwashed, and ungroomed as a charm against their safe return. He would be richly rewarded if they came back unharmed; executed on presumption of failed duties if they did not.

Amid the sparse prose of the *Chronicle of Wei* there are several comments that would echo through the ages. The people of Himiko's realm, it said, were notably long-lived, often reaching 100 years old. When high-ranking persons walked on the road, commoners were expected to back away into the roadside bushes. Their archers held their bows "below the middle," evoking images of the distinctive top-heavy Japanese bow. And when her people expressed assent, wrote the Chinese chroniclers, they said "*Hai*"—as they still do today.

The ruler of the Chinese coasts was pleased to receive emissaries from such a faraway place, and sent a typically condescending thank-you note, in which he appointed Himiko as queen (even though she already was one), and sent her multiple bolts of wool and silk—including some crimson brocades decorated with dragons—a hundred bronze mirrors, and two long swords.

The bearer of mourning plainly did his job, because the ambassadors made it home, returning with another letter from Himiko sometime later that thanked the Chinese for their gifts. The Chinese were asked to arbitrate in a dispute between Yamatai and Kuna, although it is unclear whether a letter from a distant, unseen potentate would have any effect on a local dispute.

Himiko then died.

Classical Chinese is so terse that proximity can imply causality—the text may be intended to suggest that she died because of the dispute, meaning that the emperor's decree was useless and led to her execution in a coup. Or she may have just died before the message arrived, being notably old by this point. Either way, she was replaced by a teenage girl, confusingly recorded as "a priestess of Himiko"; the Chinese chronicles dispassionately report that a hundred women were sacrificed at Himiko's funeral.

Over the next few centuries, later Chinese chroniclers would occasionally write about the land across the sea, but it is unclear to what degree they were merely embellishing the assertions made in the *Chronicle of Wei. The Book of the Later Han* returned to the topic of Himiko, long after her death, to describe her as a shaman-queen with a thousand female attendants and a single male squire who "served her food and drink and communicated her words." This text also openly assumed that the Japanese aristocracy were descended from the Chinese First Emperor's legendary expedition—an account that was plainly believed by at least some contemporaries. Further confusion has been caused by the compilers of the *Nihongi*, who seemed determined to make their narrative fit those few moments of the historical record that could be confirmed through comparison with Chinese chronicles. Excited by tales of the witch-queen Himiko, these compilers appear to have taken the accounts of Empress Jingū, for example, and shoved them in several chapters earlier than they really should have been mentioned, so that a female ruler of Japan would appear in the same period in which such a figure was reported by the Chinese.

Archaeology offers further evidence of the life and culture of these Yamatai peoples. Excavations all over Japan, not merely in the south, point to a culture of foragers initially living close to the coasts and rivers, where their seasonal diet relied heavily on marine produce in the winter months. The seafood, however, would suddenly decline. The late Jōmon period saw a drastic fall in the number of indigenous inhabitants, caused not by war but by a drop in temperature that restricted access to the two main foodstuffs that sustained them in the winter—shellfish and nuts. Northern Honshū, in particular, seemed to have suffered an apocalyptic decline in population from which it took centuries to recover. The population elsewhere rose again thanks to an increased focus on the cultivation of grains, particularly a new arrival from the mainland—rice.

The period from 250 to 700 CE, roughly concurrent with Europe's Dark Ages, is known in Japanese climatology circles as the Kofun Cold Stage, a dip in temperatures substantially worse than that known in Europe as the "Little Ice Age." Global temperatures fell, with a mysterious "dry fog" recorded in both China and Europe that reduced the impact of solar radiation for over a decade in the mid-sixth century and led to widespread famines and outbreaks of disease. Japanese weather, too, turned colder and wetter; several archaeological sites have been preserved because they were abandoned after floods.

This period dealt substantial damage to the surviving indigenous peoples of Japan, but allowed the more technically advanced immigrant communities to flourish. By 200 CE, the arrival of iron had brought swift changes to the Japanese realm. The locals continued to build with timber, but were able to access far more of it with the new efficiency of metal tools. Just as modern Japanese cutlery reflects a scarcity of metal—knives and metal implements are used in the kitchen, but not at the table—most of the Yayoi people continued to work with wooden tools, attesting to the rarity of early iron objects. However, many of these wooden tools themselves, such as shovels and rakes, became more widespread and efficient because of the availability of iron tools to make improved versions. Architecture, too, became straighter, as fences and beams were hewn with truer blades. Land was swiftly cleared, and the primeval forests were decimated in the quest for materials, but this also allowed for the development of agriculture on a larger scale.

The trees stayed on the mountainsides, where they kept the soil in place and allowed for reliable amounts of water flowing down the slopes into the new rice paddies. Japan's volcanic soil was relatively poor for agriculture, but could be tricked into producing higher yields by flooding the fields. Communities that could grow their own food could forge ahead, as could those that stored surplus produce "for evil years."

The Ise Shrine, one of the most sacred sites in Japan, is particularly useful for understanding the ancient country. Ever since the shrine was first rededicated by Empress Jitō around 692 CE, it has existed in two forms: the "original" wooden thatch-roofed building, and a copy under construction alongside. The shrine is rebuilt as an exact copy of itself every twenty years, echoing a similar narrative of demolition and renewal that seemed to accompany changes in omens or dynasties among the Japanese of the distant past. It also gives us a clue as to the architecture of ancient Japan—sturdy constructions of cypress wood above a ground of white pebbles and around a sacred central pole, with extended finials that give each roof a crossed, horned profile. It is possible that many of the buildings of the ancient Japanese capital looked like these before developments in technology and materials dragged them away from the original plans.

The Kofun period, however, takes its name from a different kind of architecture, the massive "ancient graves" (*kofun*) that dot the Japanese landscape. The simple, square burial mounds of the Yayoi period give way during the third century CE to huge tumuli featuring a distinctive combination of a rounded top connected to a trapezoid mound. From above, this makes them appear to be shaped like keyholes, and indeed they are often referred to as "keyhole tombs." Their oldest examples date from the Nara area, but in the ensuing centuries they proliferated elsewhere, implying a dominant aristocracy that took its manpower and customs further and wider.

The contents of the *kofun* would surely have much to tell us about this period in Japanese history, but their sacred status as the resting places of ancient Japanese "emperors" keeps them largely off limits to archaeological exploration. There are, tantalizingly, several similar keyhole-shaped tumuli to be found in Korea, in the Yeongsan river basin in what was once the state of Baekje, implying strong cultural connections between the builders of both.

Although Japan was already occupied from end to end, the narrative in the Yayoi period takes on a new tone. The story of what would become Japan is not now told by the Jōmon peoples, and possibly not even by their most impressive inheritors, the Yamatai. Instead, it becomes a story told by people whose arrival from the mainland is indicated by in the form of a large mound burial in the first century BCE in Kyūshū, the island closest to Korea, and a gold seal from around the same time found in the Fukuoka region.

Chinese chronicles report "disturbances in Wa" around the middle of the second century CE as these new arrivals, armed with iron that cut down both enemies and forests, began to push ever further up the coast. The corpses in their Japanese graves are notably taller than the locals, perhaps explaining why dispatches back to the mainland referred to a land of "dwarves" in the first place. There is a palpable break in the line of Japanese kings around the late fourth century, possibly related directly to unrest on the mainland that saw the collapse of the Kara state, with up to a million refugees arriving in Japan. These migrants, however, appeared to be arriving with their wealth intact, and were soon interfering with and influencing the politics and power struggles of local kingdoms. Some of the indigenous Jōmon people fled north to escape the newcomers, while others seemed to welcome them, even as they were swamped by their numbers. The archaeological record reveals a double impact—first of a huge influx of these new bloodlines, forming 73 percent of the population in some areas—and then of the inevitable increase of the newcomers' numbers as they bred both among themselves and with the locals.

Where Chinese chronicles once described everyone on the islands as "barbarians," now there is a new narrative of civilization in the hands of these fresh arrivals, pushing back against the barbarians of the periphery. For centuries thereafter, there would be a frontier in the north—a place where young men might carve out a career on the marchland; where "barbarians" on the edges were divided into the good ones who had assimilated and the bad ones who pushed back. The long march northward would only come to an end in the nineteenth century, when the Japanese staked their claim on the last stretch of wilderness in the far northern island of Hokkaidō. There, the local Ainu people bore an unsurprising resemblance to the original inhabitants of Japan in many of the accounts from the ancient past, now eking out an existence on the very edge of the land that was once theirs.

By the early third century, the keyhole tombs had made it as far as the Kansai plain—the heartland of Queen Himiko's legendary kingdom. Notably, they contain very few shell bracelets; the old ruling class had been supplanted. Mainland technology and genes soon wormed their way into the local elites. Deforestation rapidly escalated as these newcomers pursued new housing, new land cleared for crops, and new social projects such as dams and dikes.

It is likely that the confused historical record obscures a dual struggle for influence, as the old kingdoms jostled for power and the newcomer elites fought for recognition not only in the community of local kingdoms, but also back on the mainland, where they intervened in Korean politics.

Owing to the muddled condition of Japanese annals, the real dates are impossible to determine. Chroniclers, like readers, are apt to be confused by repetitive accounts of wars across the straits and kings begetting heirs, and are frustrated even further when a quick count soon establishes that these sovereigns appear to have superhuman lifespans, coming to the throne in adulthood and still somehow managing to rule for over a century. Your guess is as good as mine as to how historical a figure the dragon-slayer Yamato Takeru was—probably not all that much, although his son Chūai is another generation closer to the time when the annals were set down. It was the biographers of Chūai's widow, Jingū, however, who really muddied the waters. The *Kojiki* reports her setting sail for Silla on the Korean peninsula with an invasion fleet, which speeds across the strait, borne on the backs of helpful fishes and a generous tailwind. The ruler of Silla, seeing this unlikely entourage approaching, does not even bother to fight, but swears allegiance to Jingū, pledging himself as a mere stable-boy to the sovereign of "Heaven," and vowing that "each and every year, for as long as heaven and earth remain" he will send ship after ship in a constant rotation of tribute, specifically in horses.

The whole story is foggy with poetic license, and so wracked with portents and sorcery, along with strange turnabouts of fate, that one might just as easily interpret it as an account of *a Korean invasion of Japan*, but it does seem to bear a much closer resemblance to Japanese attitudes substantially later than the chapters in the *Kojiki*. Move the stories of tribute and alliance later—to, say, 369 CE—and they suddenly bear a much closer resemblance to cross-straits actions reported in Korean annals, as well as in the attitudes and proclamations of the man who was supposedly Jingū's long-lived grandson, Emperor Nintoku (r. 313–99), who apparently died at age 145. Nintoku was a particularly powerful sovereign who commissioned a number of large public works, including dams to divert troublesome rivers. He also famously permitted his subjects a three-year moratorium on their duties, allowing his own palace to fall into ruins, its thatched roof leaking, while the rest of his country prospered. Such a story sits at odds with the material evidence of huge public projects, not least the 2,000 laborers who spent sixteen years building his supposed gravesite—the Daisenryō Kofun, the largest of all the "keyhole" tombs—in what is now Ōsaka.

The Daisenryō Kofun is, in fact, supposedly one of the three largest tombs in the world, matched only by the famous grave of the First Emperor of China and the Great Pyramid in Egypt. Today it is set in a central pond that is itself ringed by two additional moats. Like many other surviving *kofun* tombs, it cuts a lush, viridian shock of the ancient past into the modern landscape. It is not open to the public; visitors are permitted to approach no closer than a shrine on the outskirts that looks across the pond. It takes an hour to walk around it, but all you see is a thickly wooded hill across the moat. The best view you will have of this and similar *kofun* will be from the air as your plane approaches Kansai or Itami airport. You see the endless metropolis stretching toward the hill and then a sudden stark, unexpected flash of green, unbuilt upon, so thickly overgrown with trees that no human can pass. The road curves around it; the locals ignore it. It is as if a piece of Japan had been walled off and abandoned 1,500 years ago, left to the wild.

The Yamato state was powerful enough to establish cross-straits relations with the Korean state of Baekje by 369 CE, in which year there is a record in Baekje's imperial chronicles of an imperial gift bestowed upon the "ruler of Wa." It was an unwieldy ceremonial seven-branched sword. Korean chronicles also report multiple raids by the people of Wa; either pirate attacks or sanctioned military incursions, or both. Japan's own chronicle, the *Nihongi*, is similarly focused on Korea during the period, noting that the state of Silla was expected to provide tribute to Japan, and that its failure to do so led to punitive raids around 365.

The Gwanggaeto Stone, a monument unearthed in 1883 in what is now northeast China, refers to several events in the fourth century that suggest increased Japanese involvement on the Korean peninsula. It claims that around 391 CE, the "Wae robbers" came across the sea, "destroyed" the kingdoms of Baekje and Silla, and had to be met with armed resistance from the kingdom of Goguryeo.

Unfortunately for all concerned, the provenance of the Gwanggaeto Stone is caught up in the politics of the time in which it was discovered, a mere two years after the face of Empress Jingū, or at least an artist's best guess at it, had appeared on the newly issued one-yen banknote. The stone was found by a Japanese military officer, who was accused by later Korean scholars of doctoring the stone with a chisel to imply a significantly greater "Wae" presence on the mainland than was originally intended. It certainly seems odd that the stone would talk about the Japanese having "destroyed" both Baekje and Silla when both kingdoms were plainly not destroyed at all; and strange indeed that the same sentence has two missing characters, suspiciously etched away by unknown forces, which presumably once mentioned the state of Kara. It seems far more likely that the Japanese simply served as troops that came to the aid of one Korean kingdom in its battles with the others.

The stone goes on to record some two dozen castle names, each presumably the site of a battle, before Baekje formed a new alliance with the "Wae" in 399 in an attack on Silla, for which Goguryeo was called in to the rescue. This would seem to dovetail with Baekje's own annals, which record that King Asin's eldest son, Prince Jeonji (Straight-Branch), had been sent to Yamato as part of a hostage exchange. This Jeonji would return home in 405 after his father's death with an honor guard of a hundred Japanese troops—which turned out to be more than merely ceremonial when the prince discovered that his uncle had seized the throne. Jeonji and his Japanese escort then camped on an island, waiting for matters to take their course. During this interval, in an odd moment of historical inaction, the "populace of the kingdom" then killed the usurper for him. The same story, in a garbled form, appears in the Japanese *Nihongi*—but 120 years too early, adding further fuel to the idea that the dates in that narrative are all over the place. In repositioning the life of Empress Jingū, the compilers of Japan's chronicles seem to have also dragged the lives of her son and grandson far away from their original placement.

The *Kojiki* similarly has a lot to say about Korean matters, seemingly out of chronological order, noting, "Also, many people came across the sea from Silla. Thus the mighty one…conscripted them to build dikes in the manner of overseas and thereby made 'Baekje Pond'." The story matches neatly with the tales of dam-building and large public works in the realm of the emperor Nintoku, who died in 399, but similarly places them over a century too early. Also placed way too early in the *Kojiki* is the account of a Korean prince called Sunspear arriving in Japan with strings of jewels, mirrors, and scarves with magical powers.

The Baekje annals are a veritable Yamato love-in during King Jeonji's reign. In 409, the Yamato court sends King Jeonji a gift of "night-shining pearls" (thought to be a poetic term for any kind of glittering gem). In 418, Jeonji sent Yamato a gift of ten rolls of white silk. And horses—always horses, a promise backed up by the archaeological record of Yamato graves.

Although imperial graves may not be opened, some were stumbled across by accident and subjected to rescue archaeology in modern times. Early tombs from this period contain peaceful items: comma-shaped stones denoting authority, forked ceremonial swords, and mirrors from distant China. Some of the latter may even have been the self-same mirrors mentioned in the *Chronicle of Wei*, passed on as heirlooms and eventually buried with particular aristocrats. But from around 500 CE, the contents take a turn for the warlike. We suddenly find aristocrats buried with axes and swords, armor and helmets. From the 450s onwards, the graves of Japanese aristocrats are also found containing saddles, bridles, and other items associated with horses—both horses and cattle having been introduced from the mainland.

Nor should we assume that the newcomers considered themselves to be forever free of their mainland attachments. There is evidence in chronicles from both sides of the Korea Strait that the Yamato people traded with their cousins for military manpower, scribes and ironware. Yamato's Hanzei emperor (r. 406–11) applied to the Chinese court to be officially called the "Supreme General Who Maintains Peace in the East, Commanding with a Battle-Ax All Military Affairs in the Six Countries of Wa, Baekje, Silla, Imna [Mimana/Kara], Chin-Han, and Mok-Han." This suggests that, for a moment at least, a Japanese ruler considered himself to be the overlord not only of Japan, but of much of southern Korea. The Chinese fobbed him off with just plain "General Who Maintains Peace in the East," but did eventually grant a similar title to his son, the Ingyō emperor (r. 412–53), shortly before his death.

By the sixth century, the administration in Yamato was robust enough to plan ahead for disaster relief—the first reference to public granaries in the *Nihongi* dates to 536 CE, the year in which the European chronicler John of Ephesus wrote: "The sun became dark, and its darkness lasted for eighteen months." Korean chronicles spoke of a decade of wars and invasions. In Japan, the aged Senka emperor issued a telling decree: "Food is the basis of the Empire. Yellow gold and ten thousand strings of cash cannot cure hunger. What avails a thousand boxes of pearls to him who is starving and cold?"

His words, in the *Nihongi*, allude to starvation conditions on the Korean mainland, and the prospect of a new refugee crisis calling for food supplies to be sent to north Kyūshū. Soon afterwards, the Japanese annals record ambassadors from the mainland offering "tribute," and conversations among the Yamato courtiers about the prospect of seizing the opportunity to invade the mainland.

In 552, the king of Baekje caused a stir by sending some *special* gifts across the strait: a bronze statue of Buddha chased in gold, along with attendant banners; and a stash of sutras, the precious Chinese translations of the original Buddhist scriptures. This was not the first time that Buddhist items had reached Japan, but previous missionaries or contacts had achieved little. This king was looking for some serious cooperation in his quarrels with the neighboring kingdom of Silla, and plainly hoped that Buddhist artifacts would go down well overseas as emblems of belonging to some sort of club. Buddhism, of course, was all the rage in China now, and was seen as a symbol of contemporary sophistication.

The arrival of this embassy sparked an explosive scandal, which is likely to have had very little to do with religion and everything to do with the one-upsmanship of certain noble families at the court who were seeking rank and position and arguing over whether intervention or isolation was the best policy toward the Korean peninsula. Emperor Kinmei's ministers immediately began bickering about omens and portents and perceived threats to the local religion, suggesting the continuing existence of ancient enmities and rivalries at court, shakily held alliances and dynastic pacts stretching back into the mythical past.

Emperor Kinmei, says the *Nihongi*, was enchanted by the foreign paraphernalia, pronouncing it to be "of a severe dignity which We have never seen before." Sensing an opportunity, Soga no Iname—who was not only the emperor's pro-intervention chief minister but also the father of two of his wives—agreed with his august opinion and noted that Buddhism was swiftly attaining prominence on the continent as the religion of choice. If Buddhism were welcomed at the court, it could lead to closer contacts with the mainland.

But Soga was not the only wily schemer who saw his chance. Representatives of two other clans, the Nakatomi and the Mononobe, sensed that the emperor was inviting dissenting opinions. Whereas the Soga clan had strong connections to the mainland, and still had relatives and contacts there, their rivals were drawn from clans "descended from the gods," who were likely to have been connected to the indigenous people assimilated by earlier invaders. The Mononobe regarded themselves as the armorers of the court and loyal warriors who had been first to support the legendary emperor Jinmu in his conquests. This made them staunch supporters of Japan's indigenous religion, and they were horrified at the thought of introducing a new idol to the country when there were already "180 gods of Heaven and Earth, and the gods of the Land and of Grain" to consider. "If just at this time we were to worship in their stead foreign deities," they cautioned, "it may be feared that we should incur the wrath of our national gods."

Still wavering, Emperor Kinmei decided to have the best of both worlds, and ordered the Soga clan to take the Buddhist statue and worship it for a while, to see what happened.

Unfortunately for the Soga clan, while their leader was busy setting up a temple and burning incense to his new idol, a plague broke out. His rivals were swift to point this out to Emperor Kinmei, who finally made an actual decision, ordering that the hapless statue should be thrown into a canal and the temple razed to the ground. Omens, however, continued to be unhelpfully vague, since the flames from the temple then spread to the great hall of the palace.

Worried now that he had incurred the wrath of Buddha, Kinmei flip-flopped again, and was ready to receive reports of mysterious chanting heard across the waves at Izumi; he also ordered the carving of two new statues from a piece of camphor wood that had supposedly washed up on the seashore.

It was Kinmei's grandson, Prince Shōtoku (574–622) who would really integrate Buddhism firmly into the Japanese state, along with many Chinese organizational ideas. Although he boasted a degree of Soga blood, which helped him in his dealings with that clan, Shōtoku was also a member of the imperial family. His reforms were aimed at slapping down the continued meddling in government by the feuding Soga and Mononobe families. The imperial family needed to maintain its link to the Sun Goddess by keeping its blood as pure as possible. This was already developing into a tradition in which each emperor's chief wife was liable to be his own half-sister. Many emperors hence only had a single imperial grandfather, with inbreeding often even closer, depending on the families of the grandmothers.

Such dangerous family planning seems to have been designed to keep non-imperial relatives from exercising undue influence, although instances inevitably arose when a direct-line heir was not available, occasionally presenting the threat of outsider bloodlines sneaking in.

Kinmei's son, for example—the thirtieth emperor, Bidatsu (r. 572–85)—was married to his own half-sister, whose mother hailed from the Soga family. After a messy series of intrigues over his successors, and the assassination of an emperor who tried to stand up to the Soga family, Bidatsu's widow-sister was enthroned as Empress Suiko (r. 592–628).

Her accession masked ugly competition behind the scenes, with her chief minister and uncle, Soga no Umako, in an uneasy standoff with her nephew-regent Prince Shōtoku. It would erupt again after her death, but for as long as she was in power, Japan enjoyed thirty-five years of peace, concurrent with renewed and strong contacts with China's Sui dynasty, the first family in centuries to claim overlordship over all of China.

Suiko's reign got off to a bad start, with an earthquake in Nara that led to further mutterings about grim portents. Before long, however, increased contacts with a resurgent China brought powerful influences to her court.

Her leading adviser, Prince Shōtoku, is one of the iconic figures of Japanese history—his image graced the 5,000-yen banknote for much of the later twentieth century. In any other state, he might have been ideal sovereign material, but he lacked the double imperial-line descent required of an unassailable ruler. He is the subject of breathless hero-worship in ancient chronicles, although his real-world achievements are difficult to pin down. If we are to believe the chronicles, Shōtoku was an unearthly child prodigy who had the power of speech at birth, and who grew up to become a multitasker who could somehow hear ten petitions at once and rule on them simultaneously. Shōtoku was intimately associated with the arrival of Buddhism in Japan, and also with the establishment of firmer contacts with China. It is this latter achievement that is liable to have caused much of his popularity, as he would have been seen as the figurehead of an era that flooded Japan with new inventions, sophisticated luxuries, and the beginnings of literature. Chinese civilization, previously glimpsed only in the form of mirrors and tall tales, seems to have spread throughout Japan at a fast rate, spearheaded and remembered today as "Buddhism," but likely to have been associated at the time with uncountable trade goods, new toys, and fads.

Buddhism itself offered a radically different set of beliefs from those previously practiced by the locals—not the least with its offer of a concept of salvation rather than a nebulous, unappealing eternity in the underworld. Shintō—which seems to have only been adopted as a term at all around this point in order to distinguish it from the new import—was still very much concerned with reverence for spirits and the placating of supernatural forces. Buddhism, however, introduced the notion of karma, and the idea that all living creatures were living a cycle of life after life, the state of their being largely determined by whatever merit they had won for themselves in their previous existence. To new aspirants, such claims might be misread as the offer of eternal life and an improvement in personal circumstances—for women to be reborn as men, for men to return wealthier or more powerful, so long as they appeased the Buddhist deities, soon to be seen as incarnate within the many new temples springing up all over the country. None of this had much to do with true Buddhist philosophy, but as in China itself, translation errors and philosophical misunderstandings would characterize much of Buddhism's early dissemination. Meanwhile, Buddhist practices would override much of the old order. As cremation replaced burial as the prevalent funeral practice, giant grave mounds fell out of fashion, with much of the effort previously expended on tombs redirected into the construction of elaborate Buddhist temples. The very architecture that defined the era became a matter of temple precincts and palaces inspired by Chinese designs.

Shōtoku's love of things Chinese also extended to managerial strategies. It was under his tenure that the archipelago stopped being an inefficient, haphazard federation of occasionally hostile states and was transformed into a single unified polity with a reigning sovereign. The old tribal rivalries and ethnic tensions would, arguably, endure for another thousand years, but they would henceforth happen below the throne, acted out as a matter of loyalty to the emperor.

It was Shōtoku's reforms, inspired by China and aimed at reducing the powers of the great families, which truly forced an organizational structure on the Japanese state. He established a court ranking system with a dozen grades, which clearly stipulated that positions were not hereditary; henceforth, it would theoretically be easier to keep nepotism from the government.

He also introduced a seventeen-point constitution, which was less a blueprint for government and more a set of requirements for loyal courtiers. Drawing heavily on Confucianism, Shōtoku insisted that courtiers avoid open conflict, adhere to their job descriptions, and offer true and full obedience to imperial commands. "In a country, there are not two lords," he writes sternly; "the people have not two masters. The sovereign is the master of the people of the whole country." This might have set the tone for the rule of an absolute monarch, although Shōtoku immediately undermined himself by also insisting on the power of consultation and consensus. "Decisions on important matters should not be made by one person alone. They should be discussed with many." Although it might have seemed like a contradiction, Shōtoku's maxims, taken as a whole, would eventually come to imply that the emperor was a divine, inscrutable, and symbolic head of state whose assent—tacit or otherwise—was required for all decisions to be made by his court, but whose ministers were no longer necessarily hereditary nobles. Shōtoku introduced a Chinese-influenced sense of decorum, demanding that all entrants to the palace should drop to their knees and press their hands to the ground before walking on.

Several parts of Shōtoku's constitution were overwritten by the clearer wording of later decrees, but even in modern Japan, legal scholars have been heard to argue that if his words have not been contradicted by a later revision, they still stand after nearly fourteen centuries.

Some words endure even more obviously. Until the regency of Shōtoku, the sovereign had been known as a king, great lord, or similar title. Following on from his constitution's insistence that the ruler was the symbol of heaven, Shōtoku began using the term *tennō*, "heavenly sovereign," usually translated as "emperor." All previous sovereigns were upgraded retroactively.

Shōtoku also wedged Buddhism firmly into the state organization by demanding that officials recognize the "three treasures"—not the mirror, sword, and jewel of ancient legend, but the Buddha, the law, and the [Shintō] priesthood, establishing a tripartite appeal to divine authority. Shōtoku promoted further contacts with Chinese Buddhists, inaugurating several major temples and offering tax breaks to selected artists who were able to paint devotional icons. Empress Suiko, as his mouthpiece, commanded her subjects to make large images of the Buddha in copper or embroidery, but also decreed that the gods of "heaven and earth" should not be neglected. She might have been a figurehead, but Empress Suiko still enjoyed some power, and took the opportunity to remind her subjects of the country's ancient collaboration between male and female powers. It was Buddhism, however, that attracted the attention of neighboring states—the sections of the *Nihongi* referring to her reign and Shōtoku's regency are riddled with references to grand embassies from China and Korea arriving with golden gifts and holy scriptures and being greeted by fleets of sailboats and brightly adorned troops of cavalry.

Shōtoku's constitution would form the basis of future consultations on the way to run the country; it was accompanied by a number of other reforms that added to its effect. One was the adoption of the Chinese calendar, which divided time into twelve-year cycles multiplied by five elements to create units of sixty years. A further "long count" in Chinese history held that every twenty-one cycles—which is to say, once every 1,260 years—there would be an event of earth-shattering transformation. Clearly, later chroniclers decided that Shōtoku's reforms were just such a momentous event, establishing 601 CE as the "year zero" in Japanese counting, but also spurring authors to presume that the last momentous event must have been 1,260 years earlier. This, perhaps, explains why Japanese annals begin with the seemingly arbitrary date of 660 BCE, implying that Shōtoku's regency was the best thing that had happened to Japan since the mythical time of the first, legendary Emperor Jinmu. A prophet might foretell that something similarly momentous would happen to Japan 1,260 years later, around 1861 CE—and by chance, such a prediction would only be a few years out.

One of the first acts of Shōtoku's new nation was to pack an ambassador off to the Chinese to ask them to stop calling his people "dwarves." The idea of a land of Wa, the prince thought, was insulting and belittling, and he would really much prefer it if the Chinese started referring to them with a little more respect.

An embassy sent to China decided to put this into effect in 607 by pointedly ignoring a previous missive that had hailed the ruler of Wa. Instead, it extended an ill-advised greeting from "the Son of Heaven in the land where the sun rises…to the Son of Heaven in the land where the sun sets." This scandalized the Chinese, not only for the implication that the island nation was somehow rising and ahead of China, but for the claim that the ruler of the islands was an emperor of equivalent standing to theirs.

Considering Japan's position on the eastern horizon relative to China, and the country's claim as the chosen home of the descendants of Amaterasu, Prince Shōtoku's ambassadors regarded the "land where the sun rises" as a far more suitable name for their country—in Japanese, "Nippon." In modern Mandarin, this is pronounced "Riben," but in Tang-dynasty Chinese, it would have sounded more like "Yatbun." A thousand years later, misheard as "Cipangu"—put through a Portuguese mangle into Spanish as "Japón"—it would give us the name by which we know the country today. From this point on, the land was called Japan.

CHAPTER 3

THE SHINING PRINCE: MEDIEVAL JAPAN

The guest protocols of China were elaborate and complex. All foreign visitors, even kings, were obliged to perform a series of actions designed to show that the sovereign of China was the ruler of the world, and they his loyal subjects. The Japanese—a thousand miles from home, from a land that was little more than a fairy tale—were no exception. The gifts they presented would be vetted by imperial flunkies, and anything deemed offensive or worthless to the Xuanzong emperor would be tossed aside in advance.

As was customary, Xuanzong would receive his visitors in the small hours of the morning. In the heat of the Chang-an summer, this was probably a mercy, but Ōtomo no Furumaro, the vice-ambassador from faraway Japan, was less keen when the event occurred on New Year's Day.

Awake before dawn, his breath freezing in the air, he made his way with his entourage to the majestic Daming Palace in the north of the great city of Chang-an, entering through the southern gate and crossing the vast square of the outer court. Hanyuan Hall towered above him to the north, sitting atop a mountain of twinned "dragon-tail" staircases. It was designed to impart the feeling that visitors were literally ascending into the sky to commune with the ruler of the world.

The assembled dignitaries waited in silence in the cold. In earlier generations, some might have chatted or joked, sneaking warm buns out of their sleeves, or shaken their limbs to keep warm. But the officers of court ceremony had become increasingly strict, and threatened to punish any who deviated from the correct ritual. Even when Xuanzong was not present, protocol demanded they should act as if his spirit was among them.

Just to make their position abundantly clear, foreign diplomats were housed for the ceremonies in tents pitched in the courtyard, surrounded by the pomp of the Chinese court—antiquated war chariots; ranks of Chinese guardsmen with fearsome halberds; lines of bells, drums, and chimes. The Xuanzong emperor would arrive in a palanquin, clad in striking scarlet robes with his face partly obscured by the curtain of beads that hung from his crown, while his court musicians played the Music of Grand Harmony.

The music stopped when he sat on his throne. A new melody would start up—the Music of Leisure and Harmony—signaling that the dukes, princes, and kings of subordinate countries should take their positions. A herald then commanded them to fall to the floor and kowtow twice to the emperor. They were obliged to perform such obeisances every time they received anything from the emperor, be it a kind word or a cup of wine brought by scurrying servants.

Ōtomo no Furumaro had been briefed about all of this and was ready to play the game, although as he arrived that cold winter day, he was scandalized by what he saw. An ambassador from a Korean state was in the prime position, directly beside the emperor's throne. In the quiet of the courtyard, while they waited for the emperor's arrival, Ōtomo whispered in disapproval at General Wu Huaishi, who had the misfortune to be standing nearby.

"Silla pays tribute to Japan," he hissed. "Since ancient times, Silla has been a vassal of my ruler. But you put their ambassador closer to the emperor, and us on the wrong side of them. How is this righteous?"

General Wu was a swift tactician. He had to be—not only on the battlefields of his younger days, but in the intricate placements of court ceremony. The rules of the Chinese palace had to reflect the positions of the world, with the Chinese emperor central and his subjects aligned in proper order of protocol. Some might have regarded Ōtomo's complaints as disruptive and rude, but General Wu saw them as earnest entreaties that the ceremony should proceed according to the truth of All Under Heaven. If Silla had been wrongly placed, then it would have been discourteous for Ōtomo *not* to point it out before the emperor presided over an incorrect ritual. In the scant moments before the Xuanzong emperor was due to arrive, he ordered the retinues from Silla and Japan to swap places.

There was a flurry of rustling robes as the ambassadors darted to their new positions. Such incidents were not unknown at the court, and had even resulted in ambassadors coming to blows, but the Sillan envoy seemed to know his place, and he rushed down the line with little more than a glowering glance at Ōtomo.

The Xuanzong emperor arrived, oblivious, and took his position at his throne to the usual orchestral accompaniment. The time then arose for the ambassadors to present him with their tribute.

Ōtomo was now the first, dropping to his knees and touching the ground with his forehead, not once, but twice.

"The outer subject of the Land Where the Sun Rises dares to present such a gift," he proclaimed, as his servants marched forth with their approved items to be handed to the emperor's own servants.

Then, as was customary for New Year's Day, he shouted the words "Long Live the Emperor!" three times.

He had just announced to everyone that Japan knelt before the glory of China. But the Japanese people back home didn't need to know that. His complaint over positioning had also announced to every other country that Japan was superior to them—bigger that Silla, better than Parhae, more loved than the Caliphate. He'd make sure *everybody* knew that.

After Prince Shōtoku's death in 622, his former Soga allies were left without stern opposition, and were increasingly pushy in their manipulation of the imperial family. Within a generation, they were attempting to replace the imperial line with their own—a plot that risked compromising Shintō belief in its entirety, since the emperors held their position in part because, as direct and pure descendants of the Sun Goddess, only they were able to communicate with her.

Before his death, Prince Shōtoku heard the news from China that the Sui dynasty, in which he had invested so much faith and hope, was already falling apart. The Sui emperors had driven their people to the edge with wars of conquest and sweeping reforms, spending money that they did not necessarily have. But Shōtoku also lived just long enough to hear that all was not lost; the Sui emperors had been replaced by their cousins, the sons of the duke of Tang. This new Tang dynasty would be substantially more enduring, and would lead to many more contacts across the strait. A strong, unified China, however, could mean a China with a greater interest in political expansion. Sure enough, it was not long before the Tang Chinese were interfering in the squabbling kingdoms of the Korean peninsula, forming an alliance with Silla and allowing the small state to push against Japan's ally, Baekje.

Back in China, the poster boy of the early Tang dynasty was the emperor Taizong (r. 626–49), supposedly the second ruler of his line, but actually so proactive in his father's revolution that he was just as much the founder of the dynasty. Although he was not his father's eldest son, Taizong had secured his position in the succession by declaring war on his own brothers and leading armed soldiers against them in a palace putsch. It should, perhaps, come as no surprise that the story of his palace coup would reach Japan, along with all the more genteel elements of Chinese civilization such as Buddhist statues and sutras.

Although there was a precedent for such behavior in Japanese history, and the country had no need for Chinese inspiration, the story of Taizong may have been a template for the enemies of the

Soga clan. Prince Shōtoku's constitution did not prevent enemies of his clan from having his son murdered. But in 645, the long domination of the Soga family was brought to a crashing halt by a Japanese prince who barged into his mother's throne room to murder a Soga paterfamilias at the imperial court. When his assassins hesitated, Prince Naka no Ōe took matters into his own hands, badly wounding the hapless Soga leader in front of the empress before pleading his case. When the shocked Empress Kōgyoku backed out of the room, supposedly to consider his appeal, the prince's allies finally plucked up their courage and hacked their victim to death.

Kōgyoku was a widow on the throne, powerless without the support of the Soga, who were outnumbered now by her son's allies among the Nakatomi clan. She tried to abdicate in favor of her son, but the prince instead made her put her brother on the throne so that he could continue to run things without the burden of ceremonial responsibilities. It was under his regency that Japan received another basket of radical decrees, the Taika Reforms, taking Shōtoku's constitution out of the realm of airy theory and into more concrete, practical solutions.

Taika means "great change." Although the reforms were credited to a specific emperor, they derived much of their power from the observations and ideas of an entire generation of Japanese scholars who were newly returned from two decades of studying in China and involved in the establishment of a university in Nara. A series of proclamations, issued on New Year's Day of 646, established that all land was now the property of the emperor, and that its administrators ruled it merely on his sufferance. This was perhaps the most revolutionary change, although many of the provinces didn't notice for a while. The reformers did not dare to unseat local headmen, but instead rebranded both them and their responsibilities. Instead of running their own, autonomous holdings, the headmen were now obliged to send quotas of tribute to the court.

Census takers and recordkeepers were appointed to keep tabs on the use of what was now understood to be imperial land. As appointees, long-term rulers of various districts could now be fired if they failed to fulfil their duties, which now included the sending of taxes and conscript soldiers. This last item was to prove to be the most controversial, and seems to reflect a growing fear among the Japanese that they would soon face conflict in Korea and a possible invasion from the mainland. Able-bodied men between the ages of twenty and fifty-nine were registered as soldiers, although this was often the sum total of their military "'service," and they returned home again to their fields. The new rule was so unpopular that many young men effectively abandoned their homes in order to avoid being drafted.

Ten years later, upon the death of her replacement, Kōgyoku would be placed back on the throne and renamed Empress Saimei. It was only with her death in 661 that her murderous son finally ascended the throne himself after a generation of ruling from behind it. Now in his forties, the former prince Naka no Ōe adopted the imperial name Tenji (r. 661–72). As Japan's thirty-ninth emperor, Tenji faithfully adhered to the codes set by his predecessors, largely because he had been their secret instigator: the Taika Reforms are remembered as being acts of his mother, even though he was instrumental in their imposition.

The kingdom of Baekje fell in 660, embroiling the Japanese in a long scheme to back their allies on the mainland by lending military support to an attempted restoration. Empress Saimei had in fact died at a temporary capital on Kyūshū while supposedly overseeing the plans for the great expedition; Tenji was only crowned after bringing his mother's remains back to the central plain.

In August of 661, Tenji sent out a fleet carrying 5,000 soldiers ready to support the restoration of his chosen Baekje pretender. Several months later, another 37,000 soldiers were committed to the operation, which would at least explain what happened to all the conscripts netted in the Taika Reforms. It was, however, arguably to be the biggest military disaster in Japanese history until the Second World War. Despite vastly outnumbering the ships and men from

Silla and Tang China, the Japanese armada wasted its manpower on ill-judged assaults, and was soon boxed in on the river Geum, where its numerical advantage was squandered. Accounts differ as to the scale of the defeat, but mainland chronicles estimated 10,000 Japanese dead and 400 ships lost. "The flames and smoke rose to scorch the heavens," reads one of the last entries in the *Baekje Annals*, "while the ocean's waters turned as red as cinnabar."

Baekje was gone, drowned beneath the onslaught of Silla and Tang China. "Although an end had finally been made to the destruction caused by war," observed the *Baekje Annals*, "every household in the land had been touched by tragedy, and corpses still lay strewn about like scattered straw."

"There is nothing more to be done," reads the *Nihongi*. "This day the name of Baekje has become extinct." There are those who believe that the people of Baekje and the people of Japan had such a close ethnic and linguistic affinity that they were indistinguishable from one another. The fall of Baekje led to one last influx of several thousand refugees from the mainland, including the surviving members of the Baekje royal family, who were welcomed as noble relatives. Their ranks were carried across to the Japanese court, and their descendants formed a new clan in Japan, the "Kings of Baekje" (*Kudara no Konishiki*), whose leaders would be significant players in Japan's subsequent northern frontier wars. Thereafter, however, Japan was cut off from its main source of mainland culture. Several decades of absorbing every aspect of Sino-Korean society came to a sudden halt, while the Japanese considered the likelihood of a counterattack from across the Korea Strait.

In fact—and not for the last time—the breadth of the Korea Strait proved just wide enough to prevent military actions, and the Japanese were left in peace. By the 670s, Silla and Tang China had gone to war with each other; Silla had forced the Chinese out of Korea; and the flashpoint lay between those two powers, on their shared border, rather than being directed across the Korea Strait at Japan. The Japanese, however, took more than twenty years to work this out, and spent the next generation making preparations for an invasion that never came.

In 667, Emperor Tenji moved his capital up to Ōtsu on the western shore of Lake Biwa. The Japanese capital moved fifteen times in the seventh century, in part because early Japanese towns relied heavily on wood as building material and fuel, and the depletion of nearby forests may have made it more economical to simply switch locations every few years. But Tenji's move, which took him into the ancestral heartland of Korean émigré clans loyal to the throne, may have also been a strategic move, creating a more defensible position to ward against possible invasion from the mainland.

We must read between the lines of Emperor Tenji's odd behavior in the seventh century, as he appeared to broker dynastic ties with his own half-brother, a man who had shocked the court at Tenji's own coronation banquet by pointedly stabbing the floor with a spear. Tenji had grabbed at his sword and had to be restrained by his chief minister—hardly a sign of a happy family. As if the imperial clan were not already perilously inbred, Tenji arranged marriages between many of his children and their own cousins, seemingly in an attempt to establish a new tradition. Tenji wanted his successor to be *entirely* imperial, descended in both the maternal and paternal lines from former emperors without any outside influence.

He didn't get quite what he wanted. The half-brother himself seized the throne from Tenji's son and heir, ruling from 673 to 686 as the fortieth emperor, Tenmu. He was married to his own niece, Emperor Tenji's daughter, who would succeed him in her own right to reign from 686 to 697 as Empress Jitō. Under their reigns, Buddhism was pushed even further onto the Japanese people, in part as a new means of establishing control in the outlying regions: temples were set up; repeated rituals that also emphasized the power of the sovereign were promoted; and the copying of sutras was promised. By the time Empress Jitō died, her court was directly funding 545 temples in the Yamato region.

The Tang dynasty did not merely inspire Japanese princes to take matters into their own hands and Japanese empresses to rule in their own name. It also led to one of the farthest-reaching and longest-lasting cultural impacts upon Japan. Instead of the trickle of rumours and artifacts from Korea, the Tang dynasty led to direct Japanese contacts with the Chinese capital at Chang-an (modern Xi'an), and an onslaught of culture and trends.

Although both China and Japan would continue to evolve and develop in subsequent centuries, the height of the Tang dynasty had a lasting impression on the Japanese. Many elements of Japanese culture, even today, have strong ties to the Tang. The modern Japanese readings for Chinese characters are often archaic, closer to medieval pronunciations than modern Mandarin. The architecture of Japanese temples—everything from Tōdaiji in Nara to many holy places of Kyōto—rests heavily on the style of Tang-era buildings. In China, the later Song dynasty would bring the chair into household furnishings; in Japan, people continued to sit on the floor the way they had in Tang times. If you want to know how a Tang dynasty princess dressed, look no further than the silks and elaborate coiffure of the Japanese geisha, who emulate the height of Tang fashions. For centuries to come, Japanese women would shave off their eyebrows in the Tang style, painting on delicate "moth brows" higher up their foreheads. They augmented this look in a more particular Japanese way by dyeing their teeth black with a cocktail of iron filings dissolved in vinegar; until the nineteenth century, these were the defining mark of an adult woman. Some elements of Japan's national sport, sumō, match descriptions of wrestling matches in medieval Chang-an; today's wrestlers are attired like the circus strongmen of the Tang dynasty.

While Japan's borrowing of Chinese culture was all-encompassing, it was also tied to a specific time period. As noted by Ivan Morris in his book *The World of the Shining Prince*, visitors from later Chinese dynasties would be likely to regard Japan as laughably backward, clinging to fashions and mannerisms that were centuries behind the times, with an intelligentsia communicating in a quaint pidgin of real Chinese. A kinder observer might note that the Tang dynasty is widely regarded by many scholars as a cultural peak of Chinese civilization; maybe the Japanese decided that if it wasn't broken, there was no point in fixing it.

In 684, Emperor Tenmu issued a proclamation that would have repercussions for centuries to come, establishing that local rulers needed to maintain a militia that could be put to use in the service of the throne.

> The arts of war are necessary for heavenly governance. All civil and military officials should employ soldiers and learn to ride on horseback. Be careful to provide an adequate supply of horses, weapons, and articles of personal costume. Those who have horses shall be made cavalry soldiers, and those who have none shall be infantry soldiers.

Tenmu still fretted that an invasion might arrive from China, but already a generation had passed with no sign of any retaliation. Regardless, his reforms established the first glimmerings of a military class that was, if not professional, then certainly in possession of some semblance of uniform training and ability. Among the clans of the outlying regions, and even closer to the capital, the nature of fighting men began to diverge into the relatively poor farmer-soldiers, who left their fields to fight as commanded; and an equestrian elite that could afford the maintenance and operation of horses. A "knightly" class was beginning to emerge.

Further afield, provinces that still appeared to be on the edge of barbarism were urged to send symbolic tribute to the sovereign—sometimes in the form of food, but also occasional "singers, dwarves, and jugglers." Even the Emishi turned up on the Yamato plain, ready to perform some of their tribal dances and recognizing the monarch as a powerful figure, if not their actual sovereign just yet.

From 700 to 1300, the climate of the Kofun Cold Stage gave way to what is known worldwide as the Medieval Warm Period. Winters gradually became milder; summers in Japan were frequently so hot that they brought on droughts. The population of Japan seems to have remained relatively stable throughout, with the birth rate offset by occasional epidemics of smallpox and influenza, as well as the direct and indirect effects of the aforementioned water shortages.

Despite Buddhist proscriptions, there are plenty of indicators that many Japanese, even in the administration, were clinging to the old-time religion. One report suggests that enemies of one empress tried to kill her with a curse, stealing some of her hair and stuffing it into a human skull as a form of deadly magic. Deer bones and antlers were still used in rainmaking ceremonies. Archaeologists have uncovered horse sacrifices from the 690s, intended to hold off floods and famines in a particularly bad decade. In 705, as the new Fujiwara capital struggled to maintain its status beneath an onslaught of overwhelmingly bad omens, a human sacrifice was made to a local river god. In 710, the capital was moved, yet again, to Nara, a purpose-built gridded city that was a direct imitation of the Tang dynasty's distant Chang-an. Perhaps in recognition of a more humane age, human sacrifices gave way to symbolism—the ground beneath the city is peppered with clay statuettes, seemingly buried as a form of sympathetic magic.

Conditions favored the conversion (or re-conversion) of wilderness into arable land, allowing for an increase in population, but also the development of rapid wealth and power for anyone at the periphery overseeing the repurposing of such tracts of land. The victors in the struggles of the Kofun period, now installed in the imperial court, clung to the luxuries of their existence in the capital, seeming ignorant of the trouble that was fermenting on the frontier.

A particularly damaging smallpox epidemic from 735 to 737 severely depleted the rural population, prompting the government to relax land redistribution schemes. Farmers were encouraged to stay on their land by the prospect that it would be theirs to tend permanently, leading to an inflation of landholdings and entitlements. A "farmer" who did well could become substantially more.

He could secretly buy up his neighbors' lands; he could hire help so that he was no longer the man who was physically tending the crops. He might even be able to afford horses and armor, upgrading himself into the lower levels of the aristocracy. If he was really smart, he could strike a deal with a nearby Buddhist monastery and officially "donate" his land to them, secretly retaining his land with the additional bonus of tax-free status as "temple land." It's easy to see how, within a few generations, the newly established monasteries were able to expand their reach and influence through the efforts of both the devout and the sneaky.

In an effort to keep things going in the countryside, numerous manors (*shōen*) were assigned to low-ranking members of the imperial family, who also enjoyed tax-free status. Here, too, the system was open to abuse, with local wheeler-dealers striking a marriage deal with any newly arrived imperial scion, thereby attaching their lands to his to wriggle out of paying any tax. An additional advantage of the *shōen* was that its manager had the right to refuse access to government inspectors without an imperial warrant. Once again, within a few generations, many of these simple farming concessions had expanded from manors into veritable baronies, their managers enjoying the wealth and status brought about by substantial holdings. They literally lorded it over their tenant farmers, turning lands that had once been regarded as temporary projects into permanent inheritances.

As tax revenues dropped back in the capital, the government began looking for means of cutting costs. With no sign of a Chinese invasion, it seemed as good a time as any to end compulsory conscription of troops. Henceforth, if any fighting needed to be done, soldiers would be sourced from the lords of the manors. This obliged the lords to take a greater interest in training and provisions in their domains, and encouraged many of them to begin maintaining a permanent private militia of guardsmen and enforcers. Meanwhile, honest families, tending the dwindling numbers of taxable lands, found themselves paying ever-higher taxes to offset the government's reduced revenue. Many fell into poverty; some turned to crime, while others swelled the ranks of the new militia, which was becoming increasingly necessary as the crime rate soared.

In 784, the fiftieth emperor, Kanmu (737–806) announced the relocation of the capital to yet another site, safely out of the way of interfering Buddhist monasteries and the still-powerful sway of certain families with mainland origins. However, the construction of this new capital at Nagaoka (Long Hill) met with a series of disasters, culminating in a scandal wherein the emperor's own brother was implicated in the murder of the chief aristocratic overseer, who was himself accused of taking bribes. The local river, which had been advertised as a boon to transport, turned out to be dangerously flood-prone and a breeding ground for a series of diseases. Guilty consciences at court ascribed the problems to the restless ghost of the emperor's brother, who may have been framed, and who had certainly died in suspicious circumstances on his way to exile. When Kanmu's own son fell ill, the angry ghost was appeased by being proclaimed an emperor in the afterlife, five years after his death—under the name Emperor Sudō, he remains the only sovereign crowned posthumously.

Emperor Kanmu also presided over another great redaction of the Japanese records, insisting on a review of all existing genealogies and a purge of those deemed to be unacceptable. All copies of one particular imperial genealogy were ordered to be burned; possession of another was now a crime. Kanmu may have been diligently removing forgeries from circulation, although it seems more likely that he was concerned about implications in these documents that certain Korean families *also* claimed descent from a solar deity.

The capital was moved again in 794 to still another site, which was also conceived in imitation of Chang-an. The setting remains beautiful to this day, surrounded on three sides by wooded hills. In the style of Chinese capitals, the new city had an east market and a west market, and was split in two by a wide boulevard named after Chang-an's great Avenue of the Vermilion Sparrow (Suzaku-ōji), which ran all the way from the imperial citadel in the north of the city to the main gate in the south (Rajōmon, later more famously known as Rashōmon). The gate, however, was merely a symbolic structure—the capital never had a city wall. Rather than risk another flooding waterway, the town instead diverted the water from the nearby Duck River (Kamogawa) into a canal that could be more easily controlled.

In the layout of this new capital, we see the aspirations and awe of envoys like Ōtomo no Furumaro, emulating the glories of the distant Chinese capital for a court that could only marvel at their tall tales of giant staircases and soaring audience halls. Heian, as it was originally known, would remain the capital of Japan, but for a brief hiatus in the twelfth century, for the next thousand years, to the extent that it is still known, even today, simply as the "Capital City": Kyōto. Heian has also lent its name to the Heian period of Japanese history, which lasted from the city's inauguration in 794 up to the erosion of its power center in 1185.

Shortly after the founding of Kyōto, Japanese Buddhism underwent one of its greatest transformations. Monks returned after study in China, having learned more accurate interpretations of the scriptures and gained a better sense of the relative values of certain sutras. Buddhism in Japan until this point had been confused, based on whatever materials leaked through from the mainland. Keen to reduce the power of self-appointed experts in Nara, the Japanese court openly promoted these new arrivals, including Saichō (767–822), a proponent of the Chinese Tiantai (Jp. Tendai) school that argued for the prominence of the *Lotus Sutra*. Unlike certain earlier Buddhist sects, Saichō's school offered the prospect of salvation for all, since all living creatures possessed the essence of Buddha. This promise made Saichō's school incredibly popular, although it was not the only one.

Kūkai (774–835) arrived from China with another Buddhist sect up his sleeve. His was called the "True Word" or "Mantra" (Shingon). Like Tendai Buddhism, it argued that its beliefs were based on a more direct interpretation of scriptures that the Japanese had so far misunderstood. But Shingon's version of this truth was a world away from Tendai's, instead focusing on the first and greatest of all Buddhas, the Dainichi Nyōrai, whose powers supposedly trumped those of all subsequent incarnations, and through whom the path to enlightenment could be invoked by the use of cantrips and spells—the aforementioned "true words." Shingon also seemed to offer its members the prospect of material benefits in this life—although enlightenment was still an ultimate goal, Shingon faithful could also expect help from various deities and saints. Precisely who or how is difficult to say, since Shingon jealously guarded many of its inner teachings. Ironically, both these forms of Buddhism took root in Japan as they were being purged and persecuted in China, where the Tang emperor Wuzong had launched a massive campaign to cast out an unwelcome foreign (i.e., Indian) religion. This is liable to have contributed to a sudden rise in newly arrived Chinese scriptures, giving Japanese monks more to translate, interpret, and disseminate.

The Japanese did not initially have a written language of their own. Like almost every other nation in East Asia, they instead used Sinitic—summarizing their thoughts by using Chinese characters to represent them. Both the *Kojiki* and the *Nihongi*, for example, were written in Chinese—or rather, they used Chinese characters to fix on the page the ideas and stories of the ancient Japanese. At one level, this led to a continent-wide common language: one could write a letter in Vietnam and expect it to make sense to a reader in Japan, even if neither correspondent spoke the other's language. At that time, and ever since, this meant that words in Japanese could have multiple possible pronunciations. Words on a page can prove slippery, with two possible meanings or more.

The Japanese tried to fix this problem as time went on. The men largely clung to Sinitic writing as a mark of status and learning. Shorthand fixes were dismissed as "women's writing." As a result, the men largely kept to their aping of Chinese forms, while women flourished because the shorthand version was more flexible and suitable to Japanese. Heian women—writing for private publication, and hence untroubled by the use of abbreviations and slang—wrote their diaries in a cursive, truncated script that threw away the Chinese characters and replaced them with symbols that represented the actual sounds of the Japanese language. This writing system became known as hiragana (smooth letters), and its use is a fundamental, transformative moment in the development of Japanese culture. Before long, someone realized that hiragana could be used not only to inform readers of the correct pronunciation of a Chinese symbol, but also to conjugate it. So a simple verb like "go," which would be written with the Chinese character that the Japanese read as "*i*," could now gain suffixes that put it into the present tense, *i-kimasu*; or the past, *i-kimashita*. Instead of being a sophisticated foreign code awkwardly grasped by the Japanese, Chinese ideographs were adapted into the service of the Japanese language. To this day, written Japanese remains a combination of Sinitic and hiragana, the swirls of the native syllabary augmenting and clarifying the complex alien hieroglyphs, some 2,136 of which are still required in order to make sense of a newspaper.

Modern language learners usually memorize the hiragana as a set of sounds: "*a-i-u-e-o, ka-ki-ku-ke-ko, sa-shi-su-se-so*," and so on. In olden times, however, the Japanese used a mnemonic device. Much as "the quick brown fox jumps over the lazy dog" is a sentence that contains all the letters of the alphabet, the medieval Japanese wrote the hiragana syllabary down as a poem, which is usually known by its first three sounds, *I-ro-ha*. In its entirety, it reads:

Even the blossoming flowers
Will eventually scatter.
Who in our world will not change?
Today we cross the deep mountains of karma
But we shall not have transient dreams,
Nor shall we be deluded.

Just to complicate matters, Japanese monks developed a third writing system, largely to be used in explaining the pronunciation of terms from Buddhist sutras. Using fragments of existing Chinese characters— hence the name "katakana" (broken letters)—this additional system also remains in use today, mainly to transcribe foreign words and the noises made by beasts—read into that what you will.

The development of a literate, literary aristocracy led to an outpouring of written records, many of which survive today. We do not merely have access to the doubtful yet informative chronicles of the *Kojiki* and the *Nihongi*, but also to personal diaries ("pillow books") and anthologies of thousand-year-old poetry.

Many examples of such writings have survived, giving us an invaluable glimpse of the worldview of the extreme upper class of Japanese society. One male diarist from the 900s left an account of what was expected of a Fujiwara nobleman, mixing moments of mundane grooming procedures with arcane rituals that relied on complex astrological calculations.

On waking, he should begin his day by whispering seven times the name of his patron star. He should wash his hands, take a toothpick to his teeth, and then turn to the west to offer homage to Buddha and whichever local *kami* was his. Porridge for breakfast and then, once every three days, a comb through his long hair. Fingernails to be trimmed once every twelve days; toes, too. A bath once every five days, but only if the omens were good.

For fun, he might settle down to gaze at a Yamato-e, a highly decorated scroll that sometimes included annotations but was sometimes purely pictorial. The Yamato-e was intended to be unwound in stages, the left hand unrolling and the right hand winding back up, creating a slowly panning tableau in front of the reader's eye. Any story was revealed in a linear fashion—as if the reader were walking alongside and slowly overtaking a temple procession, for example, or glimpsing a movie that unfurled in a single long take. Many modern museums, out of necessity, exhibit such scrolls entirely unrolled as single elongated pictures. This rather removes the dramatic possibilities of unwinding it oneself, and the sense of recognition and discovery as certain characters arise and reappear.

One of our most valuable records of life in the Heian court comes from a chatty, contrary, vulnerable lady-in-waiting whose habit of writing topical lists and musings often makes her come across like a modern blogger. Common to the etiquette of the day, her true name remained unspoken in public and is hence lost, although she is usually referred to by her nickname, Sei Shōnagon (Lesser Councillor of State Kiyo's [Woman]). Some of her diary entries even appear to be what we might now call memes—snickering about a cat treated as a royal personage, or a long-forgotten in-joke about a spindle tree, enduring today as nothing but an unintelligible punchline.

Sei Shōnagon loves getting letters; she derives a nerdy joy at finding books she hasn't read before. Rude people piss her off. She can never find a truly good pair of tweezers. She hates that moment when you splash ink on a book you are copying out; that moment when you wait up all night for a man who doesn't show; or when he does and then snores loud enough for your neighbors to know what's going on.

She hates going to bed alone, and burning fine incense that makes her feel like she is a class act if there is no man to notice. When she looks in her Chinese mirror and the burnished bronze is a little cloudy, it makes her fret that she, too, is losing her looks. When an evening letter arrives from her lover, she can't wait to find a lamp, and uses tongs to snatch a lump of red charcoal from the nearby brazier, squinting in the half-light, heedless of the fire hazard.

Sei Shōnagon hates it when she hires an exorcist to deal with someone's spirit possession, only for the guy to turn out to be a drowsy charlatan. She swells with childish pride when the empress addresses her and she accidentally says the right thing in response.

When her carriage travels down a narrow woodland lane, she reaches out to touch the trees.

Haters still hated. Murasaki Shikibu (the "Wisteria Girl of the Ministry of Ceremonies), a fellow court lady who also kept a diary, couldn't stand Sei Shōnagon, but had to put up with her scribblings. A thousand years later, we are immensely fortunate to have access to the writings of both these remarkable women, who not only wrote beautifully and evocatively about their lives, but did so at the same time and place. Somewhere, sitting in a bar not far from you right now, there is a pair of frenemies just like them—one bubbly, chatty, and sensual; the other shy, plainer, but smarter. Sei Shōnagon is the hot, flirty one with a ready comeback; Murasaki Shikibu is the wallflower who thinks of something cleverer, but only on the way home. Widowed at a young age, Murasaki was introverted, introspective, icily witty but faintly repulsed by human contact, particularly with Sei Shōnagon, whom she regarded as insufferably smug, airheaded, and with an inflated sense of her own literary merits.

"If we stop to examine those Chinese writings of hers that she so pretentiously scatters about the place," Murasaki wrote, "we find that they are full of imperfections." By far the smarter one, Murasaki tried and largely failed to keep her intellect secret from her fellow court ladies, whom she rightly suspected would be at first curious, and then jealous. Murasaki, who dismissed Sei Shōnagon for her flighty interests and empty opinions, had the last laugh, being remembered as the world's first novelist for writing *The Tale of Genji* around the turn of the eleventh century.

Murasaki's book appears to have been patched together over the course of a couple of decades, serialized in episodic chapters for a small circle of intimates. Its titular hero is a minor princeling, the son of one of the emperor's lesser concubines, doomed to a life of genteel idleness and forced into several soap-opera situations involving unwelcome betrothals, doomed love affairs, and court scandals. It is likely, but impossible to prove, that some of the situations in which he finds himself were thinly disguised allusions to real goings-on in the capital.

"I have a theory," Murasaki wrote, "about what this art of the novel is...It does not simply consist in the author's telling a story." Instead, she argued for writing as a true vocation—an insurmountable urge to communicate with others.

> On the contrary, it happens because the storyteller's own experience…even [of] events he has only witnessed or been told of—has moved him to an emotion so passionate that he can no longer keep it shut up in his heart. Again and again, something in his own life…will seem to the writer so important that he cannot bear to let it pass into oblivion.

Murasaki's depiction of court life is an idealized world of courtiers dueling with witty poems, and of lovelorn princesses waiting for their Prince Charming to sneak into their bedchamber for a midnight tryst. She presents a view of an idle, timid coven of women diverting themselves with guessing games and literary competitions, largely at the mercy of a society of rapacious or dismissive men. Sometimes it's difficult to tell what's worse for one of Murasaki's women: attracting the attention of a nobleman who will force himself on her in a midnight visit, or realizing that such attentions are waning, that he has found another diversion in another palace courtyard, and that she is left literally holding the baby. The attitudes of Murasaki's characters make it abundantly clear that women in in her world are second-class citizens, "creatures of sin" in Genji's words, regarded by the menfolk as idle, ditzy decorations. Such attitudes are a world away from the ancient legends of Japan, which are thickly populated with queens and warrior-women, and seem to imply that the indigenous people accepted a power structure that regarded women and men as complementary equals. In *The Tale of Genji*, we catch a glimpse of the damage that may have been done by several centuries of immigrants from the mainland, infusing the Japanese with another Chinese import—chauvinism.

Entire shelves of books have been written about *The Tale of Genji*, and the adroit, oblique way that it purports to be about its title character, the "shining prince," while actually being about the women in his life. An early chapter features Genji and his friends idly and somewhat cluelessly discussing the types of women that exist, setting up dozens of later chapters in which he blunders into relationships with their real-world manifestations.

The sheer size of the literary record that springs into being in the Heian period, and its enduring power, has distracted many scholars from the likely truths of real life in Japan's early Middle Ages. Sei Shōnagon and Murasaki Shikibu might have been a pair of waspish girls-about-town, but the only time the common folk show up in their writings, they are dismissed as bestial, dirty, stupid worm-people, unclean and unwelcome. Kyōto itself, even in its heyday, was not quite the paradise it was claimed to be by its residents. The uniform street grid never quite achieved true symmetry, and even in Murasaki's time the western part of the city was a patchwork of burned-out city blocks, market gardens, and tumbledown ruins, undesirable by day and unsafe at night. Even modern visitors to Kyōto may sense the city's lopsided medieval growth. Almost all the major tourist sites are east of Senbon-dōri (the new name for what was once the Avenue of the Vermilion Sparrow). Even at the height of the Heian period, when courtiers regarded their capital as the center of the civilized world, half the city was a no-go area. The east side was so much more desirable that Kyōto piled outside the environs of its original layout, across the river and into the picturesque hills to form the Higashiyama (east mountain) district, which is still home to many of Kyōto's most famous temples and the Gion geisha quarter.

If the Heian courtiers could be so selective about what they saw in their own city, it should come as no surprise that many were distracted from true influence and politics. While there was indeed a boom in poetry, and a gaggle of snooty aristocrats had strongly held views about the right sort of kimono for a noonday stroll, the kind of Heian courtier with the time to write such comments was also the kind who was marginalized from the corridors of real power. The influence of the Soga clan waned, to be supplanted by the Fujiwara (the descendants of the Nakatomi clan, now rebranded with an imperial surname), a ruthless family of conspirators whose influence at court defanged many institutions to such a degree that they became pointless ceremonial bodies. Fujiwara daughters were thrown at each emperor until the union produced a son, at which point the monarch would be persuaded to abdicate in favor of his infant offspring—there was no precedent in Japan for the succession of the eldest heir; merely the one deemed most appropriate, which gave the powers behind the throne a degree of flexibility in mating their imperial candidate with a number of potential ladies. The new infant emperor would be too young to rule himself, and so would require a regent (*sesshō*)—and who better than his Fujiwara grandfather? When the emperor reached adulthood, the regent would rebrand himself as an imperial spokesman (*kanpaku*) until such time as the emperor produced an heir and the process could start all over again.

Such petty manipulations obscured a sense of desperation, as Japan's one percent clung murderously to their right to stay in the hallowed enclaves of their capital. While the diarists wrote of cherry blossoms and snowflakes, in the 700s alone the Heian court was subject to one enforced mass suicide, two armed rebellions, and a conspiracy uncovered in the nick of time—not to mention a spinster empress accused of having an affair with her chief monk.

However, considering the precarious nature of life elsewhere in the world, many chroniclers of the day still regarded Heian as a paradise. And certainly, compared to life for many commoners, the capital was heaven on earth, with plentiful food, artistic pursuits, and many amenities. It was, however, only paradise for an incredibly limited elite of some 5,000 aristocrats in the main citadel. Away from the capital, communications were slower; life was harder. Books were harder to come by, as were entertainers, poets, and the right sort of booze. For as long as you were in the imperial in-crowd, life in the Heian court was a cycle of ceremonials and rituals, banquets, and intrigues. Once you were in the capital, leaving would feel like a personal disaster.

Daughters could marry well, although "marriage" was a flexible concept in most cases, and most children were sired through more casual arrangements. Sons could achieve merit; courtiers could gain the approval and sanction of ruling emperors, but those who fell from grace could be shut out. Posted to the frontier or sent off on imperial business that required no return, they would find themselves marooned far from the delights of civilization. Not even the descendants of the emperors were immune from such periodic purges, particularly when a sovereign had multiple younger sons who themselves sired multiple offspring. Girls could always be bartered as concubines in the hope that they would make a match closer to the throne. Boys were more expendable.

Some emperors made matters even more confusing by "retiring" from their official function only to meddle behind the scenes. Emperor Heizei (r. 806–09) stepped down from the throne after a reign of only three years, believing himself to be dying from an incurable disease. He resigned in favor of his younger brother, Emperor Saga (r. 809–23), although Saga was soon also ill; Heizei inconveniently recovered, leading to a messy scramble to reinstate him that was recorded in the annals as a failed revolt. Henceforth, Japanese history would gain an entire new set of players—"retired" emperors, each with their own entourage, their own capricious changes of heart regarding their favorite bedmate, and their own opinions about which of their grandchildren would make the most suitable sovereign.

Around 814, Emperor Saga tried to save the court some money by downgrading some of his unruly brood of forty-nine children from courtiers to commoners, bestowing them with the new surname of Minamoto (House of Origin) and further increasing the number of new *shōen* manors in the countryside. Several subsequent emperors similarly lopped off their minor family branches, also rebranding them as Minamoto. In such pruning we see the outer manifestation of intense politicking at court, and the aftermaths of dozens of forgotten love affairs, promises made and broken, or favorites proclaimed and disowned, among both wives and sons. Unlike the Christian world, where an "eldest son" was usually a clear-cut proposition, the Japanese court featured a whirl of competing eldest sons from different mothers. Imagine the spousal Sudoku of King Henry VIII, multiplied tenfold by a far more pragmatic attitude toward marriage and legitimacy, among an entire entourage of pushy families, every one of them hoping that the next emperor would be a child of their clan.

Both emperors Heizei and Saga, however, placed a high value on the chief of their personal guard, a man called Sakanoue no Tamuramaro, who had won fame for himself on the borderlands, fighting against the Emishi. In that role, he had been appointed as the emperor's "barbarian-suppressing supreme general," or *sei-i tai shōgun*. A relatively new post (Tamuramaro was only the second to hold it), this title allowed a general to enjoy sweeping powers on the frontier so that the court could be spared the hassle and time-wasting of communicating with representatives several days' ride away.

In 825, Emperor Saga's successor repeated the trimming exercise, downgrading some of his nephews (the grandsons of Emperor Kanmu), and giving them the surname Taira (a reference to the capital from which they had just been banished). Several of his successors also added to the House of Taira over the next few decades, creating a new class of younger, hungrier subjects with chips on their shoulders and a desire to clamber back up the ladder. The Minamoto and the Taira were soon out in the provinces hoping to make a name for themselves, fighting in the ongoing frontier clearances that Emperor Kanmu had set in motion, jockeying over who might be appointed to military positions that could lead to re-enoblement.

It may come as a surprise that the Emishi, dismissed in so many accounts as dumb barbarians, should need all that much suppressing, but the size of the military response managed by Tamuramaro and several of his colleagues points to a substantial, powerful presence at the edges of the growing realm of Japan. In fact, the period beginning in 774, in the time of Emperor Kanmu's father, through to 812, partway through the realm of Emperor Saga, includes not only the to-ing and fro-ing over the establishment of three different capitals, but an entire generation of conflict on the borders, known in Japanese as the Thirty-Eight Years' War. While the courtiers of Heian wrote poems about the moon and seduced each other's mistresses in their refined capital, their soldier class was in a permanent state of conflict on the distant frontier.

There were fortunes to be made. Whereas southern Japan was a patchwork of small counties, the provinces of the north show up on maps as substantially massive additions. If a warrior could hold onto it, a marchland at the edge of Emishi territory could generate significantly more wealth than one of the smaller baronies of the civilized south.

Court annals largely describe such matters as responses to Emishi raids. This, however, was far from the truth, as Japanese settlers were pushing into Emishi lands. Some Emishi fled north to Hokkaidō; others accepted the new arrivals at their word: that they were peaceful farmers who would cause no trouble. These farmers would arrive with a military presence in a nearby fort, and wasted no time into classifying the locals into "peaceful" Emishi, who cooperated and coexisted with the new arrivals, and "wild" Emishi, who fought back.

Such tensions are liable to have characterized every step of the Japanese advance up the archipelago from the moment that mainlanders first arrived in Kyūshū in prehistoric times. The only difference with these last conflicts is that the historical record is slightly clearer about the situation. "Peaceful" Emishi were regarded as subjects of the emperor—an assumption that could serve to drag the invading warriors even further into local politics, with some Emishi undoubtedly allying themselves with the new arrivals in order to gain some military muscle in settling local scores. Others would enjoy the benefits of trade, only to go "wild" sometime later when a local commandant informed them of their previously unmentioned or misunderstood tax obligations. Such complexities rarely made it back down south, where the situation in the borderlands was merely reported as a matter of raids by "wild" Emishi against peaceful Japanese settlers.

Nor were the Emishi easy targets. They had an intimate knowledge of the local land and access to good weapons. They were accomplished archers and excellent horsemen, and some of their leaders ran rings around the stiff stratagems of the Japanese generals. One of the most famous Emishi leaders, Aterui, scored a crushing victory at the Battle of the Koromo River in 788, where although only some two dozen Japanese soldiers fell in an ambush, more than a thousand drowned as they tried to retreat through the river.

In fact, it was the conflict with the Emishi, coupled with the geographical conditions of Japan's frontier, which largely created the enduring image of the Japanese warrior. Over the course of many decades not only of warfare but of far longer periods of peaceful interaction, the Japanese and the Emishi substantially cross-pollinated each other; you might say that by the time the fighting was over, it was difficult to tell them apart. Old-fashioned Chinese military technology simply wasn't suited to Japan. There was rarely enough flat ground for chariots. Crossbows fell into disuse, lacking adequate spare parts or maintenance. The Emishi preferred curved swords that allowed for better slashing from horseback, and the Japanese started using them themselves. Shields—more like portable planks that archers would erect in front of them as a form of cover—were next to useless on rough terrain, particularly in forests, where the enemy was not playing by any recognized rules of engagement. Components of metal armor— both the plates and the wires that held them together—would rust and chafe in the humid climate. Instead, the Japanese began to adopt a lighter, more flexible protection that used interlocking pieces of hardened leather and lacquer, with boxy shoulder-guards designed to impart a degree of the old shield coverage even when a rider on horseback was drawing back his bowstring. The helmet, meanwhile, was given a hard lacquer top and a flared neck guard, in order to offer the maximum protection against enemy archers when charging straight for them, head down, on horseback.

Eventually it became clear that there was no Chinese counterattack coming from the mainland; military conscription was suspended in the south by the end of the eighth century. The only battlefields for several generations were found in the north, entirely transforming the Japanese idea of warfare to an Emishi-focused mode. If there was any fighting to be done, it was usually in the hands of a provincial officer favored by court officials—more often than not, a Taira or Minamoto cousin—who would be expected to supply his own manpower to deal with any problem; this motivated the provincial leaders to maintain their own armies. Such manpower was usually divided between a permanent entourage of full-time warriors and an outer labor pool of farmers and vassals who lived in the surrounding area, but could be called upon in times of need.

Soldiers were withdrawn from the frontier to serve as watchmen and constabulary; ten thousand friendly Emishi, the sons and relations of numerous pacified tribesmen, were scattered across the south, sent there as hostages. They brought with them their light, boxy armor, their top-heavy longbows, and their curved swords. This, it was soon understood, was what a warrior looked like.

The Taira and the Minamoto, those spare sons of remote branches of the imperial family tree, married into the Emishi much as their ancestors had clearly done with the native peoples in the south. Taira and Minamoto sons were born with half-Emishi blood; Emishi son-in-laws were given the Taira or Minamoto surname in order to obscure their lowly origins. They grabbed large holdings of land for themselves, and became veritable lords on the remote and uncivilized borders and newly cleared marchland. Although the sophisticated courtly life stopped at the Uji bridge outside Kyoto, there was some sense among the courtiers that they had distant cousins on the far-off frontier, grubbing out a harsh existence at the edge of the world. Such men and their families were largely forgotten and ignored, although a lucky few, like Tamuramaro, returned to the capital, where they were feted for their achievements and rewarded with noble titles and court positions.

By the end of the ninth century, such men appeared to have adopted a new term for themselves that played both upon their wish to be seen as loyal retainers of the central court and on the court's desire to regard them as mere hirelings. They called themselves "those who serve"—the samurai.

CHAPTER 4

A GAME OF THRONES: MINAMOTO VS. TAIRA

There was a time—only a year earlier, at the time of his triumphant entry into the capital—when Yoshinaka had commanded 50,000 warriors. Those were the days. He had scoffed at the effete courtiers and taught them a few lessons in so-called etiquette.

Yoshinaka had clambered into the palanquin any way he saw fit. If he needed a bowl to drink, he would just take one from an altar. If he needed something done, he would just shout at the closest courtier. He had no time for the careful rituals and picky ceremonies of the imperials. There was work to do.

But now he was on the run, commander of just a few hundred horsemen, pursued by his own cousins in the Minamoto family. A roadside scuffle reduced his numbers to fifty, then a mere dozen.

One of them was a woman.

Critics are divided as to why Lady Tomoe should show up in *The Tale of the Heike* as Yoshinaka is fleeing for his life. Perhaps, as modern feminists hope, she is more typical than the historical record lets on. Traditions imply that samurai women are only expected to fight in the last-ditch defense of the homestead, but perhaps things were different in the twelfth century. Perhaps Tomoe, with a bow taller than she was and a sword that she swung with two hands, was just one of many samurai women who fought on the front line. Modern archaeology has uncovered mass graves on samurai-era battlefields in which up to 30 percent of the bodies were female. Were female fighters more prevalent than Tomoe's lone appearance suggests?

The Tale of the Heike begins in sexist terms, speaking of Tomoe's great beauty, her white skin, her long hair...and then, as if shaking himself awake, the author suddenly returns to matters of greater importance: her skill at archery; her abilities at breaking in horses and riding on rough terrain; the fact that, even though she was a woman, she was a front-line captain in Yoshinaka's forces. "She was a warrior worth a thousand," says *The Tale of the Heike*, "ready to confront a demon or a god."

The awe with which the teller of tales appears to have regarded Tomoe does not come across in Yoshinaka's own dialogue. As his forces decline and he finds himself leading little more than a fugitive platoon, Yoshinaka knows that his days are numbered. He knows that he is not going to make it out of the forest alive. And so he turns to Tomoe and tells her:

> You are a woman, so be off with you; go wherever you please. I intend to die in battle, or to kill myself if I am wounded. It would be unseemly to let people say that [Yoshinaka] kept a woman with him during his last battle.

Yoshinaka has already been presented as a buffoon, committing a series of ridiculous gaffes in his brief sojourn in Kyōto. Perhaps Tomoe is included as an example of just how clueless he is—letting a *woman* fight on the frontline? What savages these Minamoto clansmen must be, if even their womenfolk wrestle in the mud for trinkets of power!

Why does he want Tomoe to run away? It is usually assumed that he still has some unreconstructed macho sense of honor, the first stirrings of *bushidō*, what would be later known as the Way of the Warrior. It would be dishonorable to die with a woman present. Perhaps Tomoe was just a plaything; perhaps she was one of the *shirabyōshi* "sword-dancers"—military-themed strippers who enjoyed something of a fad in the age of the samurai.

Or perhaps Yoshinaka cared for her deeply. The wording of his command for her to leave is open to interpretation. "*You are a woman, so be off with you; go wherever you please.*" In other words, anyone and his henchmen will be sure to recognize a male warrior on the run, even if he cast off his armor, even if he threw away his sword. They will see who he is from his haircut and his scars. *But you, Tomoe, you can melt away into the forest. With a dab of mud and a switch in clothing, you'll look just like any other peasant girl, and the enemies will be none the wiser. You'll have a shot at living. There is no need for me to cause your death, too.*

An alternate version of the same story has him actively threatening her with punishment beyond the grave. If she does not do as he says, he tells her, he will revoke the bonds that join lord and vassal for three iterations. In other words, if she obeys him on this occasion, he promises they will be reunited in the next life, perhaps with their roles reversed. But if she refuses to leave, their souls will never meet again.

Tomoe allows her horse to slow, dropping back in the party of fleeing samurai. Before long, she and her mount are alone on the forest path, the sound of Yoshinaka's squadron already faded away in the green distance.

Sadly, Tomoe wishes for one last battle.

Then she hears the thunder of hooves.

A troop of thirty horsemen is in pursuit, chasing after Yoshinaka, led by the samurai Morishige. As he passes, Tomoe rides her horse straight into his, grabbing the surprised leader and dragging him across her saddle. She draws her dagger and knifes Morishige in the neck, savagely twisting his head from his shoulders.

Spattered in warm blood, she holds his head aloft, a trophy that in better days would have been retained to show to one's lord for rewards and prestige. But Tomoe has no lord any more, not in this life, so she hurls the head into the trees and whirls her horse around to gallop away.

The Tale of the Heike does not say whether Morishige's men give chase or not. Do they break off the pursuit of Yoshinaka, or do they even notice that one of their men is down? Regardless, Tomoe and her horse fly between the trees as she tears off the bulky, blood-drenched panels of her armor. She throws her helmet into a ditch, she loses her sword. By the time she rides out of the forest, she is a merely a woman on a horse…then she loses the horse, washes in a stream…and fades into the countryside.

Yoshinaka was right; he would never make it out of the woods. His horse gets stuck in the mud, and he leaps off with his own sword in his mouth to guarantee he won't hit the ground alive.

As for Tomoe, some say she was unable to stay away from the battlefield, and would become the wife of another samurai and the mother of a famous strongman in the following generation. Others said that she went into seclusion and died in her nineties as a Buddhist nun. Another story claims that she hunted down Yoshinaka's pursuers, stole back her lover's severed head, and was last seen cradling it in her arms, walking out to sea.

In 1068, the Fujiwara were successfully played at their own game. The seventy-first emperor of Japan, Go-Sanjō (1032–73), was the first emperor in 170 years not to have immediate connections to the Fujiwara family. Consequently, his career was initially blocked by the Fujiwara faction at court, but the death of his predecessor without a direct heir suddenly propelled him to the throne. He immediately set about annoying the Fujiwara clan, overriding his *kanpaku* (spokesman) and calling for an audit of *shōen* estates and provincial governors. Inconveniently for the Fujiwara, the constitution set in place all those years ago by Prince Shōtoku and his successors made this all reasonable, and the threat loomed that Go-Sanjō might sweep all the Fujiwara from the court with a single edict. He was only headed off when the Fujiwara effectively threatened to go on strike—there were so many of them that their complete removal would have rendered the state powerless and unable to function.

Quitting while he was ahead, Go-Sanjō abdicated while still in his thirties, leaving the throne to his adult son, who had a Fujiwara mother and might thereby be expected to run things more in accordance with the wishes of the shadowy power brokers. But Go-Sanjō was young enough to be able to interfere himself, and his chosen successor, the seventy-third emperor, Shirakawa (1053–1129), was demonstrably old enough and able enough not to require a regent.

Go-Sanjō's run of luck ended with his death, at the suspiciously young age of forty, shortly after taking holy Buddhist orders. Shirakawa, however, would continue to play his father's game, himself abdicating only fourteen years later and then entering a monastery to embark upon his own scheme to steer events from behind the throne. Owing to the location of his hideout, this process became known as "cloistered rule" (*insei*); it would be used by many of his descendants.

For Shirakawa and his immediate heirs, cloistered rule was a success. More by luck than judgement, Japan enjoyed a period of peace and prosperity, and the stranglehold of the Fujiwara on government appointments was broken. But in divorcing his descendants from collusion with the Fujiwara, Shirakawa cut the imperial family off from its main supplier of muscle—and cloistered emperors had no army of their own. In order to secure their position with force, many of his descendants would lean upon the loyalties of their hungrier, less-established cousins from the frontier—the likes of the Minamoto and Taira clans, long excluded from court life, but always keen to find a way back in.

Many years after the events recounted in this chapter, scribes set down a collection of epic tales about the early part of the great struggle for mastery of Japan. It is a wholly different Japan from the image presented by Murasaki Shikibu, as if the weepy romance of *The Tale of Genji* suddenly gained a distaff war-movie sequel. Genji was a fictional creation likely to have been distantly inspired by real people, created over many years by a female author in the court. Two centuries on, his complement is the rise and fall of an entire rival clan, born from the same kinds of family politics and pruning that shunted Genji from the spotlight, memorialized in a huge and occasionally untrustworthy saga of battles and betrayals, seemingly written by a committee of excitable men. But even *The Tale of the Heike* cannot resist beginning on a melancholy tone. Although later chapters are full of glorious deaths and stirring heroism, its opening pages lament the pointlessness of it all, foreshadowing the desolation of its own finale:

> The Gion bell tolls, sounding the knell that all things must pass. Like the colors of the summer camellia, prosperity is ever followed by decline. The proud do not endure; they are like a dream on a spring night. Even the mighty meet with destruction, until they are as dust before the wind.

Sometime around the year 850, Japan had ceased to be a nation with an insecure frontier. There was a trading post on the southern tip of Hokkaidō during this period, but Japanese rule did not extend far beyond it. The Korea Strait separating Japan from Korea, along with the Tsugaru Strait between Honshū and Hokkaidō, functioned as an effective barrier for potential large-scale trouble. Unlike China, from which much of its model government was derived, medieval Japan did not really have a border problem—there was no serious chance of foreign invasion or of disaffected noblemen forming alliances with foreign tribes. Japan was neatly cut off, which allowed its system to prosper and flourish without further adaptation. China's Tang dynasty was deteriorating, and when it fell, the Japanese did not rush to communicate with its successor states—although China was not entirely forgotten, the great influx of Chinese culture was shut down. The only drawback here, for a system that relied on pushing its dregs and spares onto the borderlands, was that without any new lands to be won, the Japanese would soon start fighting each other over the lands they already had.

Inevitably, the *shōen* estates and the farthest marchlands assumed the status of autonomous counties or baronies. In particular, the Taira and Minamoto families, united by their mutual ancestry and shared experience of exile, came to dominate many of these outer estates, turning the edges of the nation into a patchwork of holdings with allegiance to either Red (Taira) or White (Minamoto). To this day, these two colors remain a symbol of polar opposites for the Japanese; teams in game shows are divided into Red and White, and the colors of the Japanese flag even represent the standoff. From the tenth to the twelfth century, these two clans experienced a series of huge reversals and resurgences in an era that some commentators call "feudal Japan."

Others vigorously deny the classification. It is easy to see elements of feudalism in medieval Japan, but the term is unpopular with many historians. There is an easy temptation, particularly in popular accounts such as this one, to over-translate all terminology into European equivalents, talking of Japanese dukes and viscounts, barons and knights. British parallels are particularly alluring—an island kingdom at the edge of a continent, with a monarch ruling by divine right over contending noble houses…But even though the samurai pledged allegiance to a semi-divine emperor, each emperor's real-world power was highly limited. European schoolchildren might learn about the deeds of their great kings and queens, but Japanese schoolbooks often gloss over the emperors in favor of the real rulers—the regents who held power through several reigns, the shōguns who effectively ran the country in the name of their bosses, or the relatively lowly princelings who achieved something concrete while their imperial siblings were kept busy with rituals and ceremonies. It was, in theory, possible that any lord might lose his manor overnight and be ordered to hand over the keys to a successor newly appointed by the government. The real question in Japan, as ever, was who the government actually was: all orders were given in the emperor's name, but true power resided in the ability to gain that particular stamp of approval.

In many ways, this is what the samurai houses were fighting over. It no longer mattered quite so much if they had access to the luxuries of the court—many of them were living very well on their own estates. But now they required greater influence at that same court in order to make sure that everything they had built over generations was not taken away from them because a minister had fallen out of favor, or because the arrival of a pretty concubine had propelled her father into a new ministerial role at court and ousted his predecessor. Whereas the samurai families had once been "servants" of the court, they now increasingly tried to make the court serve them.

There was, at least on paper, no need for the Taira and Minamoto to be at odds with one another. They were, after all, both supposedly loyal to the same emperor. In the early days of their ascension, they were not even clearly divided into Us and Them—multiple branches of both Taira and Minamoto were often pitted against others of their own surname. Inevitably they would clash over allegiances and the nature of their service. The Taira lost their Kantō power base after one of their major lords, Masakado, proclaimed himself to be independent. That in itself might have been enough to plunge Japan into civil war in 940, but the problem was dealt with by his own clan—the Taira pretender was defeated by his own Taira cousins. The scandal cost the Taira their hold on the Kantō plain, but left them eager to prove to the emperor that Masakado was the exception rather than the rule. They were swift to volunteer for piracy suppression operations in the Inland Sea and on the western coast, in which capacity they were even obliged to sail against a Fujiwara sea-lord who had also decided to defy the central authority. Back in Kyōto, the emperor was pleased with their loyal service; his Fujiwara in-laws, not so much. Luckily for them, they could find some military champions of their own among the Minamoto.

The greatest expansion of the Minamoto came under the leader Minamoto Yoshiie (1041–1108), who made a name for himself carrying out dirty work for the capital's prominent Fujiwara family. After he led a campaign to neutralize rebels in the Kantō region, the court found a way to wriggle out of paying him off. Instead of complaining, he reached into his own treasury for the money. This made him popular not only with his own troops, who now trusted him more than their government, but also with many newfound allies, who flocked to associate with him and extended the reach of his already-large holdings.

As the generations passed, the tensions caused by the samurai families became increasingly obvious. Two year's after Yoshiie's death, his son started a revolt in the provinces that was put down by a Taira general. His grandson Tameyoshi almost caused the downfall of the entire clan in 1156, when he backed the wrong side in an imperial power struggle.

Bear with me. We'll slow down for a moment and look at the origins of this one crisis just to get a sense of the complexities and hidden conflicts that would characterize dozens of similar intrigues throughout the period. We won't do this for the next thirty emperors, many of whose situations were no less confusing, but the roots of what became known as the Hōgen Insurrection are a textbook case of the intricacies of court politics—a multisided standoff with half a dozen factions. The conflict dated back to the seventy-fourth emperor, Toba (1103–56), who spent his whole childhood and teens as the ruler in name only, while his "retired" grandfather ran the state from a monastery. At age twenty Toba himself retired, leaving the throne to his own infant son, the seventy-fifth emperor, Sutoku (1119–64).

With up to three imperial predecessors still at large, Sutoku stood no chance at all of making his own decisions; he passed a frustrating, boring twenty years as emperor in name only. He, too, looked forward to the day when he could skip the court with his own entourage, but his father was still very much hands-on. Retired Emperor Toba was still only in his thirties, and had recently become a father again. Favoring the new child's mother (a Fujiwara) over Sutoku's (another Fujiwara), Toba shunted his son off the throne and had the new successor, Konoe (1139–55) crowned as Japan's seventy-sixth emperor.

Stories would be told about the incident for centuries afterwards. Later authors would create an entire supernatural scandal around the events, claiming that Toba had been bewitched and cursed by an evil twin-tailed fox spirit. The spiteful creature had originally come from China, where, in the glamorous form of a famous beauty of ancient times, it had caused the downfall of an ancient king. It had moved on to India, where it had similarly caused havoc among impressionable men. Now it was in Japan, where it adopted the sensual form of Tamamo-no-mae, an impossibly beautiful servant girl at Toba's monastery. Toba, who was at least officially a monk now, engaged her in conversations about philosophy, in which her replies came with citations from ancient scriptures no human girl should have known.

Toba fell ill, and his condition progressively worsened, until a bold fortune-teller said the words no other courtier would utter: that his mistress, with her odd mastery of scripture and her propensity to glow in the dark, was not a Buddhist saint at all, but a malicious demon who intended to kill Toba and supplant him. Tamamo-no-mae supposedly disappeared at this point, leading to a savage cull of foxes in the surrounding countryside until Toba regained his health.

I repeat the story here not for its historical accuracy, which is nonexistent, but for the glimpse it offers of the whispers and petty jealousies of Heian life, with bedroom companions influencing political decisions, and courtiers hiding behind coincidence and innuendo in their fox-shaming campaign against some poor concubine. Tamamo-no-Mae was never seen again, although her angry spirit was said to influence many of the scandals that followed. Even in the afterlife, it seems, there were intrigues and scandals, dead emperors and wronged courtiers who might be persuaded to avenge forgotten insults. It was, some said, the curse of Tamamo-no-mae that brought down Toba's young proxy, Konoe; the young boy was always sickly, and reigned for barely more than a decade, dying at the age of seventeen, before he had the chance to sire an heir of his own.

The year was 1155. Retired Emperor Sutoku hoped to regain the throne, but Retired Emperor Toba still had seniority, and managed to recommend that his own fourteenth son, Sutoku's brother, should be crowned as Japan's seventy-seventh emperor, Go-Shirakawa (1127–92). Sutoku had hence been passed over in the succession three times—forced to abdicate against his will, and then replaced by two of his siblings when he regarded himself as a prime candidate for restoration. There was also a scurrilous rumor, never quite discounted, that Toba hated Sutoku because he wasn't really his son at all, but the secret love-child of Toba's father, sired on Toba's wife in some tawdry incident.

If all that looks confusing, it's only half the story, since these feuding emperors were themselves merely the outward manifestation of another conflict underway over who got to be the emperor's chief minister. In fact, it hardly mattered who the emperor was; the real issue was who his *mother* was, with the various fallings in and out of imperial favor masking internal conflicts within the Fujiwara family, which had supplied most of the brides and concubines, and hence most of the regents.

Nobody dared challenge the decision directly, and the new emperor Go-Shirakawa, a man who had never expected to be emperor and rather seemed taken by surprise by the whole thing, endured a tense first year on the throne, ending in the summer of 1156 with the death of his father Toba. Toba had taken two months to die, on a sickbed attended by hushed whispers and intense conferences, in a mansion guarded by stern samurai.

It was Toba who had held everything together, and whose factions had crushed any resistance. With him gone, Sutoku was the new senior retired emperor, and he was ready to pounce.

Emperor Go-Shirakawa knew trouble was brewing. Three days after his father's death, his officials were ordering samurai to steer clear of the capital. Two days after that, known associates of Retired Emperor Sutoku were directly ordered not to recruit troops. Forty-eight hours later, samurai loyal to the incumbent emperor and samurai loyal to the retired emperor clashed in open combat on the streets of Heian.

It was a landmark moment. The intrigues of the court had erupted into open violence, and had done so not at the border, but within the very capital itself. That, at least, was how things felt to the court at large—the attentive reader will recall that some of the courtiers' own ancestors were not above stabbing their enemies to death in the emperor's presence in ages past—but it seems that many of the contemporary courtiers had come to believe their own hype, and were ill-prepared for violence returning to their doorstep.

The samurai in play amounted to several hundred on each side, but the only prize was Go-Shirakawa himself, who might be persuaded to abdicate if he fell into the hands of his brother's rebels.

There were Fujiwara courtiers and Minamoto samurai on both sides of the conflict. Unfortunately for the pro-Sutoku faction, their nominal leader, Fujiwara Yorinaga, was very much an armchair general whose ideas about warfare were based solely on the idealized, rather ceremonial events described in old stories and songs. His Minamoto advisers, veterans of many an asymmetrical skirmish in the northern wars, suggested that the best thing to do was to start a fire at the emperor's residence, which was sure to lead their target to flee in his palanquin with a small group of bodyguards. They could then overwhelm the guards, seize the palanquin, and thereby obtain control of the only figure who could order the enemy to stand down. The conflict would be over before it started, with minimal loss of life.

Yorinaga was not interested. The whole thing sounded sneaky and underhanded to him, and he very much preferred to imagine things the way they were in the old songs, with a few hundred samurai marching out to a nice area of flat ground, stating their names and lineages, and then taking each other on in single combat until the victor was revealed.

It does not seem to have occurred to Yorinaga that if his own samurai had come up with the idea for such a ruthless, surgical strike, then the enemy, whose samurai hailed from a different branch of the same family, was liable to have a very similar idea. In fact, his enemies had already apprehended one of his men, who had spilled all their plans, leading the incumbent emperor to authorize the seizure and search of Yorinaga's house.

At dawn on the eleventh day of the seventh lunar month, 1156, the emperor led his court in prayers while his loyalists converged on Yorinaga from three directions with several hundred mounted men. Within an hour, there were flames and smoke in the east of the city. The battle was bloody but brief, although its aftermath would stretch on for two generations.

Several of the rebel leaders were killed in the skirmish. The pretender Sutoku was packed away into monastic exile on a remote island, where he lived for another eight years, muttering curses against his enemies, and, it was said, forming a malicious faction in the afterlife with the fiery fox spirit Tamamo-no-mae. In subsequent years, his angry ghost would get the blame for many famines, earthquakes, and misfortunes, becoming one of the great bogeymen of Japanese history.

For centuries, the Kyōto aristocracy had boasted of the civilized nature of their capital. It was a mark of the drastic changes in attitudes and expectations that the uprising ended with a round of beheadings. Courtiers had prided themselves on the peaceful capital for the last three and a half centuries—nobody had been executed in Kyōto since the failed coup of Retired Emperor Heizei in 810. Now, Sutoku's surviving supporters were executed, sometimes in cruel situations in which their own relatives were ordered to carry out the task.

In the most infamous case, the Minamoto loyalist Yoshitomo was ordered to behead his own father. He was unable to carry out such a terrible command, but one of his lieutenants, seeing that a Minamoto would die at the hands of a Taira unless he took action, did the deed himself. Shortly after he had spared his lord from committing patricide, the loyal lieutenant killed himself in contrition.

It was by no means the first reference to suicide in the tales of the samurai, nor even in the events of the Hōgen Insurrection. But it is during this failed rebellion that the chronicles of the samurai first start referring not only to suicide, but to a particular kind of suicide. The cult of the samurai had already begun to take on certain new elements. One was the desire to wear flashy armor, decorated with striking icons or tied with distinctive color strings, in order to make it clear who was winning fame on the field of battle. Samurai helmets, in particular, became notorious for their ostentatious adornments; these have included, among many other things, a giant snail shell, insect's wings, antlers, devil horns, sunbursts, and rabbit ears. The samurai had started to develop a sense of themselves that placed them on a hierarchy of bravery and battle prowess, and that meant it was necessary for their victories to be obvious to all. A side effect of this ease of identification was that it would also be clear who was running away. The distinctive nature of samurai battlefield adornments promoted a gung-ho sense of always charging, never retreating.

There were times when victory was impossible. Samurai might be surrounded with no possible retreat. They might be disarmed. They might find themselves just about to fall into enemy hands, where they might suffer the further shame of being used as hostages or bargaining chips, or tortured for information. Or, like Yoshitomo's lieutenant, they might find themselves in an impossible situation, where they had done the right thing by their lord but could not possibly be expected to go on living after having done so.

Instead, they chose to kill themselves, but not with the throat-slitting or defenestration favored by women in search of a quick death. Instead, they killed themselves in the most painful way imaginable, by slicing open their own abdomen as a mark of their bravery and inner strength—the belly was thought to be the seat of the soul, and hence also a mark of sincerity. Cutting the belly, seppuku (more vulgarly, *hara kiri*) was a one-way trip to agony. There was no cure; only a slow, lingering death. The decision to slice open one's abdomen was also a get-out clause for one's underlings—they would not dare lift a finger against their master, but would be justified, once he had voluntarily wounded himself in such a fashion, in ending his suffering by beheading him.

Over the years, seppuku would take on new rituals. Samurai would wear a white kimono, symbolising death and purity. They would write a death poem, ensuring that parting words, criticisms, or curses were encapsulated in repeatable form. The nature of the wound would become deliberately cruel, with "tradition" demanding four cuts through the abdominal muscles—*shi*, meaning four, being a homonym for death, but also demanding incredible determination and strength of purpose in the self-harming samurai. Seppuku started as a battlefield compromise—a last resort by besieged men in burning castles, determined not to surrender to enemies who would torture and humiliate them. But once it became enshrined in tradition, it became the default means of repentance, and even criticism. It faded out after the era of the samurai, but still occasionally returns to haunt the country.

If this seems shocking to the modern reader, we should bear in mind that religious belief played an important part. Buddhism had taken hold, but with a certain nihilistic angle. The concept that "all life is suffering" had been embraced by the Japanese with a melancholy sense of poetry, as well as a certain sense that the end of the world was nigh. Certain Buddhist scriptures predicted the rise, peak, and subsequent fall of the Buddha's teachings: five hundred years of struggle for success, a thousand years of worship and achievement, and then five centuries of worsening conditions as things fell apart. It was, hence, widely believed among the medieval Japanese that they were living in the "Latter Days of the Law" (*mappō*). Any natural disasters, reversals of fortune, or atrocities could be written off as further evidence that the teachings of Buddha were under attack, and that any ends available would justify the means of sustaining them.

One particular Buddhist sect, the Essence of the Pure Land (Jōdo Shinshū) gained ground in medieval Japan. Pure Land Buddhism regarded the country's troubles as yet another example of the Latter

Days of the Law, in which it was almost impossible for anybody to engage in correct Buddhist devotion. In a sense, Pure Land Buddhists all but gave up trying, instead paying a new form of devotion to Buddha that recognized that things were terrible—people were trapped in cycles of toxic karma, eating meat, drinking booze, fornicating, and otherwise coping with the onrushing end of the world—but that it was still possible to at least make it obvious to Buddha that you bore him in mind. You would do this by chanting "*Namu Amida Butsu*" (I take refuge in Amida Buddha) as often as possible, as a little spell to hold back the worst of the world. Most importantly, Pure Land Buddhism was a sect that offered the chance of rebirth in a Buddhist paradise to absolutely everybody. It was not restricted to monks or the rich who could afford costly demonstrations of devotion; literally anyone could find refuge in the Pure Land—even warriors.

Buddhism was actually abundantly clear about killing people being a sin. "A disciple of the Buddha," said the fifth-century *Sutra of Brahma's Net*, "should not possess swords, spears, bows, arrows, pikes, axes, or any other fighting devices. Even if one's father or mother were slain, one should not retaliate."

It was, however, the Zen flavor of Buddhism, originating in the Shaolin Temple in China, which achieved prominence among the samurai. Yes, killing people would bring about bad karma, but what about standing up for what was right, if that involved breaking a few heads? What about killing an assassin hell-bent on killing one's lord? In such cases, presumably we would not be talking so much about bad karma, but about the least-worst.

Zen found plenty of adherents in Japan's warrior class, in part because of some of its teachers' habit of cutting through knotty issues of philosophy with seemingly dismissive put-downs. In fact, there was substantially more to it than that, but the nature of certain Zen parables and questions for meditation did lend itself well to a breed of anti-intellectualism. The Chinese Zen master Linji, for example, once famously said, "If you see the Buddha on the road, kill him." He meant that the earnest Zen scholar should question all presumptions, and never lean on credentials or blind faith. But in the hands of the samurai, this became a recipe for a nihilistic battlefield philosophy.

It is often necessary to read between the lines in comments from the history books about "Buddhist monks" in medieval Japan. We already know, for example, that certain retired emperors were shaving their heads and ruling "from the cloisters," even though their lives (and loves) continued in much the same way as they did in lay life. We also know that wily landowners were evading their tax responsibilities by "donating" their lands to Buddhist monasteries. With such deceptions at all levels of Japanese religious life, it should come as no surprise that there was an entire class of Buddhist "monks" who were little more than shaven-headed militia employed as military muscle to deal with their institution's widening secular responsibilities. Even legitimate temples got in on the act, employing mercenaries to protect them from their newly proactive rivals.

Despite proscriptions against violence in other areas of Buddhism, and indeed within Zen itself, the interpreters of Zen among the samurai came to regard it as a warrior's creed. Meanwhile, monasteries of doubtful provenance—some established as tax refuges—were prepared to offer prayers for the soul of a samurai who killed in the name of justice. Although not quite like the selling of indulgences in a European sense, it did give rise to a warrior class whose members felt that their religion *entitled* them to fight.

It was during the time of the wars of the Taira and Minamoto that Zen Buddhism first began to take hold in Japan, brought back to Japan, like so many other things, by monks who had studied in China. Zen was an offshoot of Buddhism that emphasized self-reliance. As brought to China by the monk Bodhidharma, Zen was a teaching "outside the scriptures"; sometimes this was interpreted as an extremely brawny, no-nonsense dismissal of much scripture and philosophy in favor of sparks of insight and moments of direct action.

Zen Buddhism hence threw away many of the accretions of Buddhist religions in favor of the cultivation of enlightenment (*satori*)—a perpetual moment of clarity. The version brought to Japan by the monk Eisai (1145–1215) was keen on short, punchy aphorisms designed to function as tools for thinking. Known in Japanese as *kōan*, these parables have come to characterize much Zen thought, as acolytes meditate on such questions as "What is the sound of one hand clapping?"; "What is the face you had before you were born?"; and that old favorite from Tang-dynasty China, "If you see the Buddha on the road, kill him."

Later sects postdating the Taira-Minamoto war would introduce other ideas, such as *zazen*, "sitting meditation," in which the aspirant emptied his mind of all thought except for a single mantra or goal. This was particularly appealing to the samurai, who loved the idea that there was no difference between life and death—there was only the singleminded pursuit of one's mission.

Buddhism, particularly Zen Buddhism, soon turned in the hands of the samurai into an elaborate game of death in which killers accepted the risk of bad karma balanced against the accrual of merits for loyal service and just actions. As Buddhism splintered and evolved in Japan, there were plenty of sects that could offer warriors the chance to buy off bad deeds with donations and penances, and priests who spoke of the wheel of reincarnation. The samurai believed that the relationship between a lord and vassal was, if not immortal, then sure to last for at least three lifetimes. Die well in this life, and you were assured of respawning at a higher social station, under better conditions, perhaps even having been dealt a better hand. Die badly or with dishonor and you might not return as a samurai at all, but as a peasant, or a woman or an animal. In the multiple reversals of fortune and wars over nothing that would come to characterize medieval Japan, a "good death" became one of the primary aims of a samurai life.

And the result? As implied by the opening lines of *The Tale of the Heike*, you might say that it was all for nothing. Go-Shirakawa, the reigning emperor in whose name so many fought and died, sat on the throne for barely two years before deciding that he, too, would abdicate in favor of his own teenage son, the seventy-eighth emperor, Nijō (1143–65).

Go-Shirakawa would remain the main power broker for the next thirty years, through the troubled reigns of five successors. He gained such a reputation among historians for cunning plans and dastardly schemes that he is still referred to as the "Grand Crow-Demon" (Dai Tengu) or even the "Shadow Lord" (Anshu). Meanwhile, there were mixed feelings among his supporters in the skirmish. Taira no Kiyomori (1118–81), the scheming, moustachioed courtier who brokered the power behind the scenes, gained an impressive promotion and a nearby coastal fief to rule over. Minamoto no Yoshitomo, however, who had done the actual fighting in a conflict that had cost him the deaths of his own relatives—sometimes at his own hands—received much less. As far as the court was concerned, he was a loyal servant being granted some great concessions of noble rank and title. Yoshitomo felt that Kiyomori was getting the glory for his own hard work, and that once the fighting was done, the courtiers had suddenly remembered again how much they despised the samurai.

The Fujiwara, meanwhile, were up to their usual tricks, making sure that the new emperor had a Fujiwara bride. The one they found had previously been the child-bride of her new husband's uncle, the sickly teenage emperor Konoe. Kiyomori made sure one of his own daughters was married to the new emperor's chief minister, and, it seems, dismissed Yoshitomo's complaints that he was not getting what he deserved.

Yoshitomo took action in January 1159, waiting until Kiyomori and his cronies were on a pilgrimage. His men snatched both Emperor Nijō and his father Go-Shirakawa, who were then obliged to sack many of their ministers and replace them with appointees favorable to the Minamoto clan.

This was by no means the first time such a power grab had occurred, but the outcome was different. It used to be that whoever had lost the upper hand would run for the provinces, to lean on their power base there. But Kiyomori had observed the fate of such former figures: absent from the capital, they had been branded by the captive administration as "rebels," which led all loyal samurai to take arms against them. Kiyomori had seen several such examples in recent memory, and was determined not to be another one. Accordingly, instead of running for the coast of the Inland Sea, he rode straight back to Kyōto, daring his enemies to make their move.

Kiyomori and his Taira samurai were unable to act for as long as commands were issued in the name of the emperor—the confidence of the samurai had yet to achieve that arrogant tipping point whereby they acted out of regard for what the true emperor's orders might be. Instead, the capital endured a tense ten-day standoff of messengers and conferences, with a substantial number of samurai at battle readiness. Four years earlier, the troops fielded had numbered in the hundreds; tellingly, there were now thousands ready to strike.

The impasse was broken through subterfuge. Two aristocrats switched sides and dolled up the teenage emperor Nijō in makeup and women's clothes, sneaking him out of his palace in disguise and whisking him away to Kiyomori's compound in the middle of the chaos caused by a convenient fire at the palace. Go-Shirakawa was even bolder, sneaking from the palace by simply dressing in commoner's clothes and riding out the gate.

Now the power shifted once more. Emperor Nijō issued a new proclamation naming Kiyomori's residence as the "new palace"—effectively declaring a state of emergency that implied anyone in the original palace was an imposter or rebel. A force of some 3,000 Taira cavalry, with at least as many foot soldiers in support, was already marching on the former imperial palace, leading to a running battle in the streets of Kyōto. Depending on whom one believed, either the Taira were chasing the Minamoto across town, or the Minamoto successfully pushed the Taira back to Kiyomori's mansion. Either way, Yoshitomo's only chance of survival was to snatch back his imperial bargaining chips before they could officially declare him to be an enemy of the state.

But it was too late. Yoshitomo had been outmaneuvered, and now it was his turn to flee, splitting up and leading a dwindling band of faithful samurai in a fighting retreat amid a driving midwinter snowstorm. Few of them lasted more than a few days, with even their allies turning against them. Yoshitomo himself was murdered while bathing at a house that he believed to have been run by friends.

Yoshitomo's newest mistress, the twenty-year-old Tokiwa, took a different route with her three young sons, leading two by the hand with the third, a new-born baby, nestled against her chest beneath her robe. She was soon apprehended and brought before Kiyomori, who informed her that the menfolk of the Minamoto were being purged from the Earth. He did, however, have an offer for her that she could not refuse. Her three sons would be spared if she sent them away to a monastery...and agreed to become Kiyomori's concubine.

The Taira were appalled that Kiyomori could even consider such an offer. His own stepmother warned him that Yoshitomo's children were sure to grow up with a desire to avenge the fall of their clan. But Kiyomori was arrogant in victory, utterly convinced that he had stripped the Minamoto of all their power. Raping their leader's woman would be the final insult.

Tokiwa would live another three decades, although Kiyomori soon tired of her; she ended her days married to a Fujiwara courtier. Kiyomori, meanwhile, achieved all his desires, and was the first samurai to be made chief minister in 1160. Not long afterward, his sister-in-law attracted the eye of Go-Shirakawa, fell pregnant, and persuaded the retired emperor that the child of their union should be the next infant sovereign requiring a regent. The boy was crowned as Emperor Takakura in 1168, and would eventually marry Kiyomori's daughter. Kiyomori then "retired" from his official posts, enjoying the glory but rejecting the responsibilities that might actually be required to carry out those roles. What could possibly go wrong?

In fact, things had already started to go wrong, on a dark, snowy night when Emperor Takakura's regent, Fujiwara Motofusa, found his retinue's path blocked by a bunch of teenage samurai. The regent's men demanded that they move, but the samurai, celebrating after a day's hawking and hunting, told them to shove it. The regent's men dragged them from their horses, and the lead teenager—another of Kiyomori's grandsons—went home and whined to his dad about it.

His father, wise to court etiquette, immediately apologized to the regent, but Kiyomori had other ideas. He rounded up sixty country samurai with allegiance directly to him, and ordered them to avenge the "insult" to his grandson. They lay in wait for the regent's entourage, ambushed their target on the road, wrecked the carriage, and cut off the hair of the captured guardsmen. The humiliated regent arrived at the palace in a cart dragged by one of his retainers, the oxen having been cut loose.

In the aftermath, the grandson was packed off to the provinces, and the perpetrators of his vengeful drive-by were dismissed. But the incident had made Kiyomori ample enemies among the Fujiwara. The fateful nuptials of Emperor Takakura and Kiyomori's fifteen-year-old daughter were only a few days later; although they would eventually produce the Emperor Antoku in 1178, they occurred amid an atmosphere of resentment.

The child-emperor Antoku was the culmination of all Kiyomori's scheming, and also the seed of his downfall. From being stripped of imperial status, the Taira were just about to supply Japan's next ruler. In bundling Antoku onto the throne, Kiyomori made a permanent enemy out of Retired Emperor Go-Shirakawa, who was far too wily a politician to say anything in public. Instead, Go-Shirakawa got his own son, Prince Mochihito, to proclaim that Antoku was a usurper and that *he*, Mochihito, was the rightful heir, and to call on any samurai with a sense of justice to come to his aid.

In the beginning, he had few supporters. In fact, he spent the remainder of his short life on the run, protected by a small group of loyal guardsmen and "warrior monks" (some of whom were former Minamoto who had taken holy orders to avoid persecution in pro-Taira times), pursued out of Kyōto by samurai loyal to the Taira. He made it as far as the bridge at Uji, falling off his horse six times.

His men pulled up the planks on the bridge to delay their pursuers, and commandeered the nearby Phoenix Hall temple to give the pretender a rest.

It was, however, a fatal delay. The pursuing enemy samurai plunged straight into the rushing waters of the river—200 men and horses were swept away by the current, but plenty made it to the opposite bank, their fellow samurai providing cover with a hail of arrows from the far side. One warrior, the fighting monk Jōmyō, did not bother with the river, but made an acrobatic barefoot assault across the scaffolding of the bridge. *The Tale of the Heike* reports him reaching the other side ready for action, firing off all twenty-four arrows from his personal supply (killing twelve men and wounding eleven—even a breathless story allowing for one miss). He then grabbed his spear, killing another five men before it broke. Drawing his sword, he dispatched another eight opponents before snapping his blade on the helmet of another, and dropping it into the river. Then he drew his dagger—at which point *The Tale of the Heike* appears to lose count. It does, however, return to Jōmyō when all the fighting is done, counting sixty-three arrow dents in his armor, five of which have pierced the leather, although none of them seriously.

The fighting spread to the Phoenix Hall, with many of the Minamoto loyalists choosing to make a last stand, dooming themselves in order to allow Prince Mochihito to escape. *The Tale of the Heike* offers a catalogue of last stands and acts of seppuku, although at least one samurai lived to fight another day. The warrior monk Tayū Genkaku somehow fought his way back to the bridge, jumped into the river, and hit bottom in his heavy armor before clambering out on the Kyōto side, hurling insults at his enemies, and commencing the long, damp trudge back to the capital.

But all the heroism amounted to nothing. The prince's foster brother, trembling amid the duckweed in a roadside ditch, saw a troop of Taira samurai heading home, bearing the headless body of Prince Mochihito on a window shutter. The prince's head, along with the heads of some 500 of his allies, was taken to Kiyomori's mansion by the evening, where victory celebrations soon soured, as nobody could be found to make a positive identification.

Since he had been sequestered for years in a remote palace, living largely in the company of an entourage who were now dead, nobody knew what Prince Mochihito actually looked like. Tense hours passed while the Taira scoured the capital for someone who could identify him, eventually dragging in the mother of one of his children, whose distraught reaction was all that Kiyomori really needed to see.

And there things really ought to have ended, with the pretender dead—except the momentum of Mochihito's rebellion kept on without him. Despite his protestations that Mochihito was dead, Kiyomori still had to contend with the news of Minamoto armies assembling to the east. Those three surviving Minamoto boys were now all grown up, married into Kantō plainsman aristocracy, and ready for revenge. Their cousin, too, a man called Yoshinaka, had been adopted into the Kiso clan, and hence had not shown up as a Minamoto clansmen when the purges were all the rage. Now he, too, rediscovered his Minamoto roots and came after Kiyomori.

Kiyomori did not live to see the endgame he had set in motion. Bedridden and in his sixties, he died in 1181 as Minamoto forces advanced on the capital; his grandson, the Emperor Antoku, was moved for safety's sake to the Taira heartland on the coast of the Inland Sea.

The Minamoto flooded into the capital, where they were welcomed by the scheming retired emperor Go-Shirakawa. Although Antoku was still on the run with the sacred imperial regalia—the mirror, the sword and the jewel—the Minamoto wasted no time in proclaiming that he had abdicated, and that his half-brother, Go-Toba (1180–1239), the son of a Fujiwara mother, was the new emperor. In the battles that followed, the Minamoto would hound the Taira across the Inland Sea until their final showdown at sea at Dannoura in 1185.

Realizing that all was lost, the last of the Taira began jumping into the sea, their armor dragging them straight to the bottom. Kiyomori's widow, Tokiko, turned to her grandson, the six-year-old Emperor Antoku, and told him to say prayers to the east, toward the Shintō shrine at Ise, and west toward the homeland of Buddha.

"Beneath the waves lies our capital," she said. Then, hugging Antoku close to her along with the ancient sword Kusanagi, she hurled herself into the sea.

The conflict between the Taira and the Minamoto was finally resolved, with the Taira almost entirely wiped out and excluded from the capital. Scattered survivors, including Antoku's mother, who was pulled by her hair from the water by sailors using a rake, would live on as impoverished local fishermen or religious devotees. The sacred mirror and jewel were, at least officially, retrieved by divers, although the sword Kusanagi was never found—Japanese authorities are deliberately vague about it; although a sword still forms part of the imperial regalia of Japan, the one carried most recently during the coronation of Emperor Heisei in 1989 is believed to be a replica.

The Minamoto were victorious…but—as with every other event in *The Tale of the Heike*, as foreshadowed by its opening lines—it was all for nothing. In the aftermath, the Minamoto turned on each other, as the eldest surviving son of Yoshitomo, Yoritomo, unleashed his simmering resentment against his half-brother Yoshitsune, who had been instrumental in many of the Minamoto victories of the war with the Taira. Yoritomo largely stroked his chin and looked at maps in his distant headquarters at Kamakura, a fort chosen for strategic reasons—it was approached by seven roads, every one of them traversing steep, defensible mountain passes. But it was Yoshitsune who was on the front line—often against the wishes of his fellow Minamoto generals, but winning forever the support of his men.

Yoshitsune is another of the iconic figures of Japanese history whose life story has lent itself well to legend. From his first appearance in Japanese stories (and indeed, in this book), tucked into his mother's robe as she flees in a snowstorm, to his legendary tutelage at the feet of crow demons in the hills outside Kyōto, he has gained an enduring presence in Japanese plays, books, and movies. It is Yoshitsune, so the legend goes, who bested the warrior-monk Benkei on Kyōto's Gojō Bridge; who seduced a nobleman's daughter so he could read her father's copy of an ancient Chinese military manual; who led a foolhardy cavalry charge down a steep cliff, surprising the enemy by hitting them from behind their camp at Ichinotani. It was Yoshitsune who lit fires on the landward side of the Taira base, frightening his enemies into taking to their ships and thereby setting up the ultimate showdown at Dannoura.

Yoritomo hated that his half-brother was getting all the credit. He seemed to find fault in every one of Yoshitsune's victories, criticizing him for minor details like escaped prisoners, rather than praising him for his incredibly effective strategies. Yoshitsune even managed to charm Go-Shirakawa, the retired emperor, although Yoritomo regarded that as yet another example of scheming. On the apparent belief that his half-brother was planning to betray him, Yoritomo ordered his arrest, ending the war with a tragic coda in which the greatest Minamoto general became a fugitive in the north, fleeing his own family.

Yoshitsune the loyal lieutenant was eventually hunted down and killed, his henchmen and son murdered, all so Yoritomo could feel secure. "Sympathy for the lieutenant" (*hōgan biiki*) remains a popular term in Japanese for championing the underdog. Yoritomo was left with a large holding of his own lands along with the lands of Minamoto vassals and over 500 estates taken from the defeated Taira. It made him a substantial rival for the imperial court itself, which for its own part now lacked any military allies on which it could call for assistance.

With the Minamoto now dominating the court, and with the death of the manipulative retired emperor Go-Shirakawa in 1192, his grandson the child-emperor Go-Toba was persuaded to recognize the possibility of another war breaking out against unknown enemies of the state, and appointed Yoritomo as Shōgun. Despite the continued use of the archaic title for "suppressing barbarians," Yoritomo was more of a government-appointed autocrat, running Japan in the emperor's name under a state of martial law. The term he used, which would be used by his successors for the next seven centuries, was intended to imply that this situation was merely a temporary fix until the trouble had died down: the authorities came to be known as the *bakufu*, or "tent government," taking their name from the *baku* windbreaker behind which samurai generals would hide from enemy archers while plotting their next move.

You would be forgiven for thinking that it was a happy ending for the Minamoto, but they had taken heavy losses in the war, not helped at all by Yoritomo's paranoid postwar purges. Ruling Japan from Kamakura, Yoritomo became the first leader of the Kamakura shōgunate, which would technically run Japan in the emperor's name for the next 200 years—except much of his military success had been funded by his father-in-law, Tokimasa, leader of Kamakura's Hōjō clan. After Yoritomo's death in 1199, his sons were swiftly elbowed aside in favor of "regents" (*shikken*) from the Hōjō clan. It was these regents who held the true power of the Kamakura shōgunate thereafter, while the Minamoto disappeared in a bout of stabbings and assassinations—Yoritomo's son, the shōgun Sanetomo, was assassinated by his own nephew, who was then executed for murder, bringing the line to an end while the ghosts of the Taira laughed on the bottom of the sea.

Exactly what kind of unrest was the Kamakura shōgunate expecting? The biggest problems they might expect to encounter often seemed to come from the imperial family itself, whose members did not take kindly to being the puppets of their leading general. Crowned during the conflict as a three-year-old child by the Minamoto in 1183, Japan's eighty-second emperor, Go-Toba, was forced to abdicate in 1198, but remained inconveniently alive for the next forty-one years, watching from the sidelines as his sons were pushed onto the throne and then off again in the service of the shōgunate's power games.

In 1221, Go-Toba made his move. Without waiting for the shōgunate to recommend its own candidate, he put his two-year-old grandson on the throne. He then invited all the important samurai in the vicinity of Kyōto to a celebration.

It was a brilliant strategic move. Those who accepted his invitation were clearly willing to support him in any further resistance to the shōgun. One prominent lord did not show up, and soon died under suspicious circumstances—by implying even for a moment that he disapproved of Go-Toba's actions, he had signed his own death warrant. The others were ready to hear Go-Toba's new proclamation in the style of his ill-fated ancestors: that anyone who was truly loyal to the emperor and the court should rise up against the Kamakura usurpers. The Hōjō clansmen were officially declared outlaws, and disaffected samurai in the Kyōto region began to flock to Go-Toba's banner.

Well, maybe not "flock." Go-Toba attracted a few followers, but the bulk of Japan's samurai were persuaded to support the so-called outlaws. Hōjō Masako, Yoritomo's widow, rallied the troops by reminding them of the improvements they had enjoyed under the *bakufu*. She proclaimed that this was a crucial turning point in history, where the samurai could choose either to remain masters of their own destiny, or to return to the days when they were mere patsies for the court. She must have struck a strange figure addressing the samurai—her head was shaved, as was the custom for widows, leading to her nickname among the samurai: *ama-shōgun*, the Nun Shōgun.

A Kamakura army marched on Kyōto, scoring a string of successes against the lesser numbers of Go-Toba's followers. Go-Toba went to the fighting monks on nearby Mount Hiei, pleading for them to come to his aid, but they refused, unwilling to take on the shōgunal forces. The imperial forces made their last stand at the bridge over the river at Uji before giving up and fleeing. Kamakura forces occupied Kyōto, and Go-Toba and his "retired" sons were exiled to remote islands. The grandson became known as the "Dethroned Emperor," having ruled for barely two months, the shortest reign in Japanese history; he was not even recognized as an emperor at all until the nineteenth century.

The defeat of Go-Toba's attempted restoration played into the shōgunate's hands, allowing for the confiscation of some 3,000 estates that could be used to buy favor with the samurai faithful. It secured the shōgunate two generations of relatively stable rule until the 1270s, when the conquest of China by the Mongols led to the threat of an invasion by Kublai Khan.

CHAPTER 5

ASHES OF VICTORY: THE WARRING STATES

Lady Nijō's diary, *The Unasked-for Tale (Towazugatari)* begins on New Year's Day 1271, when the retired emperor Go-Fukakusa drew her father aside for a mumbled conversation. Not yet fourteen years old, Nijō did not comprehend its tone, or the meaning of Go-Fukakusa's words when he said that he now desired "that which I have set my heart on for so long."

Nor did Nijō seem to truly appreciate the signs in her correspondence over the next few days—a mysterious gift of tissue paper and elaborate clothing, accompanied by a poem that spoke lasciviously of wanting "to lay my sleeves on yours."

Nijō had two unknown suitors, and if she thought one of them was the thirty-year-old Go-Fukakusa, who had quit the throne fifteen years earlier, she did not let on. Her memoir, written decades after the events described, insists that she was innocent, unheeding of her family's giggles and nudges, and perplexed at her father's excited preparations for an imperial visit at their mansion.

"Remember," her father said to her, "a court lady is always gentle and obedient."

It seemed to the teenage Nijō to be a statement of the blindingly obvious.

Her chambers had been seeded with particularly heady incense, and she drifted off to sleep that evening.

When she woke up, Go-Fukakusa was lying next to her. She got up to run away, but he held her down and creepily announced that he had been waiting for this moment since she was born. He said more that night, but the words flew far over Nijō's head. All she could recount in her diary was that she was "too upset" to follow his meaning, and became increasingly tearful.

Eventually, somewhat irritated at her lack of understanding, Go-Fukakusa got up and left, muttering that she had not "returned his love" and that she was "cold-hearted." Their friendship, he scowled, had proved useless after all, but he entreated her to act normally, so that people would not talk.

A passive-aggressive love poem arrived shortly afterwards, commenting that he could still smell her scent. When she didn't respond by noon, a second poem arrived by messenger, more conciliatory in tone, threatening to die in sorrow if she ignored him.

Nijō wrote back with surprising, uncanny self-assurance, with a poem of her own that blamed Go-Fukakusa specifically for her unease. Then she went back to her mat to sleep, still deeply troubled by the previous evening's events.

Go-Fukakusa returned to her father's mansion that night.

She heard him sliding back the door to her room, and chirpily addressing her prone form with a half-hearted query about her health.

Nijō did not dare to move. She lay there, paralyzed with fear, while Go-Fukakusa lay down beside her, pressing against her, telling her of the depth of his feelings.

When she still did not reply, he raped her.

"This night," she wrote dispassionately many years later, "his behavior was really quite atrocious, and soon my thin robe was ripped at the seams. He did just as he pleased with me."

Lady Nijō's diary is a captivating document. It is disingenuous to impose our own modern values on the fate of a young girl 750 years ago, but her measured account of experiencing the former emperor's attentions offers a frank glimpse of court life during the

Kamakura period. She struggles to enunciate feelings of astounding modern resonance—victim-blaming, gaslighting, Stockholm syndrome, and ultimately codependency. Buried between the lines of her diary is a subtle but horrifying implication—that Go-Fukakusa might have been the secret lover of her late mother, and that had been waiting for thirteen years for the chance to have sex with his own daughter.

"Not by my own will," she seethed, "was my girdle undone." She wrote this in a poem addressed to the retired emperor himself, a truly foolhardy declaration of anger. Her relatives tutted among themselves, and regarded her behavior as damagingly self-regarding and ungrateful.

Nijō remained a prisoner of her situation. Pregnant with Go-Fukakusa's child, she began an affair with a childhood friend. Later on, she conceived a second child with the friend in secret, which would scandalize her fellow courtiers. Her relationship with Go-Fukakusa blew hot and cold, as he occasionally took interest in her life, and offered sympathies on the death of her father, but more often developed new obsessions. Their child died in infancy, which caused both of them to seek a little distance. Sometimes Go-Fukakusa even roped her in to his latest seductions, using her as a go-between with whatever hapless courtier he was planning on mounting next.

Lady Nijō's diaries never mention the Mongol invaders on faraway Kyūshū. Still only seventeen years old at the time of the first Mongol attack, she was more worried about keeping her second pregnancy secret from Go-Fukakusa, setting up an elaborate scheme whereby she lied about the time of her child's conception, gave her newborn daughter up for adoption, and then claimed to Go-Fukakusa that the child had been his, but was dead. At the time that samurai were fighting for their lives and leading suicide squads into the midst of the storm-tossed enemy fleet, she wrote of the lining of her dress and the sight of the trees on a nearby hill. She watched Go-Fukakusa copying out the *Lotus Sutra*, using his own blood for ink, but this was not some elaborate ritual to stave off enemy attack—it was a penance designed to ease the imperial succession.

Lady Nijō even records a meeting with her grandfather, the minister of war, who was surely spending his every waking hour fretting over the country's apocalyptic defense. But the subject of her meeting was a request for some new robes.

This is where we came in, with the two great Mongol-Chinese-Korean fleets attempting an invasion of Japan, turned back by the brave resistance of the samurai, who were for once fighting a foreign enemy instead of each other. But the resistance to the Mongols, although successful, ended with a vast expenditure of resources and no real means of rewarding the participants with booty or confiscated lands.

One of the few groups that did benefit from the Mongol attacks was a new Buddhist sect led by a cantankerous fisherman's son called Nichiren (1222–82). Nichiren had become disenchanted with Pure Land Buddhism, although he agreed with its assertion that humanity lived in the Latter Days of the Law, and that the best that the faithful could hope for was some fragmentary, partial appreciation of Buddhist belief. He also lifted from the Tendai sect the idea that the *Lotus Sutra* was the most crucial distillation of the teachings of Buddha. He focused on the *Lotus Sutra*, and encouraged his followers, Pure Land–style, to constantly repeat the phrase, "I take refuge in the Supreme Law of the Lotus" (*Namu myōhō renge kyō*).

Nichiren's power base was in the Kamakura area, and many of his early converts were from the samurai class. Perhaps they warmed to his belligerent nature—Nichiren saw himself as a reincarnation of a demigod of action, and was something of a blood-and-thunder preacher, ever ready to denounce other Buddhist sects as purveyors of false religion. "In the beginning of the Latter Days of the Law," he wrote, "slanderous priests will fill the entire world, so that all heavenly gods will be enraged and comets will appear in the sky and the earth will shake like the movement of huge waves."

Nichiren was arrested on several occasions and exiled twice. He was even slated for execution, only for his would-be killers to be spooked by what seems likely to have been a passing meteor in the dawning sky shortly after he had prayed for deliverance at a shrine to the war god Hachiman.

Japan, he predicted, would face even worse troubles unless it adopted his version of Buddhism as the one true faith. Nichiren foretold that unless the Shōgun beheaded his religious rivals, Japan would fall prey to foreign invaders.

> Nichiren is the pillar and beam of Japan. Doing away with me is toppling the pillar of Japan! Immediately you will all face the "calamity of revolt within one's own domain," or strife among yourselves, and also the "calamity of invasion from foreign lands." Not only will the people of our nation be put to death by foreign invaders, but many of them will be taken prisoner.

For this, some were ready to claim that he had predicted the Mongol armada, although he was really referring was two of the seven archetypal disasters mentioned in the ancient *Medicine Master Sutra*, a portentous document that also spoke of pestilence, storms and droughts.

Technically speaking, if Nichiren had prophesied anything, he had said that the Mongols would *win*. In the years that followed, his rather vague pronouncement would become garbled, until even his enemies in Japan seemed to believe that he had somehow foreseen the destruction of the Mongol fleet. The tale grew with the telling, and many Buddhist temples came to believe in the prophecy of the Mongol invasion, as well as the idea that the incursion had been repelled not only by the military resistance of the fighters on the beaches in Kyūshū, but also by the prayers of the country's Buddhists. It was not merely a wind that had smashed apart the Mongol armadas: it was a Divine Wind, a Kamikaze, demonstrating that Japan was the privileged "land of the gods." This phrase, in fact, first achieved popular currency during the Kamakura period (1185–1333), where it began a genealogy of the emperors that was aimed at sorting out the succession issues which would characterize the end of the era.

Although the Mongol invasions would create ultimately fatal instabilities, and there were several uprisings requiring military action, the Kamakura period nevertheless saw new flourishing in the arts. Not that the Kyōto courtiers thought so—an older but no less forthright Lady Nijō, now a pilgrim struggling to overcome depression, found Kamakura to be laughably backward, built with no thought given to *feng shui* principles and populated by hicks who had no clue about the correct etiquette or garb for visiting a shrine.

"I found this to be an altogether unattractive sight," she sniffs. Her disdain arguably tells us less about the backwardness of Kamakura, which had evolved from a military camp, and more about the Kyōto elite's continued belief in their own superior status. While Lady Nijō made arch comments about the awful manners and lack of class of the Kamakura people, those same former soldiers were becoming patrons of new and influential arts.

It was, for example, during the Kamakura period that carpenters, metalworkers, and masons who had previously been devoted to the fulfillment of military orders were able to rededicate themselves to sculpture. They found ample work to keep themselves busy, not merely because of the number of temples destroyed in the war, but also because so many of the victorious Minamoto wanted to alleviate their karma by sponsoring religious enterprises. Many of Japan's greatest "old" examples of Buddhist temple statuary date from this period, including the 13.35 meter (33 feet) Great Buddha at Kamakura, which was built in the grounds of a Pure Land temple and has attracted admirers ever since—not the least Rudyard Kipling, who buried an ode to it in the chapter openings of his novel *Kim*:

> And whoso will, from Pride released;
> Contemning neither creed nor priest,

May feel the Soul of all the East
About him at Kamakura.

Lady Nijō does not appear to have been so impressed with the Great Buddha at Kamakura, not bothering to say anything about it on her trip. The only statue she writes about at length is that of Go-Fukakusa, enshrined in a Buddhist temple after his death, where she wept profusely during a ceremony in his honor.

Noticing her visible distress, a high-ranking priest asked her who she was, but she declined to reveal her past as an imperial concubine.

"My father has just died," she lied—or did she?

Only a couple of pages later, her diary stops abruptly, with her self-effacing comment, "I cannot aspire to having left to posterity anything worth reading." Then she is silent, although a scribe's note from several centuries later has been appended to the manuscript, reading: "The rest seems to have been cut away with a sword."

The Kamakura period also saw a creative peak in sword making. Japanese swords had often been appreciated as fine artifacts, but a century of actual warfare had honed requirements to extreme levels. The contact with the Mongols, in particular, had confronted swordsmiths with the fact that many samurai had previously fought largely with arrows rather than swords. Mongol armor was thicker and harder, and was met by the swordsmiths by a new trend in thinner blades with a triangular cross-section, which might be more likely to punch through tougher armor.

It was not merely a case of evolving technology. The Kamakura smiths also benefited from an aristocracy that valued weapons but no longer required them to be churned out in quite such high quantities. For a century before (and, as it would turn out, for a century afterwards) battlefield conditions required swords that were made efficiently and quickly, in anticipation of high turnover, breakages, and losses. Now the swordsmiths could afford to take it easy, to experiment with new ideas, and to take money from their patrons, who were no longer troubled warriors but relatively wealthy men of leisure commissioning new family heirlooms or impressive curios.

In the Kamakura period we see refinements to the curved blade of earlier wars; the edge was tempered, and several variant hardnesses of steel were used, folded hundreds of times. The weapon could be honed to razor sharpness while remaining flexible enough to take some punishment. Blades were tested by their ability to cut through something with the consistency and resistance of a human body; this would sometimes involve testing on them corpses or even live human subjects, with convicted criminals meeting unpleasant fates in the service of science. It was not unusual for a sword cut a man's body from shoulder to navel in a single strike. The best were certified for cutting through several bodies at once.

Despite their demonstrable practicality, many such swords were unlikely to see real action, and instead were cherished as family heirlooms. They hence gained an entire subculture of fittings and trappings, including ornate scabbards, highly decorative hand-guards (*tsuba*), and exotic materials binding the hilts.

The good times, however, did not last for long. The Hōjō clan juggled as many of their problems as they could after the damaging costs of the Mongol defense with a series of bodged financial decisions. Although their Taira enemies were long gone, they still had to deal with the enmity of the imperial court, which had never forgiven them for the suppression and exiles of the earlier restorationists. The imperial family played a long game, waiting a whole century for another try, before the ninety-sixth emperor, Go-Daigo (1288–1339) made his move in 1331.

Emperor Go-Daigo made no secret of his dislike of the Kamakura shōgunate, and plotted to seize power back from them, effectively restoring *himself.* He was, however, betrayed by one of his Fujiwara ministers—nobody noted the irony of a Fujiwara turning on the throne—and fled for a countryside stronghold, taking the three sacred treasures with him.

Within the year, a samurai army had marched on Kyōto and Go-

EMPEROR JINMU Jinmu, the first legendary emperor of Japan, as depicted in an 1891 print from Adachi Ginko's *Stories from Nihonki*. The depiction makes some attempt at invoking his prehistoric status with rough-sewn clothes and a rough-hewn bow, but the ornate sword is far more anachronistic.

(Wikimedia Commons, posted by Artelino.)

EMPRESS JINGŪ Kamakura-period sculpture of Empress Jingū by Kyokaku (1326). Jingū claimed to be possessed by the Japanese gods, led an invasion of Korea, and returned to give birth to a new emperor who had supposedly gestated in her womb for three years. *Photo: Reiji Yamashina*.

Empress Jingū as she appeared on the one-yen banknote (1881) in an idealized representation by Edoardo Chiossone, an Italian engraver who designed most early Japanese currency. *Photo: World Imaging*.

NINTOKU'S TOMB Daisenryō Kofun, a fine example of a Kofun-period "keyhole tomb" that is said to be the grave of Emperor Nintoku. The site, which is thickly covered in trees and surrounded by a three moats, was excavated in 1872, uncovering a stone coffin and grave goods, some of which are now exhibited at the Boston Museum of Fine Arts. Pottery shards found on the site have led to doubts about the tomb being Nintoku's, as they date from the fifth century CE, after his legendary reign. *Photo: Osaka Info.*

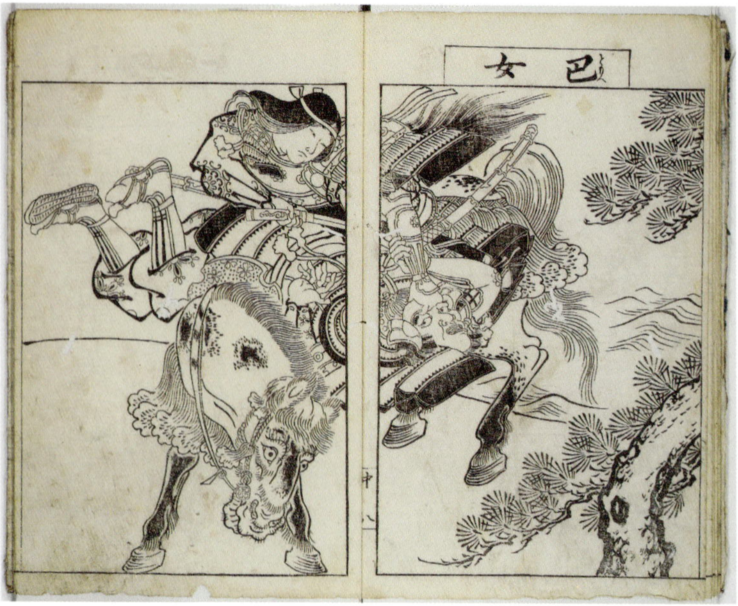

TOMOE GOZEN Tomoe Gozen, the woman warrior, leaps onto her enemy's horse and slashes off her foe's head in a two-page illustration from Tsukioka Settei's *Onna buyū yoso-oi kurabe* (Comparisons of Female Heroes, 1766). *Photo: Private Collection.*

SAMURAI ARMOR Detail of the elaborate furnishings on a suit of samurai armor, including the ornate faceguard, a half-moon insignia, and the reinforced helmet designed to protect against enemy archers when charging, head-down, on horseback. *Photo: Kati Clements.*

TANEGASHIMA Artist's depiction of the Portuguese sailors who first brought matchlock firearms to Japan. They landed on the southern island of Tanegashima, from which the weapons take their name in Japanese. *Photo: Private Collection.*

THE GREAT BUDDHA AT KAMAKURA Located on the grounds of the Jōtoku-in Buddhist temple in Kamakura, this 121-ton bronze-cast Daibutsu (Great Buddha) was funded by public donations and completed in 1243. It was originally housed in a wooden hall, but after three such buildings were destroyed by storms and tsunami, it has been open to the elements since 1498. This has caused its original gold-leaf coating to wear away, exposing the underlying bronze. *Photo: Kati Clements.*

KINKAKUJI The grounds of this palace, originally a villa in northern Kyoto, were sold to the shōgun Ashikaga Yoshimitsu in 1397. The building was converted into a Zen temple in accordance with his last will and testament, and has come to be known as Kinkakuji, or the Temple of the Golden Pavilion. The striking golden building survived the Ōnin Wars and the Second World War only to be burned down in 1950 by a mentally disturbed monk. The current building, a 1955 restoration, was controversially given a thicker, more enduring coating of gold leaf that may make it gaudier than the original. *Photo: Kati Clements.*

COMMODORE PERRY Matthew Calbraith Perry, commander of the "Black Ships," is commemorated in a statue in Hakodate, one of the treaty ports opened by his famous mission to Japan. The flag from Perry's flagship was taken from the US Naval Academy Museum in 1945 and brought to Japan, where it was flown on the *USS Missouri* during the signing of the Japanese surrender. It is still displayed at the *Missouri*'s current berth in Pearl Harbor, Hawaii. *Photo: Kati Clements.*

SAIGŌ TAKAMORI Statue of Saigō Takamori, the leader of the Satsuma Rebellion, in Tokyo's Ueno Park. The sculptor, Takamura Kōun, relied on picture references of Saigō prepared by the engraver Edoardo Chiossone, who himself cobbled together an image based on Saigō's living brother and cousin. Despite such vague references, Chiossone's image of Saigō has become the default for all Japanese representations since. *Photo: Kati Clements.*

FUMI-E A bronze "trampling image" or *fumi-e* depicting the crucifixion, its original details worn away by countless feet. Japanese subjects were obliged to prove that they had no Christian sympathies by walking across such icons, often as part of New Year's festivities at Buddhist temples. Christianity was not legalized until the 1871 proclamation of religious freedom that formed part of the Meiji Restoration reforms. *Photo: Kati Clements.*

SAILOR SUITS After the reforms ushered in by the Meiji Restoration, Japanese schoolchildren adopted uniforms that were in fashion in Europe. Japanese schoolgirls continue to dress in Victorian-era "sailor suits" to this day. *Photo: Kati Clements.*

ADMIRAL TŌGŌ Statue of Admiral Tōgō Heihachirō, the "Nelson of Japan," at the dockside in Yokosuka. Behind him is his flagship, the *Mikasa*. Tōgō was a teenage samurai at the bombardment of Kagoshima by the Western powers, and went on to fight in the Meiji Restoration, study in England, and return to rise through the ranks of the Imperial Japanese Navy. His greatest victory was against the Russian Baltic Fleet, which sailed around the world only to be sunk in the Korea Strait at the Battle of Tsushima in 1905. *Photo: Kati Clements.*

NAGOYA CASTLE Built in 1521, abandoned in 1582, and restored in 1610, Nagoya Castle was one of the most important fortresses in Tokugawa-era Japan. It was destroyed during an air raid in 1945. A thoroughly restored version was opened to the public in 1959, now boasting concrete foundations and internal elevators. Like many castles in Japan, Nagoya's is iconic but arguably a product of modern times. *Photo: Kati Clements.*

WHALE MEAT Canned whale meat, whale jerky, and even whale curry may be bought on the streets of Yokohama. Despite repeated bans on commercial whaling by the International Whaling Commission, Japan persists in "scientific" culls of whales; much of the meat from these ends up being sold as food. *Photo: Kati Clements.*

A 2000 yen banknote from 2000 depicting a scene from *The Tale of Genji* (left) and its author Murasaki Shikibu (lower right). The images on this note replicate paintings from twelfth and thirteenth century scrolls. (Bank of Japan)

UCHIKO-ZA KABUKI THEATER IN UCHIKO, EHIME PREFECTURE. Dating from 1916, the theater is famous for Kabuki and Bunraku performances. The stylized pine tree on the backdrop is a carryover from the

Noh tradition. It represents the presence of the divine and the sanctity of the performance. *Dreamstime © Sean Pavone*

FROM THE FIRST ISSUE OF MARUMARU CHINBUN, a weekly magazine established in 1877, originally satirical in the manner of the British *Punch*. In its earlier years it was aligned with the Freedom and People's Rights Movement in its advocacy of social and political reform. This image essentially states the magazine's intention to keep eyes, ears and nose primed to pick up on political and social evils.

(Wikimedia Commons, originally sourced from: http://rnavi.ndl.go.jp/kaleido/entry/jousetsu140.php)

Daigo had fled. The army was led by Ashikaga Takauji (1305–58), a warlord so disenchanted with the emperor's behavior that he was prepared to back an all-new candidate. Snatching the sacred mirror, sword, and jewel from Go-Daigo, he enthroned a new emperor. However, it soon transpired that Go-Daigo had swindled Takauji by handing over fakes—the mirror, sword, and jewel were not the sacred treasures of renown; hence, arguably, Takauji's new emperor had been enthroned without any true power. We already know that the real sword Kusanagi, at very least, had been lost at the Battle of Dannoura more than a century earlier, but it was the principle that counted.

In 1331, Go-Daigo escaped from his place of exile, announcing that his successor was entirely devoid of power and authority, and that he was still the sovereign. He came up with a meaningful new era name to reflect this change in conditions. The name he chose was Kenmu—the Japanese pronunciation of "Jianwu," a 1,300-year-old reign title from China's Eastern Han, where the true ruling house had wrested control of the dynasty back from a usurper. Initially, Go-Daigo enjoyed some impressive successes, particularly when his onetime nemesis Ashikaga Takauji turned on his Hōjō masters and brought his army with him. Go-Daigo's banner also attracted one of Japanese history's most famous heroes, the samurai Kusunoki Masashige (1294–1336).

Go-Daigo plainly saw himself as the true authority and the shōguns as unwelcome meddlers, but his bold scheme does not seem to have been backed by any convincing alternative. He began with a bout of decrees that seemed intended to reestablish ancient notions of protocol, hoping to "restore" imperial authority to a time when emperors were truly in charge—an era only really known in legends. But he still needed the support of the samurai to enforce any of his decisions, and he does not appear to have appreciated how fickle they could be. He parceled out a few pieces of land confiscated from the Hōjō clan, but nowhere near enough to secure the necessary support. In his most foolhardy move, he tried to levy an extra tax on the samurai in order to pay for improvements to his own court.

In a perfect illustration of Go-Daigo's unrealistic expectations, the Ashikaga house switched sides a second time, turning back against him. With Ashikaga Takauji's army advancing on Kyōto, the loyal general Kusunoki advised the emperor that it was a good time for a tactical retreat to a nearby mountain. Go-Daigo, however, remained emotionally attached to Kyōto and refused to quit the city. Another account of the same incident has Kusunoki pleading with his emperor that Ashikaga support was not lost to him, and that a little negotiation and diplomacy might neutralize the threat far more effectively than a battle. But Go-Daigo refused to listen, instead ordering Kusunoki to meet the Ashikaga enemy on the battlefield.

It was a disaster. Kusunoki's company was swiftly hacked down to a mere fifty horsemen. Surrounded with no hope of escape, he led a fatal charge right into the heart of the enemy forces, with the words: "Would that I had seven lives to give for the emperor!"

Kusunoki's absolute obedience and unquestioning loyalty, even in the face of certain death, would eventually make him a Japanese icon. More than five centuries after his death, he would become something of a patron deity for Japan's kamikaze suicide pilots. Today, it is his statue that guards the entrance to the imperial palace in Tōkyō, frozen for all time in that crucial instant as he wheeled his horse to face the enemy.

Go-Daigo survived the Ashikaga attack, pushing himself as the true emperor, while his Ashikaga-supported rival refused to back down. This was by no means the first time that Japan had found itself with two claimants to the title of emperor, but on previous occasions, the question of who was a pretender and who was the true emperor had usually been swiftly and violently settled. History would not be so conveniently brutal in this case, leading to an embarrassing period of more than fifty years in which the claimants were split into rival courts—the northern pretenders with their Ashikaga support, and the southern line of Go-Daigo's children and grandchildren, who still had possession of the sacred treasures. Matters would not be resolved until the 1390s, when a deal was brokered for future heirs to alternate between the two families. This, however, lasted barely a generation before the northern line refused to give up their turn. All subsequent emperors, down to the present day, have been descended from the northern line.

In the meantime, the Ashikaga family filled the power gap left by the collapse of the Hōjō family. Ashikaga Takauji, now the master of Kyōto, was the new shōgun, and would pass on the position to his descendants for the next two centuries. They inherited the same financial and political problems that had hounded the Minamoto, the Hōjō, and the imperial court, and although they would eventually lay the double-emperor problem to rest, their period in office also saw a continued, seemingly inexorable decline.

The third Ashikaga shōgun, Yoshimitsu (1358–1408) achieved the most of his line, not the least by reopening trade with China. It was during the Ashikaga period that the Chinese first began complaining about increased pirate activity, identifying the expansion of an entire class of sailors and fishermen on the edge of Japanese waters, forming a mobile, marine society, their numbers swelling every time Japanese fled famines or wars at home. Like the Vikings of medieval Europe, these pirates belonged to no particular ethnicity, but had accreted through circumstance—their numbers included Japanese, but also Koreans, Chinese, and Ryūkyū islanders. In Ming-dynasty China, however, they were regarded as a problem of Japanese origin, and were referred to with an archaic term that seemed deliberately intended to sting Japanese pride: *wokou*—dwarf pirates or outlaws of Wa, the same words previously seen on the Gwanggaeto Stone as "Wae robbers."

Discussion of the *wokou* remains a politicized issue; studies of their predations usually come accompanied by much finger-pointing and posturing about who was raiding whom. Increased trade between Japan and China inevitably led to increased *smuggling*, which helped to foster a new class of maritime scoundrel. Undoubtedly there were periods when Japanese outlaws formed a major component of the pirates, but by the end of the Ashikaga shōgunate, up to 70 percent of the "Japanese" pirates raiding China were actually

Chinese. Since the Chinese authorities offered higher rewards for "Japanese pirates" than for local criminals, large numbers of have-a-go heroes on the Chinese coasts decided to claim that the criminals they had caught and beheaded were seaborne raiders. Later investigations uncovered disconcerting inconsistencies, such as a Japanese "pirate raid" that was conducted far inland by a squadron of heavily armored Chinese cavalry.

Regardless, the Chinese pushed for the Japanese to exert greater control over sailing activity in their waters, and Yoshimitsu seems to have found a way to kill two birds with one stone. He forced coastal officials to police piracy with greater efficiency, and paid for it, at least in part, by increasing actual trade. This was conducted under the guise of "tribute" to the Chinese emperor, who gratefully returned the favor in 1404 by offering Yoshimitsu the title of "King of Japan."

How times had changed! At the time of the Mongol invasion, Japan's regent had executed ambassadors and taken the country to war rather than accept such a title and the implications it carried. Yoshimitsu, however, was happy to play along with the Chinese game, particularly if it meant he could unload bulk quantities of Japanese swords on the Chinese market. For letting the Chinese ruler call him the king, when Japan still had an emperor, Yoshimitsu attracted the ridicule of many later generations.

Yoshimitsu famously built a mansion with a lavish garden, the Palace of Flowers, on Muromachi Street in north Kyōto—it is from this location that the era of the Ashikaga shōgunate, 1336–1573, is often referred to in history books as the Muromachi period. Yoshimitsu looms large on the modern tourist itinerary because of the twentieth-century replica of his Temple of the Golden Pavilion (Kinkakuji), a famous gold-covered house on the grounds of what was once his mansion in Kyōto. But his temple, while undeniably beautiful and striking, does not represent his most enduring contribution to Japanese culture. Indeed, the ghost of Lady Nijō might well have gasped in shock at such a gaudy sight—an entire building covered in gold! Yoshimitsu's true place in the history books was secured by his patronage of a father and son whose adaptations and refinements of what had once been a folk performance art would achieve new heights. Noh (literally "the Craft") began as a form of public worship, slowly evolving into a seasonal theater tradition performed by itinerant actor-families.

In 1374, Yoshimitsu was so impressed by such a performance that he offered to sponsor the troupe's star, Kan'ami Kiyotsugu. This not only propelled Kan'ami's troupe into an unparalleled run of success among the aristocracy, but helped legitimize what had previously been regarded as a low-class entertainment into an element of high culture. More crucially, the sponsorship deal lasted long enough for Kan'ami's son, Zeami Motokiyo, to grow up with an aristocratic education, steeping him in the stories and culture of the capital. That, at least, is the public version of events—it is no secret in the Noh tradition that the teenage Yoshimitsu developed something of a crush on the twelve-year-old Zeami, and that his patronage of the arts went hand-in-hand with a homosexual affair. Courtiers were horrified, not so much by the male romance, which was commonplace and unremarkable in the period, but by the gap in *class*—as in Elizabethan England, actors were regarded as little more than itinerant beggars, and here was the shōgun, welcoming one into his house and bed.

It is Zeami who is remembered as the great dramatist of the Noh theater tradition, although it is very likely that the evolution of Noh into its final form was steered by the whims of Yoshimitsu. This does not merely apply to the setting and style, but also the repertoire. "Audiences"—and by that we can infer Yoshimitsu himself—seemed very keen on stories from *The Tale of the Heike*; they were presumably eager to hear tales of the glory days of the samurai before they found themselves as frustrated accountants administrating a failing economy. We can talk about the "final form" of Noh because it seems to have changed little since Zeami's time; many of what are now regarded as its traditions may have derived almost accidentally from the conditions, composition, and performance environment of the troupe that Yoshimitsu favored.

Under Kan'ami and Zeami, Noh lost some of its original religious aspects, becoming more recognizable as a dramatic tradition for entertainment. The standard Noh stage is a platform with three sides; the backdrop a stylized image of a lone pine tree. The cast comprises a small band playing traditional instruments, and two main actors—a protagonist and an antagonist. The actors, always male, wear masks at all times, and perform in a highly stylized manner, with symbolic movements that aficionados are expected to interpret as signifiers of particular emotions. Props are limited; the set is nonexistent; and there is no curtain. Death is not an obstacle in a Noh performance. It is relatively common for a leading character to die or be killed partway through the performance only to continue on as a ghost, seeking revenge or passing on a grim message.

Noh remains an absorbing glimpse into the concerns and sensibilities of fifteenth-century Japan. Its language is so arcane and its performances so idiosyncratic that modern Japanese audiences often have trouble following it. In later centuries, it would be derided for being ossified and hidebound, imprisoned within its own arbitrary rules—but this is a major part of its appeal, presenting us with a time-capsule portrait of what entertained the Ashikaga shōgun all those centuries ago. Criticising Noh for being oh-so-fifteenth-century is like mocking Shakespeare for being too Elizabethan.

The eighth Ashikaga shōgun, Yoshimasa (1436–90), is credited with the introduction of many other iconic elements of Japanese culture, although it might be fairer to say that his era merely saw many existing trends, some started by his ancestors, solidified and codified. Zen Buddhism reached its height under his rule, springing out of the temple life and battlefield nihilism and into a pensive style that found its manifestation in new and enduring forms.

Paramount among these was the tea ceremony, an intricate, austere observance in which the preparation, whisking, and pouring of a bowl of tea becomes a ritual of contemplation—not merely of the tea itself, but of the poise of its server, the décor of the tearoom, and the sounds of nature outside. Every moment, every iota of data conveyed in movement and sound, touch and taste, becomes an instant worthy of Zen, a living poem.

Over the centuries, the tea ceremony has become something of a cliché of Japanese inscrutability. There are those who regard it as the pinnacle of Japaneseness—an exquisite, inwardly focused meditation that exalts a mundane moment to a theater of Zen prayer. Your mileage may vary; unlike Noh drama, the archaeological value of which should be manifest and apparent to all, the tea ceremony, like the pungent beverage it produces, is very much an acquired taste. A cynic might point out that, much like the Heian courtiers of old, the participants in a Japanese tea ceremony are behind the times, enthusing to a farcical degree about the preparation of a frankly medieval beverage requiring outmoded utensils and practices. Back in China, loose-leaf teas and partially oxidized oolong varieties had long since supplanted the primitive powder form of Japanese matcha, but the Japanese chose not to know this, much as they kept sitting on the floor instead of using chairs. One might even dare to suggest that the tea ceremony reflects the very particular interests of a fifteenth-century bigwig with whom nobody dared argue, like some fearsome, witless despot who decides that the pinnacle of human cuisine is the hot dog. Three centuries earlier, the pronouncements on culture of the Minamoto general Yoshinaka had the courtiers of Kyōto snickering behind their sleeves. But with the flames of urban conflict still smoldering in the distance, maybe there was nobody left to laugh at the Ashikaga clan.

On the other hand, an apologist might argue that the Ashikaga were a world removed from the boorish warriors of the olden times. The samurai had clawed their way up from the frontiers, and now enjoyed all the fruits and luxuries of a capital life. And they were not idiots—as the holders of the new wealth, they had ample time to see that their children were educated in all the refinements of Kyōto culture. Unlike many of the courtiers who scoffed at them, they could even afford it.

Such a skeptical account of an iconic ritual is a catch-22 situation for the Japanologist. Dare to suggest that we might be looking at an outbreak of the emperor's new clothes, and the Japanese will politely reply that you are clueless barbarian who does not understand the subtleties of their culture. In the centuries to come, many Japanese would regard foreigners' doubts about such pursuits as evidence of Japan's own cultural superiority. Japaneseness, it would be argued, was not something that could be bought or applied for; you had to be born into it, living and breathing the culture from infancy, steeped it in at a genetic level, before you could truly understand its depths and variations. Confess, for example, that the tea ceremony leaves you cold, and you are merely admitting to an absence of *hinkaku*—an undefinable, unknowable dignity and class that was only available to those who were born and bred in Japan. It might sound as ludicrous as waiting half an hour for a cup of horrible tea, but the *hinkaku* argument has many modern manifestations, cited in official documents on everything from the exclusion of foreigners from the upper ranks of sporting organizations to the conferral of passports on immigrants.

Regardless of where one stands on the tea ceremony (I myself am rather partial to matcha, although it still seems oddly atavistic compared to a good Chinese Tie Guan Yin), it became a transforming element of Japanese style. Its centrality to the hobbies of a certain breed of new aristocrat also fostered the development of other arts, including the arrangement of the flowers that formed the decoration nearby, and the arrangement of the view outside into pleasing forms, including a raked installation of stone and sands that would become known as a "Zen garden." Most of these installations were created by Zen monks at the behest of the Ashikaga rulers; although they are remembered today as reflections of the intellectual depths of the upper class, it remains entirely possible that the upper class had no idea what they were looking at, but played along for fear of looking stupid.

In many ways, Yoshimasa appears to have been an old-fashioned capital guy—focusing in a relentlessly blinkered fashion on cultural pursuits even as the state for which he was responsible collapsed into a protracted civil war. Japanese history books talk of his promotion of "Higashiyama culture" (so named for the "Eastern Hills" district of Kyōto where he had his own mansion), referring to the introduction of such noble pursuits as ink-brush painting and flower arranging. However, such accounts usually neglect to mention that Higashiyama was an island of civilization in a capital that was largely ruined under Yoshimasa's watch.

Not all of this was Yoshimasa's fault—he had a run of bad luck from 1459 to 1461, with a series of natural disasters that placed additional strain on provisions. The harsh winter that began 1461 caused an estimated 82,000 deaths in Kyōto, mainly from cold and starvation. Taxes during the Ashikaga shōgunate rose to a crippling height of 70 percent; no wonder Yoshimasa's reign saw eighteen peasant revolts. But this was only to be expected; the Ashikaga shōgunate had merely seized control of the foundering Kamakura shōgunate, and had unsurprisingly inherited most of its problems. Yoshimasa's most creative remedy was also an example of him at his most corrupt: supposedly in response to peasant protests, he issued proclamations canceling their debts. The fact that he had to do so repeatedly—roughly once every two years throughout his reign—suggests that the cancellation of debts did nothing to alleviate the systemic problems that had created them in the first place, such as food shortages and damage to local infrastructure. One might also argue that it simply pushed the problem onto a different sector of society, away from the immediate threat of the peasant uprising onto a smaller but equally angry group of moneylenders. Yoshimasa also profited personally—he only canceled a debt if 10 percent of its value was paid to him, effectively allowing his peasants to steal from their creditors and then pocketing a tenth of their gains. Increasingly, he was forced to rely on local enforcers, the daimyō (great names). Although the term has come to have a cachet of nobility in Japanese, having shifted over the centuries to refer to a feudal lord, its rise in the Muromachi period suggests a wiping out of the old order and the sudden rise of new strongmen. Where there were once noble houses and great clans, now power rested with whoever fought hardest for it, regardless of their origins.

Meanwhile, Yoshimasa's advisers, each of them the head of a samurai clan, fell out over who would be the best choice to replace him. In more stable times, this might have been decided over a cup of tea, but after years of famine and unrest throughout the country, tempers flared into a full-on conflict.

The Ōnin War, spanning from 1467 to 1477, brought home the violent conflict of the samurai to the capital itself—not in the isolated arsons and street fights of earlier eras, but with full-blown battles fought in what had once been the bastion of peace and tranquility. Not even Ashikaga enclaves were safe—most of the buildings in the grounds of the Temple of the Golden Pavilion, once cherished by Yoshimasa's great-grandfather, were burned to the ground along with a third of the rest of the city. It effectively ended the Ashikaga shōgunate, since Yoshimasa's successors would all prove to be puppets of other clans. But it also ended Kyōto for decades to come, leaving the city a burned-out husk infested with roving gangs of looters.

The Ōnin War also marks the beginning of Japan's protracted civil war, plunging the country into a period of unrest that would not truly come to an end until 1615. Japanese history books call this the Sengoku Jidai, deliberately using a term that alludes to the "Warring States" of China in the ancient past. The term first crops up in comments made by the aristocracy of the day, and seems to reflect their belief that, like China in olden times, Japan was stuck in a cycle of endless conflict, awaiting the rise of a great leader who could hammer the country into a unified whole. The term also rather implies that the monarch is entirely powerless, and that only a new system can solve the problems the country faces.

The shock and awe of the Ōnin War partly derives from the terrible irony that after centuries of fighting to get back into the capital, the samurai had successfully done so only to ruin it. It also reflects the fact that most of the chroniclers of the disaster were monks and literati based in the Kyōto region who felt its ruination most keenly.

However, the fall of Kyōto was merely the most obvious sign of a general nationwide collapse. The Ashikaga clan's hold on its outlying provinces became increasingly theoretical, as local power brokers saw few reasons to obey the law. Many became increasingly assertive, and the wiser Ashikaga leaders learned not to issue any orders unless they were sure their underlings felt like obeying them. It is during the Ōnin War and its aftermath that we first hear the term *gekokujō*—"the low dominating the high," implying that the aristocrats have lost their way or lost sight of true issues, and that it is their supposed underlings who must take the initiative. This situation led to many coups on the outlying provinces, propelling a number of minor clans into power on many of the semi-independent estates. The later Ashikaga could not even control the provinces close to Kyōto—hardly surprising, when these were the same places supplying their "advisers."

The last few Ashikaga shōguns were not even allowed in Kyōto; they "ruled" the city that was supposedly their capital from another town. Just like the emperors, they were forced to abdicate before they were old enough to do any good, serving as shōgun in name early on, while the toughest of their advisers held the real power.

Such reversals of fortune, switches in sides, and double-crosses would forever change the nature of Japan's version of chess, the board game *shōgi*. Until the late Middle Ages, it had been a relatively tame variant of the great strategy game. During the Warring States period it transformed, as did so many imports, into something uniquely Japanese. Whereas pieces in traditional chess are considered dead once removed, in *shōgi* they are merely captured, and can be restored to the game on the side of their new master. *Shōgi* pieces reflect this by all being of the same color—their loyalty is revealed only by the direction they face. A *shōgi* game can appear all but lost, only to be saved by the sudden arrival of turncoat pieces leaping into the fray in an unexpected location. This change in the rules is attributed to Japan's 105th emperor, Go-Nara (1495–1557), who presided over many of the worst reversals, betrayals, and flip-flops of the Warring States period.

There were parts of Japan where nobody paid heed to the local lord at all. Several regions where a particular brand of Pure Land Buddhism reigned supreme unified along religious lines; in these areas, local samurai banded together with Shintō priests and powerful local Buddhist monasteries to form mutual defense organizations. Effectively, this turned parts of the country into independent states outside the authority of emperor and shōgun, ruled by councils of commoners. Deriving their name from their "single-minded" (*ikkō*) faith, they were known as *ikkō ikki*—"leagues of one mind" or "federations of purpose."

History, as always, is told by the winning side. Japanese history until the twentieth century is very much a tale told by the samurai, about the samurai. Although there were undoubtedly samurai who rose up from the common population to become aristocrats, they did so by accepting and embracing the rules and protocols of the elite. But the *ikkō ikki* were something different—best described, perhaps, as religious enclaves pushing a radical alternative. Born from peasant mobs, rejecting both the disdainful emperors and the predatory samurai alike, the *ikkō ikki* were seen as dangerous experiments that had to be wiped out before the virus spread, fanatics loyal to a Buddhist patriarch who promised, or at least appeared to promise, an afterlife in paradise.

Kaga, for example, on the west coast of Japan, enjoyed almost a century as the "Peasants' Province" after a collective of monks and farmers first supported a local warlord during the Ōnin War and then ousted him shortly afterwards. The area became a haven for rebels and outcasts, and was embroiled in several factional disputes over the ruins of Kyōto, where its priestly rulers had originally come from. However, Kaga backed the wrong side, and was wiped out in the Warring States conflict.

The nemesis of the *ikkō ikki* was Oda Nobunaga (1534–82), the first of the three Japanese generals who would eventually unify the nation. Nobunaga had lost two brothers in battles against the *ikkō ikki*, and was merciless in his war against them. His samurai were seen hunting *ikkō ikki* members for sport in the forest—where once they had chased wild boar, they now hunted down pockets of peasant rebels, executing men, women and children. In the course of his ascent to power, backing one faction in the struggle over the last Ashikaga pretenders, and eventually supplanting them, Nobunaga would also destroy the *ikkō ikki* fortress at what is now Ōsaka in a prolonged multiyear siege. In his later years, with half of Japan united under his rule, he built himself a wonderful castle overlooking Lake Biwa at Azuchi near Kyōto, and made plans to bring the rest of Japan to heel. He was, however, brought down by one of his own generals, who ambushed him at a Kyōto tea ceremony, leading to his angry seppuku as the building burned down around him.

The most famous story of the three generals—Nobunaga, Hideyoshi, and Ieyasu—was not told until the 1800s, when it appeared in the compendium *Kasshi Yawa* (Night Tales of the Kasshi Era). There's no indication how many years the story was told and retold before it was set down in its enduring poetic form, but today it is so ingrained in Japanese culture that it tends to appear as a simple three-line proverb, without any mention of who is speaking.

> If the cuckoo does not sing, kill it.
> If the cuckoo does not sing, coaxe it.
> If the cuckoo does not sing, wait.

Barely ten years separate the birth dates of the three generals who would finally end the constant warring in Japan. It is hence entirely feasible, although rather unlikely, that all three of them might have been present one day in a garden or an orchard and noticed a *hototogisu*, or lesser cuckoo.

When the cuckoo fails to sing, it's Oda Nobunaga, the tyrant of Japanese history, who speaks first. A violent man who saw his first battle at age thirteen, he had supported the last Ashikaga shōgun only to overthrow him when he outlived his usefulness. It was Nobunaga who declared war on the fighting monks of Mount Hiei when they threatened his Kyōto power base, and ruthlessly conquered half of Japan by the time he was assassinated by one of his own generals. It is hence Nobunaga, the force of nature who lives only for war, who is heard to decree that the cuckoo must die.

Toyotomi Hideyoshi (1537–98) speaks next. A new-made man who had risen swiftly through Nobunaga's ranks as a foot soldier and a specialist in siege warfare, his nickname in his younger days had been the Monkey, for his simian face. Nobody would dare call him that in later life, as he avenged Nobunaga's death and carried his campaigns to the edge of Japan and beyond. It was Hideyoshi who would unite all of Japan in his campaigns of conquest, and who would begin the efforts to demilitarize the nation with his Sword Hunts, confiscating weapons from peasants who would surely no longer need them. It was Hideyoshi who organized a census in 1590, confident that all Japan was his and that the time had come to turn a machine of military conquest into one of national government. Under Hideyoshi's rule, the value of any lord's holdings was determined in rice—the tonnage it was expected to generate in a given harvest—a portion of which had to be paid to him. As his reign proceeded, he tore down castles in pacified areas, issued new coins, and proclaimed his ownership of the land's silver and gold mines, as well as strict controls over foreign trade. Faced with a huge faction of idle samurai, it was Hideyoshi who cunningly shipped some 158,000 of them abroad—for it was Hideyoshi who proclaimed Japan's new frontier in Korea, declaring that his forces would cross the Korea Strait, seize control of the entire peninsula, and then, ultimately, march on China.

It was a ludicrous and unlikely enterprise, but one into which the samurai threw themselves with gusto in 1592. Historians are still divided as to whether Hideyoshi had gone insane and wanted to proclaim himself the ruler of the world, or whether his grand scheme was the ultimate in political calculation, pushing the deadly energies of the samurai class into a foreign war that would keep them busy for years. Unlike the Kamakura shōgunate, which had failed to reward its warriors with new lands, Hideyoshi offered them the rest of the world, and packed them off to die fighting for it. An entire generation of samurai that might have turned on Hideyoshi instead spent the next six years plotting, maneuvering, fighting, retreating, and counterattacking, while Hideyoshi went into quiet retirement and built himself a lavish palace at Momoyama in Kyōto (the endgame of the Warring States unrest, from 1573 to 1600, is sometimes called the Azuchi-Momoyama period, named for the residences of Nobunaga and Hideyoshi). Owing to Hideyoshi's common origins, he was never proclaimed shōgun.

And so, in the folktale about the bird that will not sing, it is Hideyoshi who suggests that they should just offer it the right encouragement, leaving only Tokugawa Ieyasu (1543–1616), the man who would reap all the rewards of his predecessors' campaigns. Since his teens, Ieyasu had played an active role in the battles that tore Japan apart, and suffered many of their consequences. His father was killed when he was only six years old. He had become a staunch ally of Nobunaga and risked his life in many conflicts. He had weathered a stormy scandal in which his own wife and eldest son were executed on Nobunaga's orders, suspected of plotting a coup. In the wake of Nobunaga's death, Ieyasu had stayed put, waiting to see who would win in Hideyoshi's latest war, swiftly offering support to Hideyoshi only when it was clear that he would be the victor.

In the folktale of the bird that will not sing, it is Ieyasu who patiently waits, just as he waited out the worst of the final battles of the Warring States era. When Hideyoshi died in 1598, the distracting war in Korea was called off, and Ieyasu became one of the five-man council of regents sworn to uphold the inheritance of Hideyoshi's infant son. But Ieyasu was now the single most powerful landowner in all Japan, and he secured support from several other major power brokers. When the most senior regent died in 1599, Ieyasu mobilized his forces to seize the castle belonging to the infant shōgun.

Japan was soon split between his supporters and his opponents. But the southern domains most likely to oppose him had been severely depleted fighting Hideyoshi's foreign wars. Matters came down to a battle, in 1600, at a rain-soaked crossroads in Sekigahara surrounded by muddy fields. Ieyasu began the battle outnumbered almost two to one, but Sekigahara was a crossroads in more than one fashion—a fork in the road of Japanese history that would define allegiances and positions for generations. Making a fateful decision when the battle was already underway, one samurai lord switched sides, compromising the defenses of Ieyasu's enemies. Before long, four other generals declared for Ieyasu like devious *shōgi* pieces reversing direction, and the tide turned in his favor.

It would be three more years before the mop-up operations and final flurries of resistance were stamped out, but Sekigahara was the great determinator, and is still remembered as the battle that divided the nation. Loyalties on that day would determine social positions for centuries to come. Those who had supported Ieyasu wholeheartedly would become major players in the new order. Those who had switched sides to join him on the day of the battle would be granted grudging rewards and minor positions. Those who submitted to him only after the battle would forever be regarded as outliers. Those who had opposed him were crushed, their leaders executed and their lands reassigned.

In 1603, Ieyasu had himself proclaimed shōgun. He was able to do this because he had taken the name Tokugawa in his twenties, thereby implying that he was descended from the famous Minamoto clan, and of sufficiently high breeding to qualify to be the grand general of all Japan. Two years later, he "resigned" in favor of his adult son Hidetada. By doing so, he was able to rule from the shadows like many a shōgun of old, but by putting a capable adult in charge—Hidetada had already led armies for his father—he avoided any possibilities of dispute and usurpation. Having grabbed the shōgunate for himself, Ieyasu secured it for his descendants, who would hold it until 1867.

The story of the bird that would not sing is not the only variant. There are other versions of the same tripartite problem to be found in Japanese proverbs. Nobunaga, people say, was the miner who quarried the stones; Hideyoshi was the mason; but Ieyasu built the house. Or—perhaps most evocatively—Nobunaga made the pie, Hideyoshi baked it, but Ieyasu got to eat it.

CHAPTER 6

TIME WARP: 200 YEARS OF ISOLATION

They leave town before dawn, trembling a little in the cold night air, clutching their cloaks to them.

Ohatsu sees the frost by the roadside and comments grimly to Tokubei that people will compare them to it. But he is not listening to her; instead he has looked back toward the dark merchant city of Ōsaka, listening for the bell. It has struck six times; not long from now, the sun will rise.

The two shuffle across the bridge at Umeda. Tokubei likens it to the mythical bridge of magpies that forms once a year to allow two stars in the night sky to see each other again.

The teenage Ohatsu blushes at the thought.

"I will be your wife forever," she assures him.

Some of the taverns are still open for business. There are shouts and laughs from a lantern-lit window as they pass, and the chorus of a popular song, a ditty about someone in the media—an actor or a merchant whose love affair has made them the talk of the town.

"It always seemed that such things happened to other people," says Tokubei. "Tomorrow they will sing songs about you and me."

Ohatsu's eyes brim with tears. Her hands fumble at her Buddhist rosary, her thumb and forefinger rubbing and pushing each of the 108 beads in turn.

"I will never let you go," she sobs, and the pair of them, hand in hand, head up into the forested hill at Sonezaki.

Crows in the trees look down at them impassively. Tokubei glares at them but they do not move.

"Is this a good place?" asks Ohatsu innocently, peering through a thicket at a clearing wet with early morning dew.

Tokubei shudders and moves on, pushing deeper into the forest.

He strides into another clearing, washed with moonlight, and seems to make his decision.

Ohatsu gasps, pointing through the trees. There is an apparition, a ball of soft light, a will-o-the-wisp. It is the light, perhaps, of another soul, of someone else who haunts this grove.

"I think we have company," she whispers, but the light is gone. There is an odd tree in the clearing—a pine and a palm that have somehow grown entwined and inseparable.

"This shall be the place," says Tokubei.

They embrace in the forest clearing. Tokubei's hand snakes around to unfasten his cloak. Ohatsu pulls off her outer robe to reveal her finest kimono. Although she is no virgin, she is still a modest girl. She is worried that they will be discovered with their clothes in disarray, but Tokubei is ever resourceful. He can tie her to the tree with her blue sash, so that she won't be found in a revealing position.

"You think of everything," she beams as he pulls the sash tight.

It is, if anything, a little too tight, but Ohatsu doesn't mind. She doesn't plan on breathing for much longer anyway.

"My parents died when I was young," muses Tokubei. "I'll see them soon, but I feel sorry for my uncle, who will end up cleaning up this mess."

"You're the lucky one," observes Ohatsu. "I haven't seen my parents for months, but they are still alive. The news about us will get back to their village soon enough. They will be awfully unhappy to hear about what's happened to me. But it can't be helped."

Tokubei is crying now. Ohatsu is afraid he will lose heart.

"Better get on with it, darling," she says. "Hurry up and kill me."

"I take refuge in Amida Buddha," sobs Tokubei. "I take refuge in Amida Buddha."

He stabs out with his dagger, but strikes the tree, once and then again. He cannot bear to look at her. A third wild slash hits home, and he drives his knife deep into his lover's throat, twisting and pulling it free as her blood pulses out. She chokes on her own blood; she writhes against her bindings. He dares not look in her eyes lest he sees regret.

But then her body slackens, the blood flow slows, and he realizes that she is gone.

"Let's draw our last breaths together," he says to her still-warm body.

He reverses the knife and drives it deep into his own throat so hard that the blade almost snaps. His head slumps, his eyes grow dim, and then nothing stirs in the forest clearing.

There is the sound of a distant bell, mournful in the distance, and the sun begins to rise.

"Nobody is there to see it," says a disembodied voice to the watching crowd. "There is none to tell the tale but the wind that rushes through Sonezaki Wood, carrying the message far and wide."

There are sobs and sniffs from the audience, as the girls dab at the tears on their cheeks. There is the clink of a tea bowl as someone sets it down a little too hard.

"High and low," continues the narrator, "they will pray for these two lovers, who will surely be together in their next life. They have become models of true love."

Then there is silence for a few breaths.

The lovers' bodies lie still on the stage, frozen in the moments of their final agonies.

There is no movement and no sound.

The playwright, Chikamatsu, watches from the wings. At fifty, it finally looks like he has a hit.

The samurai war machine, running almost constantly for a century, suddenly ground to a halt. Matters that had been in flux for decades, such as one's position in the hierarchy—and indeed, who the shōgun was—were now fixed and immobile. But for the disinheritance of Hideyoshi's son, which led to a flurry of infighting and the Siege of Ōsaka in 1615, the outcome of Sekigahara settled matters for the next two centuries. Loyal lords who had been on the winning side at Sekigahara were known as *fudai* (legacy) daimyō—part of Ieyasu's inner circle. Lords who had only switched sides with reluctance, or on the day, were *tozama* (outer) daimyō, regarded with a degree of mistrust and either fobbed off with remote domains or put in charge of small baronies closer to the shōgun's headquarters. The prolonged period of subsequent peace helped Japan's population double from its level in 1600 to 31 million in 1721, after which point it stabilized, having reached the limits of sustainable agriculture and technology.

Oddly, one of Ieyasu's first acts on becoming shōgun was to inaugurate a new office intended to oversee and promote the study of Go. This deceptively simple game, in which black and white counters attempt to encircle and neutralize each other on a grid, had arrived from China centuries ago, but appears to have been a particular favorite of Ieyasu. His decision to institute an official Go office, and four competing Houses of Go that would contend annually for the championship, can be seen in retrospect as an early intimation of much Tokugawa policy, grabbing the skills of the battlefield and repurposing or redirecting them, however haphazardly, to function in a time of permanent peace.

Ieyasu also put his subjects' loyalty to the most severe of tests by shuffling many of their responsibilities. He switched a number of domains like pieces on a game board, forcing even some of his longest-serving generals to permanently quit their ancestral lands and relocate where they were needed. Local ties, established over generations, were cut. Christian domains suddenly found themselves with un-Christian overlords. Men who once ruled entire provinces suddenly found themselves running one-horse towns at critical road junctions, and vice versa.

Once Ieyasu had finished, his family and its branches controlled 15 percent of the land in Japan, and his close allies another 10 percent. Nor would the Tokugawa family relinquish its hold on power. Ieyasu swiftly established a hereditary shōgunate, and he would be succeeded over the next two centuries by fourteen descendants.

In 1615, shortly before his "retirement" in favor of his adult son, Ieyasu presented the samurai with a new code of conduct for a military aristocracy in a time of peace, the Various Laws for the Military Households (Buke Shohatto). These laws would be amended and augmented several more times by his successors, forming the new basis of samurai existence. In recognition that peacetime was a time of relative plenty, the Various Laws commanded the samurai to live frugally, to wear appropriate clothing for their status, and not to go crazy with entertainments. They should not shirk their military obligations, but should set aside time for training in the all-important arts of archery, swordplay, and horsemanship.

Domains, meanwhile, were subject to increased scrutiny by headquarters. Lords could not even marry their children to each other without shōgunal approval. "Rebels and fugitives"—which is to say, anyone assigned that status by the shōgun—had to be expelled or apprehended. Each domain imprisoned its residents, and lords were permitted no interaction with their neighboring daimyō without shōgunal approval. To discourage false-flag actions, even if there was a peasant uprising in a friendly neighboring domain, a daimyō had to wait for the order to come from Edo before he could cross his own borders with a task force.

As the "great barbarian-suppressing supreme general," Ieyasu and his successors as shōgun still had a primary responsibility to keep Japan safe from foreign attack. In doing so, they would initiate a series of decrees and initiatives that would result in the effective isolation of Japan from the outside world, particularly the European missionaries and traders who had been making inroads into East

Asia. During the time of the Warring States, European contacts had been useful to certain generals—not least the warlords of Kyūshū, who traded silks and precious metals for foreign firearms.

One of the great game-changers of the Warring States period was the arquebus, a primitive matchlock gun that first reached Japanese hands on the southern island of Tanegashima in 1542. The Japanese were familiar with gunpowder from China, but the new weapon, soon known as a *tanegashima* in honor of the place where the Japanese had "discovered" it, transformed the military strengths of the Warring States era.

Oda Nobunaga's most infamous victory, for example, had been at Nagashino, where he put such firearms to a new and more organized use. *Tanegashima* had been around for a generation, but Nobunaga crammed his army with musketeers fielding a boggling three thousand of them. He also put these troops to work systematically, protecting them behind a wooden stockade and rotating them in shifts so that one group could be reloading while another was firing. It no longer mattered how many years a samurai had been training in archery, or how ornate his armor was—the stockades kettled the enemy cavalry into easy targets, and the overwhelming number of gunners soon picked them off. Guns were expensive and difficult to maintain, but far cheaper in the long term than twenty years of training a samurai in the various arts of war. A peasant could be turned into a mobile cannoneer in mere days, which was one of the reasons why the *ikkō ikki* were able to rise so suddenly to present a creditable threat during the period. A hallmark of genuine antique samurai armor from the period is often the presence of a conspicuous dent in the breastplate, demonstrating that the maker tested it by firing at it point-blank with a gun before pronouncing it battle-ready.

But foreign contacts did not merely bring guns. They also brought religion. Christian missionaries soon came ashore, targeting the ruling aristocrats—particularly in Kyūshū, which was closest to their first ports of call.

Foreign observers had trouble working out just how Japan fit into European paradigms. Several referred to it as a place with sixty-six "'kingdoms," mistaking the local daimyō for kings—although, considering the precarious grasp of the shōgunate at times, this was an easy mistake to make. They also regarded Japan as a place permanently in thrall to natural disasters. In 1565, Luis Frois wrote of "whirlwinds most vehement" and earthquakes so common that the Japanese simply shrugged them off. An unknown English sailor wrote of "the wind called tuffon," which:

> ...signifieth a storme or Tempest, which you commonly find in these voiages from China to Japon. If you saile of it sometime, it is not often, it commeth and beginneth from one point, and so runneth with a continuall storme almost about all the points in compasse, blowing most stiffely, whereby the poore Sailers have worke ynough in hande, and in such sort, that not any stormes through all the oriental Indies is comparable with it...

The Portuguese Jesuit João Rodrigues wrote of the Japanese: "They are so crafty in their hearts that nobody can understand them. Whence it is said that they have three hearts: a false one in their mouths for all the world to see, another within their breasts only for their friends, and the third in the depth of their hearts, reserved for themselves alone and never manifested to anybody." This seemed to be a common criticism among missionaries, who were often frustrated by Japanese manners. "They learn from childhood never to reveal their hearts," tutted the Italian Jesuit Alessandro Valignano. "They regard this as prudent and the contrary as stupidity—so much so that people who lightly reveal their hearts are considered fools, and scornfully called single-hearted men."

Valignano, at least, thought he had hit on the reason for such behavior, identifying the effects of centuries of samurai conflict and customs:

> They have the most peculiar form of government in the world. Each man enjoys absolute power over his family and servants, and he may cut them down or kill them, justly or otherwise, as he pleases, without having to give an account to anybody. And although a man may be under the authority of another lord, he is allowed to kill his own children and servants because such matters are not the concern of his lord. Not only may a man kill his children, but he may also disinherit them whenever he pleases.

Missionaries like Valignano, however, were soon capitalizing on such powers. Valignano explained to his Jesuit masters back in Rome that there was no point in seeking out the dregs of Japanese society. It made far more sense for him to concentrate on the very top, as a daimyō convert would be likely to persuade his entire entourage to convert with him.

This, in fact, is what happened in southern Japan in the 1570s, where several prominent rulers were persuaded by the Christian missionaries to proclaim themselves and their subjects as Christians. In some cases, this was nothing but a fad, with local samurai sporting crucifixes as fashion accessories. In others, conversion was substantially more devout, soon spooking the shōgunate with the implications. Just as the peasant-led Buddhist *ikkō ikki* had offered the dangerous prospect of a new way of life, Christian missionaries worried the samurai with their stories of a God greater than any other, whose earthly representative in the distant Vatican seemed to offer a potential threat to the authority of the emperor and the shōgun.

Christianity's hold on the Japanese began to waver in the late sixteenth century, with wild swings in popularity. The greatest damage was done to it in 1596, by a Spanish sea-captain who had become angry with the looting of his wrecked cargo of silks off the coast of Shikoku, and who had threatened his rescuers with a Christian backlash. Missionaries, he fumed, were only the front line. As soon as they had enough converts, they would open the way for invading troops, and Japan would fall to a fifth column of Christian sympathizers. Stories drifting in from faraway Europe of wars fought between Christian denominations, and an entire continent split between Protestant and Catholic, made the Japanese authorities even more suspicious.

Unfortunately, it was exactly the sort of scaremongering that the Japanese establishment wanted to hear. Anti-Christian edicts formed some of the last draconian decrees of the dying Hideyoshi, but despite many persecutions and purges, Christian believers hung on in the south, hoping that fortune would swing in their favor again once the wars were over.

It didn't. Had Christian samurai fought on the right side at the Battle of Sekigahara, then the new religion might have stood a chance. Instead, there was a notable faction of Christians among Ieyasu's enemies. Only those who prominently and conspicuously repudiated their religion and hunted out pockets of belief in their domains would hold on to their power.

With the rise of the Tokugawa clan, Hideyoshi's suspicion of the Christians was reiterated. The Tokugawa clan would not be reversing his policies; instead, they pushed them harder, throwing out foreign missionaries and persecuting native believers. The gains made in Japan's Christian heartland, in Kyūshū, were swiftly stamped out. In Ieyasu's great shuffling of the nobility, Christian daimyō were deposed and replaced with stern anti-Christian lords. Foreigners were thrown out, ushered increasingly into more tightly controlled areas, until soon even the Chinese were confined to just two ports, and the Europeans to just one.

In 1634, European traders were restricted to Dejima, a quarantine island in Nagasaki harbor. Their numbers chiefly comprised Dutchmen, who had protested to the shōgun that, as Protestants, they were not subject to the whims of the pope like the Catholics. Other Europeans simply gave up—the English, for example, suspended their Japan trade of their own accord, finding new markets for their woollen goods.

The most drastic purge came when anyone with two or more foreign grandparents was ordered to leave the country. Where there had once been a sector of Japanese society with connections to foreigners, all these people were now ordered to leave. Families were split apart: half-Dutch daughters were sent to friends or relatives in Jakarta; half-Chinese sons were forced to relocate to the mainland. The rich melting pot of what had once been Japan's Christian heartland was stripped of its newfound European heritage.

Soon afterward, the Christians were purged most savagely. Increasingly harsh taxation on the old Christian communities on Kyūshū, combined with the terrible harvests of the worst of the cold years of the Little Ice Age, pushed certain farming communities a step too far. In Shimabara, where many of the aging veterans of the Korea invasion had settled as farmers, a local lord's predations against the community to pay for his new castle reached a breaking point. Locals rose up in a revolt that lasted for several months before eventually being contained and suppressed with extreme prejudice by the shōgunal authorities.

It was the supreme test of the new Tokugawa system. News reached Edo of a peasant uprising in Shimabara in 1637. Effusive in its comments about the end of the world and the establishment of a new order, the peasants' own propaganda sounded all too much like the manifesto for some Christian version of the *ikkō ikki*. All along the road between Kyūshū and Edo, samurai lords poised, ready for action. True to the new Tokugawa rules, they were unable to cross their own borders without shōgunal approval. They hence had to wait at the ready for the messengers who had passed them en route to Edo to return bearing the shōgun's orders. When the lords eventually did, they would do so only days ahead of those other samurai, closer to Edo, who had received the orders before them.

The result was a race to Kyūshū, as the lords farthest from the revolt but closest to Edo received their marching orders before the lords who were farthest from Edo but closest to the revolt. Samurai who had been spoiling for a fight for a generation piled down the road network to Shimabara, where they laid siege to the rebels in a hastily recommissioned abandoned fort at Hara. They spent much of their time squabbling about who should lead the final assault, although when it came, in spring 1638, it was nothing to be proud of. An army of bloodthirsty samurai swept through a camp of starving refugees in a day of prolonged, uncompromising butchery.

Christianity had at last been stamped out. For generations to come, there would be hunts against underground believers, and occasional discoveries of foreign priests who had sneaked into the country to administer to their flocks, but the samurai had successfully held off the greatest threat to their ideology and culture. Thereafter, they would periodically test the faith (or lack of it) of their subjects with a "trampling image" (*fumi-e*), an icon depicting Christ or the Virgin Mary that loyal subjects were expected to walk over in order to prove that they did not venerate a foreign god. The Protestant Dutch in Nagasaki saw no problem with all but tap-dancing on a mere picture if that was all it took to secure trade deals, and happily stepped on the *fumi-e* whenever ordered. Many Catholic converts among the Japanese, however, went to their deaths rather than dishonor their religion.

After the Shimabara Rebellion had alerted the shōgunate to the possible presence of a fifth column of undercover Catholics, *fumi-e* tests became a permanent feature of Japanese temple life. Buddhist temples became centers of enforcement, where local populations would be made to line up to prove they were true Buddhists. Even as late as the latter days of the nineteenth century, the poet Masaoka Shiki would refer to the *fumi-e* brought out each year at a temple near his native Matsuyama:

> At the temple
> Beneath peonies in full bloom
> We trample on the face of Christ.

The ban on Christianity was only one of the measures designed to shut Japan away from the world. Contacts were corralled into quarantines in designated harbor towns, and similarly drastic rules were imposed on the Japanese themselves. Just as the outside world was forbidden entrance to Japan, the Japanese were forbidden access to the outside world, on pain of death.

Ieyasu received approaches from Chinese embassies asking him to rein in "Japanese pirates" in south China, but such men were the flotsam of Ieyasu's own policies, outlaws pushed out of Japan by his clampdowns. He was hence uninterested in granting the request, particularly since he displayed little desire for the official acknowledgement of tributary status that the Chinese were dangling in front of him as some sort of incentive.

The approval of the Chinese emperor was simply not something that Ieyasu really required—not since the days of the feuding imperial pretenders of the Ashikaga shōgunate had there been any real need to appeal to Chinese authority. When Korea fell to Manchu invaders in 1636, the Koreans were instructed to order the Japanese to send tribute to their new masters. Instead—presumably knowing exactly where the battles would end up being fought if Japan and the Manchus went to war—the Koreans delayed until the Manchus mercifully lost interest. The Manchus invaded China in 1644, but were kept busy with that enterprise for the next few decades, by which time they appeared to have forgotten Japan anyway—Manchu policy in general avoided and tried to ignore the sea. The Tokugawa regime displayed even less interest in pandering to the rulers of China, offering no help to Ming loyalists in resisting the Manchus, and not even bothering to reestablish official diplomatic relations until 1871. The only exception to this was the Ryūkyū Island chain. The Tokugawa authorities passed the responsibility for these islands to the Satsuma clan, which had conquered them in 1609. By 1650, the Satsuma clan ruled that the best way to avoid rocking the boat was for the Ryūkyūs to pay tribute not only to the new Manchu emperor and to the Satsuma clan in Kagoshima (where a Ryūkyū prince was kept as hostage), but also to the last of the Ming pretenders hanging on in his final bastion on Taiwan. This sham continued until the 1680s, when the last of the Ming loyalists was wiped out, but the Ryūkyū Islands continued to pay tribute to the Manchus, thereby ensuring that the Satsuma clan's secret trade route into China remained secure.

Chinese traders still docked at Nagasaki, where they were confined in a special compound but still allowed to buy and sell. There was a thriving community of Chinese exiles—refugees and prisoners from the ill-fated Korea expedition, for example—kept as special artisans by certain daimyō. Chinese cultural items and books continued to find connoisseurs and readers in Japan, but China itself became a fading memory.

Japanese could not leave. Foreigners could not enter. So began the period known in Japanese as *sakoku*, the "locked country." The Tokugawa clan concentrated its energies formidably on control, stamping out dissent. Matchlock guns were locked away in castles. Foreign influences were ruthlessly purged, with knowledge of the outside world left firmly in the hands of experts in Rangaku (Dutch studies), who were authorized to deal with the men, books, and technology that could be found on the quarantine island of Dejima.

The *sakoku* era roughly spans the period of low temperatures known to climatologists as the "Little Ice Age." Winters became substantially more severe, with their worst conditions leading to several periods of famine. The worst, the Tenpō famine of 1833–39, is likely to have played a significant part in undermining the authority of the shōgun—but it is unfair to speak of the *sakoku* period as a failure merely because it eventually failed. For two centuries, Japan enjoyed a relative boom time, locked in a time warp that pretended it was still the 1630s while the world outside experienced the industrial revolution.

With peace formally declared, the samurai truly transformed into a hereditary "class," comprising some 6 percent of the Japanese population; they were imposed upon every town as an administrative sector. They dressed like the warriors of old, and the lucky ones still got to live in castles, although before long each domain was forced to reduce its castle count to a single headquarters and to dismantle and decommission any other strongholds.

The basic unit of assessment and payment was rice—or rather, the amount of rice that one's domain was expected to produce. A *koku* of rice was subject to certain fluctuations in official size, but was essentially equivalent to two or three wheelbarrow-loads—enough rice, it was thought, to feed a man for a year. A lord was handed land with a theoretical output of *koku*. He got someone else to harvest it. Samurai were paid in rice; if they wanted to convert it to cash, they needed to see a broker. But the size of a lord's tax and manpower obligations to the shōgun, and hence his status among other lords, was determined by the number of *koku* his land could produce each year. At 500 *koku*, you were a wealthy landowner with servants and some standing in the community. At 10,000 *koku*, you were low-ranking aristocracy, obliged to contribute a hundred foot soldiers to a notional battle. At 100,000 *koku*, you were a battalion commander, expected to marshal forces of some 750 pikemen, musketeers, and cavalry. However, part of the problem with permanent peace was the absence of any real opportunities to put those men to use. The samurai of the seventeenth century soon ran out of things to do, and seemed to spend much of their careers spoiling for a fight. Very occasionally, there might be a riot or uprising that required some constabulary action, but—though none dared voice such an opinion at the time—the samurai's position became increasingly ludicrous. They turned into clerks, night watchmen, and security guards, incongruously dressed for the battlefields of yore, leeching food from the surrounding community while they swaggered through it feeling assured that they held the power of life or death over the locals.

Ieyasu's reforms also introduced an innocent-sounding clause about the necessity of loyal samurai presenting themselves in Edo "for the service of the shōgunate." For most of the lords, this eventually manifested as *sankin kōtai*, a custom of "alternate attendance," whereby each daimyō would spend one year in Edo and the next back in his own lands. To-ing and fro-ing to the shōgun's headquarters forced each lord to maintain a mansion and representatives in Edo itself, and ensured there were familial hostages there, even on the off-years. It also obliged every daimyō to embark on lavish annual processions between Edo and their home domain—for the highest-ranking, a procession of some 1,500 litter-bearers, porters, footmen, and outriders was customary. Any such journey generated a mountain of paperwork and an outbreak of business opportunities all along the roads and waterways, which each local lord was himself obliged to maintain for the benefit of travelers.

Japan during the *sakoku* era was not necessarily "backward." True enough, it was not an industrialized society, but it was notably self-sufficient. The forests were well managed, the fisheries were abundant, and the farmers benefited from a double-bladed plough and a spike-wheeled potato planter. The cities were thriving, literacy was high, and popular culture was a vibrant whirl. Japanese cities were notably cleaner than their foreign counterparts, with highly evolved recycling and waste-management systems. Meanwhile, Japan's commercial sector enjoyed many innovations yet to take hold in the West, including marketing and product placement, prepackaged goods, and the advantages of the efficient system of roads and taverns. It might have evolved to aid in *sankin kōtai*, but it served the needs of the merchant class just as well.

Sankin kōtai had an enduring effect on Japanese culture. Opinion-formers from every domain served their time in Edo, turning that city—not the capital in Kyōto—into the center for cultural interchange. Even if a fashion or trend, a particular book or play, a new look, a new food, originated in the provinces, it only reached the rest of Japan through Edo. The mass movement of the lords' entourages through the countryside, sometimes from one end of the country to the other, served to encourage a nationwide phenomenon of roadside inns, stables, and brothels, along with what modern readers would recognize as the early fumblings of a tourist industry. It does not take much effort to imagine the sort of banter that might greet the weary traveler stumbling into a rest stop somewhere on the road:

> Welcome to the town of Marugame on the beautiful Inland Sea, the perfect place to water your horses and get a good night's sleep before the next stage of your journey. While you're here, why not buy one of the handmade fans for which our town is famous? Have you seen the temple at Kanonji? It's only a short ride away, and they have wonderful little bespoke amulets, available to weary travelers for only a small donation. Have you tried our signature dish? The broth for the noodles tastes *slightly* different…

Regional variations in Japan often became matters of very fine subtlety—the use of characteristic decorations, or the exploitation of a specific local product. Nagasaki got a reputation for its cakes, which could be made with the rare South Sea sugarcane brought in by its merchants. Shimonoseki became known as the place to try the poisonous *fugu* fish, the deadly venom of which could be transformed into a mouth-numbing sauce as long as your chef knew what he was doing. Edo itself became famous for rice bites, topped by or wrapped around a savory morsel, often seasoned with vinegar and swiftly assembled by snack vendors. The nature of the food seems to have been established by particular demographic conditions of the Edo area, allowing for fast and varied access to fish markets, but also a large enough throughput of customers that such delicacies would not have time to spoil. They were known as "Edo-mae-zushi" (Edo-portion vinegar-rice), or simply "sushi."

Edo styles began to drive the look of the rest of the country. The Japanese language itself became standardized and homogenized as samurai from far-flung realms congregated in Edo, swiftly learning to pronounce their words and write their characters in a way that did not mark them out as hicks. Still today, modern Japanese local "accents" are defined largely through word substitutions and occasional twangs—the basic building blocks of spoken Japanese remain clear-cut and distinct.

Even hairstyles reflected the samurai look. During the period of the Warring States, samurai shaved the front of their head in order to make their helmet fit more comfortably. One suspects that there may have also been vainer reasons for this particular style, since it clearly imitates the most common form of male-pattern baldness likely to affect a middle-aged samurai. But whatever the original intent, a shaved forehead came to be regarded as a statement of committed battle-readiness, creating a new and odd fashion that soon spread to all ranks. After all, who *wouldn't* want their helmet to fit better? This *chonmage* (cut-and-knot) style became the default appearance of the samurai class and anyone who wanted to look good—even the men in drag playing women at the Kabuki theater, who were obliged to conceal a shaved forehead behind a rather obvious purple headband. The look endured right up until the 1870s, when it was abolished by imperial decree as one of several modernization measures.

A trip to Edo was not a military campaign. Although it was a road trip of substantial time and expense, it would have been scandalous and fatal for the samurai to plunder nearby farms, and silly to travel with a year's supply of food. A merchant in Ōsaka, through which city a good half of the *sankin kōtai* processions were obliged to march, came up with a scheme to save everybody the trouble. This allowed lords to donate their tax-rice to Ōsaka warehouses; the warehouse owner would issue them vouchers that could be redeemed at other branches in Sendai and Edo. Often, that rice would still have to be moved to where it was needed, leading the same merchants to invest in new transport links, particularly shipping; other retail enterprises, such as alcohol distributors, piggybacked on these ventures. When samurai fell on hard times, the same merchants might be prevailed upon to issue loans in anticipation of the following year's harvest, or to pawn samurai possessions against vouchers that did not relate to rice at all. Despite its pretentions toward a medieval society, Japan swiftly evolved a distractingly modern mercantile economy.

This was good news for the merchants. The frankly medieval concerns of the shōgun's order put the samurai at the top of the social pyramid, and the farmers—the vast majority of the population, who generated the rice with which the samurai were paid—as the next rung. Craftsmen and artisans, who at least did something useful with their hands, were in third place, and the merchants were next, one step above the "untouchable" non-people—leatherworkers, butchers, undertakers, and workers in other trades proscribed by Buddhist tradition. One might observe that devout Buddhists weren't supposed to kill people, either, but the samurai had not given that much thought for centuries.

As far as the samurai were concerned, the merchants were mere parasites who capitalized on the peaceful realm by wheeling and dealing, taking a rake-off from the activities of good-hearted people. The merchants, however, were becoming increasingly powerful, reaping the benefits of runaway capitalism while being free of the ceremonial obligations of the samurai aristocracy. The only time they saw a rice stipend was when they changed it for vouchers and took a cut. There was no "merchant's code" forcing them to stay away from theaters. While the samurai clung to their time warp, the merchant class flourished. While the samurai postured and trained for wars that would never come, the merchants became the driving force of Japan's peacetime economy, creating a vibrant new culture of consumption and entertainment.

Although the rule of the Tokugawa clan was stern and unswerving, it nevertheless generated some new and unexpected freedoms. With the long period of wars coming to an end, a new fad flourished for offbeat and eccentric behaviors. Men dressed in foppish fashions; samurai carried ostentatious swords that would have been impossible to wield; hairstyles suddenly blossomed from practical, austere wartime cuts to outlandish bouffants. There were incidents of drunken samurai turning on each other in tavern brawls; of cross-dressing pranks that scandalized court society. It was an age of braggarts and outlaws, who were decried by conservative society as *kabukimono*—"eccentrics."

A leading figure among such hipsters was the dancer Izumo no Okuni, a semi-mythical figure about whom no definite facts are known. According to legend, she was a blacksmith's daughter and sometime shrine maiden in the late sixteenth century who drifted into a new kind of performance. Reflecting the irreverent times, she would put on parody versions of old temple dances and creative interpretations of the old *kyōgen* comedies that had previously run in between more serious Noh plays. Even offstage she dressed like a loon, in Portuguese pants and hat, carrying a golden sword and sporting the ultimate in exotic fashion accessories—a crystal rosary with a shiny gold crucifix.

Perhaps Okuni genuinely was a shrine maiden fallen on hard times and perverting the rituals she had only half learned; perhaps she was a prostitute with a series of attention-grabbing gimmicks. She soon achieved nationwide fame, putting on shows in which she reenacted stories about her late lover, a possibly fictional samurai called Nagoya Sanzaburō, whose many great deeds were soon spun into increasingly tall tales. In a crowd-pleasing twist, the ghost of Sanzaburō would suddenly leap out of the audience and dance with her, turning her grand finale into an exorcism of evil spirits and a celebration of love beyond the grave.

At some point, someone cracked a joke that played upon Okuni's eccentric nature. Her performances, it was said, were *kabuki*—a pun on their eccentricity, but also on *ka-bu-ki*, the words for song, dance, and prostitute.

Kabuki theater caught on like wildfire. Free of the constraints of Noh, it continued long past the death of its supposed founder in the early 1600s, swiftly evolving into an exciting new tradition of theater. Performers dropped the masks of Noh, instead painting their faces with garish makeup, donning flamboyant costumes that bulked them out and accentuated their strangeness. The onstage orchestra would belt out popular songs, using innovations like the *samisen* three-stringed banjo newly imported from the Ryūkyū Islands.

The Tokugawa shōgunate didn't like it. Kabuki was becoming a nexus for an entire subculture of entertainment and consumption, with the theater as the centerpiece for teahouses, taverns, and brothels. The authorities were most scandalized by the prospect that the actresses were actually using their performances to advertise their services as prostitutes, and banned women from the stage in 1629. Thereafter, female roles were played by young boys, until it turned out that they were also available for sexual services.

By the late seventeenth century, Kabuki theater was only tolerated if all the roles were played by adult men—the "prostitute" part of its name was not properly dropped until the 1800s, where it was replaced by a homophone meaning "skill." From its early beginnings on waste ground—the first shows were supposedly performed on the parched summertime river bed of the Kamo River in Kyōto—Kabuki gained a standardized theater layout featuring a runway leading from the back of the audience through the theater to stage right. Reflecting the number of supernatural effects, theaters were also built with trapdoors that would allow for the sudden appearance of ghostly apparitions.

The repertoire was an intriguing mixture of historical dramas and modern tales, many of which centered on the conflict of *ninjō* (human emotion), with *giri* (duty). The Tokugawa clan had made it plain that it would tolerate no defamatory accounts of the incumbent regime, taking any real-world political or military dramas offstage, but creating a thriving market for old-time tales of the samurai glory days, particularly the war of the Taira and the Minamoto. Safely in the past so as not to ruffle the feathers of any living samurai, such dramas occasionally alluded obliquely to current affairs, but with enough plausible deniability to keep everybody out of trouble.

Of equal importance for the Kabuki repertoire were stories of commoners—merchants and farmers, bar-girls and fallen women, often ripped from the headlines or sensationalized from urban myths.

Ghost stories were particularly popular in the summer months, where they imparted a nervous chill on hot days—jealous lovers returning from the grave, and spirits taking vengeance in the name of wronged Buddhist priests. The biggest hit of its day was *The Love Suicides at Sonezaki*, inspired by the real-world deaths of a courtesan and a clerk from a soy-sauce factory in 1703. Within a month of its occurrence, their story had been adapted as a puppet show—the *bunraku* puppet theater often being a front-runner in the arts and the source of the more lurid or acrobatic storylines adapted into other forms. By 1717, the story had been transferred to the Kabuki theater, initiating an entire subgenre of tragic love-suicide or *shinjū* dramas. The underlying message, deriving in part from Pure Land Buddhism, was that by dying together in this life, lovers would guarantee their reunion in the next.

Despite the breathless and giddy spin put on love suicides by the theater, in the real world such acts were regarded as disgraceful crimes. You would think that being hounded to one's death by unbearable circumstance and opposition would be punishment enough, but Tokugawa law demanded that the corpses of love-suicides be displayed on the Nihonbashi bridge in the center of Edo for three days. If the bodies were lost or unrecoverable, then the couple's living relatives would instead be exposed naked at the same location and forced to accept identification as criminals.

If this was intended as a drastic measure to dissuade would-be suicides from disgracing their families, it failed. Japan was plagued by a rash of copycat suicides, themselves seemingly inspired by numerous theatrical rip-offs of the original story. In 1723, the shōgunate banned love-suicide stories as a dangerous fad, although within a generation they sneaked back onstage.

Kabuki stars were the celebrities of their day, idols for rabid fans, sought after for product endorsements for everything from medicines to women's cosmetics, and the subject of lurid and occasionally pornographic speculation in the gutter press. In a triumph of what would be known in our era as mansplaining, the female impersonators, or *onnagata*, became the default authorities on femininity, lecturing women on the right way to apply makeup, wear their hair, or use a fan.

Older Japanese portraits often show aristocratic women taking pride in waist-length or even floor-length hair. In the Edo period, Kabuki performers and courtesans began to favor an upswept chignon called a Shimada hairstyle. Other women soon began to copy them, even though such hairstyles were often wigs for the original wearers. The hairstyle is most apparent in Edo-period prints, particularly of geisha, who are often distinguished by a larger number of clips in their hair—where an aristocratic lady might have one or two hairpins, a high-ranking courtesan would have a veritable sunburst of bright yellow bobbins, all the better to attract attention and make it clear that she and her servants had taken the utmost care over her appearance. Most crucially, she would make sure to display the nape of her neck, an erogenous zone which was regarded as erotically intimate.

Our best glimpse of Edo's vivacious urban culture, as well as its fashions and street views, can be found in the books and prints of the period. Whereas artists had previously relied on the patronage of the aristocracy, military, or religious orders, the Tokugawa period saw the rise of mass-market publishing, which created new readerships among the merchant and artisan classes.

The low end of the print trade was cheap and cheerful—the images would cost no more than a bowl of fast-food noodles, and the pictures themselves might be destroyed in the manner of their display—moistened and pasted to a paper wall, for example, and hence liable to be gone within a season. Some such pictures do survive today, although their appearance has often been distorted by the actions of time. Organic colors, such as reds and yellows based on vegetable dyes or crushed cochineal beetles, have faded, leaving only mineral-based hues like the imported Prussian blue.

The erotic art known as *shunga* (spring pictures) was a particularly impressive genre of Tokugawa publishing. Ironically, the fact that it was often cherished and kept hidden was a contributing factor in the survival of so many such works. Popular belief held that a *shunga* carried by a samurai would be a charm against death, or that possession of such images might serve to ward off fires. The subjects of Japanese erotica offered glimpses of the sexual lives of famous courtesans for those who could not afford them in the flesh. There were fictional or gossipy pairings of famous actors, both in and out of costume. Some purported to have medical value, offering practical introductions to the various sizes and shapes of sexual organs. Straightforward depictions of sex were accompanied by subtle references to historical personages or events, or poetry that evoked erotic allusions. In a style that sought to accentuate the focus of the participants while zooming in on the most crucial elements of an artistic scene, the genitals would often be drawn oversized.

The book world enjoyed a similar boom in novels, travel books, Confucian classics, philosophical tracts, and how-to guides. After a brief flirtation with moveable type, printers returned to a reproduction method that cut the text into a single block of wood. Unlike the Western world, where movcable type separated and then downgraded the importance of illustrations to the world of print, the concentration on woodblock engraving kept text and image closely related in Japan.

The nature of woodblock printing also allowed for certain titles to be customized—a basic mass-market edition would be produced in black and white, and a more expensive edition with extra color and better paper would be available for the connoisseur. Many editions were made for rental, peddled from door to door by traveling book dealers. Publishing of the Tokugawa period embraced every conceivable element of the printing spectrum, from flashy, fantastic penny-dreadfuls to masterful editions of poetry, samurai war stories, and religious classics.

The actual wooden blocks took up a lot of storage space, but the smarter publisher with an eye for the long term would sit on the woodblocks for as long as possible. If a certain book was a success, new copies could be run off on demand; or if sufficient time had elapsed, a book might be repackaged with a different story to accompany the images, or the face of yesterday's Kabuki star cut out and replaced with a wooden plug bearing the visage of whoever was the new heartthrob.

Although men like Hokusai and Hiroshige are the ones who get all the attention in the modern art world, we should not overlook the incredible skills and talents of the woodblock carvers themselves, who would take an original design, paste it to a block of wood, and then painstakingly cut out the image required in each color set—multiple colors requiring multiple blocks, each to be laid in turn precisely in the correct position relating to the others. The block cutters would not only reproduce the artist's design, but also the distinctive handwriting of the artist's signature and the text that accompanied it, much of which was dashed off with a lightning-fast ink brush that created delicate, swirling calligraphy. This, too, had to be reproduced exactly with a mallet and chisel.

Meanwhile, Japan's poetic tradition, which had long flourished as aristocrats dueled with words and one-upmanship, gained a new, stripped-down variant in the Tokugawa period. Whereas the great literati of old would challenge each other to keep a poetic composition going for as long as possible, creating great linked stanzas (*renga*) of up to a hundred verses to and fro, Tokugawa poets began to pare down their poems as far as they would go. Eventually, the likes of Matsuo Bashō (1644–94) dispensed with everything except the opening couplet, delivered without the expectation of any response. Bashō perfected a form of deceptive simplicity, a seventeen-beat declaration that would somehow contain a seasonal word, an apt juxtaposition of mundane and divine, and often some sort of structuring absence inviting the listener to fill in the rest of the meaning themselves. What could be more Zen than a poem that itself created a blank space for contemplation? And so was born the haiku, that literary form that lends itself so well to epigrams and calligraphy, challenging the poet to evoke a sense of wonder in just a few words.

Bashō's mastery of the form is best evoked by his sense of humor. While lesser poets looked for moments of divine inspiration or picture-book picturesques, Bashō was not above laughing at himself with slapstick glee.

> Now, then. Let's go out to enjoy the snow
> Until I slip and fall.

It is a wonderful moment, leading the reader off into a reverie of nature's beauty, only to bring them back to earth with a thump.

For the general population, the outside world was an enigma. The Tokugawa, however, kept tabs as closely as they could on the outside world, relying on scholars in the new discipline of "Dutch studies" to keep them informed about new developments. At the edges of Japan, *sakoku* was more permeable. In the remote north, it was not altogether clear where Japan stopped and the outside world began. The domain of the Matsumae clan supposedly only occupied the southern tip of Hokkaidō, but the family's trading network and contacts spread far across the island into the remote Ainu communities, who themselves traded with Sakhalin and the Siberian coast. On the Korea Strait, the Sō family on Tsushima kept close contact with the Koreans, and functioned as a gateway between Japan and a country that was similarly "closed" to outsiders during the period. And down in the Ryūkyū Islands, the locals cannily paid tribute to both the emperors of China and Japan, which allowed them to move between the two domains with relative ease.

Meanwhile, in the port of Nagasaki, many a "Chinese" visitor turned out to actually be Siamese, and every now and some of the traders among the "Dutch" were revealed to be English, French, or German. For a period, when the Dutch were cut off by the Napoleonic Wars, American ships put in at Nagasaki instead, trading under a Dutch flag.

It couldn't last. Even the Dutch tried to warn the shōgun that the world was evolving at a rapid pace. Russia, which had once been a "European" power, had expanded so far to the east that it went right past Japan to Siberia and into Alaska. The English craving for tea had led to the Opium Wars in China and the presence of the Royal Navy on Japan's doorstep. Meanwhile, the Mexican-American War, which ended in 1848, had brought the US acquisition of California. The United States now spanned "sea to shining sea" and looked out across the Pacific at a new horizon.

Not a year passed by without some sort of unwelcome coastal encounter—a shipwreck of foreign sailors, or traders trying it on. The rise of steamships was particularly dangerous for Japan, as they both brought it far closer to the rest of the world in terms of travel time and left foreign shipping hungry for coaling ports in the north Pacific.

Sometime in the late 1840s or early 1850s—so claims the Japanese historian Nitobe Inazō—a haunting song briefly achieved notoriety in Japan.

> Thro' a black night of cloud and rain
> The Black Ship plies her way—
> An alien thing of evil mien—
> Across the waters gray.
>
> Down in her hold there labor men
> Of jet-black visage dread;
> While fair of face stand by her guns
> Grim hundreds clad in red.
>
> With cheeks half hid in shaggy beards
> Their glance fixed on the wave,
> They seek our sun-land at the word
> Of captain owlish-grave.

While loud they come—the boom of drums
And songs in strange uproar;
And now with flesh and herb in store,
Their prows turn toward the Western shore.

And slowly floating onward go
These Black Ships, wave tossed, to and fro.

The "Song of the Black Ship" has attained a certain fame among scholars of the period, and is often cited as some sort of bizarre prophecy of events that would unfold in 1853. When regarded in its entirety, however, it seems to be more of a reflection of the many unsuccessful visits and offshore sightings of foreign ships, distinguished by their size and their black anti-fouling paint, in the mid-nineteenth century, leavened with rumors about such vessels' crews and their intent. Foreign vessels were glimpsed with increasing frequency in Japanese waters, despite the repeated assurances of the shōgun and his coastguards that foreign ships would never be allowed to dock outside of the Nagasaki quarantine.

That, however, was only half the story. Behind the scenes, the shōgunate was increasingly worried about incursions by foreign shipping. There were suspicious increases in the number of shipwrights at Japanese ports, and a sudden application of greater diligence on the coastal forts and gun batteries. Although the authorities in Japan continued to assure their emperor and people that all was well, there was trouble on the horizon.

CHAPTER 7

THE STENCH OF BUTTER: RESTORATION AND MODERNIZATION

It began as an unplaceable thrumming sound. When the waves were hushed, when the birds were sleeping, fishermen on the Sagami shoreline heard a new, unknown sound in the darkness. It hummed: a distant growl, as they might have imagined a tiger would sound, if its growl went on forever and somehow came from beyond the sea; but it did not come closer…instead, it passed and faded.

It took daylight for the source of the noise to come into view, moving close enough to the shore that the black clouds of its smoke were visible, first as a haze, then as belches of sooty particles.

By the time the sea air was spiced with the smell of coal tar, the ships were visible. Some of the people of Edo Bay had heard of foreign whaling ships. Some claimed a friend of a friend had seen them, but none wanted to be too specific. Familiarity with foreign ships implied familiarity with foreigners, and that was still a capital offense. Watchers on the hills spoke agitatedly of a "fire on the seas," only to realize with mounting distress that they were watching the approach of the state of the art in foreign naval might—four American warships.

They were like no ships most of the Japanese had ever seen before. Their sails were rolled up, but somehow they were still making headway against the wind, their coal engines churning great paddlewheels at their sides. The flagship, the *Susquehanna*, was twenty-five times larger than the largest Japanese vessel afloat. People called it a "castle upon the water." The ships were "as large as mountains" and "as swift as birds."

If the Japanese had been a little more clued in, they might have noticed a few asides. They were too caught up in the size of the flotilla to notice that two of the ships were actually being towed—not every vessel was high-tech. The commander, Commodore Matthew Perry, had hoped to stage a more imposing arrival, but several of his squadron's most striking ships were elsewhere undergoing repairs.

Regardless, he steamed on ahead, ignoring the shouts from irate coastguards in tiny boats, including one group that held up a sign proclaiming (in French) that he should turn away and not dare to drop anchor.

Perry dropped anchor. It was July, 1853.

It turned out that there was nothing that the Japanese could do about it. Shore batteries were silent. Samurai stared from the shore. Perry sent word ashore that he was seeking an audience.

The shōgun had known he was coming for months. The Dutch in Nagasaki had forwarded comments from their own viceroy in India that an envoy would be arriving with a letter from the president of the US for the emperor of Japan, and that he would be returning some Japanese castaways and asking for the opening of some Japanese ports.

Perry had studied the Japanese obfuscations over previous approaches, and his arrival in sight of the shōgun's headquarters was a calculated show of force. He even demonstrated his ships' seventy-three guns, firing a salute in belated celebration of American Independence Day before leaving, having promised to return the next year for his answer.

The members of the shōgun's inner circle, sitting on intelligence from their "Dutch studies" scholars, were well aware that Perry was not bluffing. They had already heard stories of the damage wreaked on China by the British in the Opium Wars, and of the resultant "unequal treaties" that forced open trading, awarded foreigners a waiver from local justice, and imposed harsh indemnities, the repayment of which weakened the national economy. Perhaps a reasonable solution would be simply to agree to open the ports and miss out the war in the middle?

This decision, however, was not in the shōgun's power to make. He was, after all, the "barbarian-suppressing supreme general"; his job description expressly demanded that he keep foreigners *out*, not grant them concessions. He asked the emperor for advice only to be fobbed off with a series of airy memorials, none of which granted him permission to shirk his responsibilities.

The Japanese were ready to read all sorts of portents into it. The medieval founder of Edo himself had supposedly once prophesied:

> To my gate ships will come from the far east
> Ten thousand miles.

The idea that there was an "east" past Japan had been ludicrous at the time. Now it turned out there was a whole continent there. This, too, was not a surprise to the Japanese upper class—the shōgun had himself seen a foreign-made globe showing Japan's position relative to the other nations of the world.

Tokugawa Nariaki, the Prince of Mito, was having none of it. "Let not our generation be the first," he wrote, "to see the disgrace of a barbarian army treading on the land where our fathers rest." Nariaki was no fool; he had a bunch of reasons why the foreigners should not be made welcome, not least the continued mistrust of Christianity and the suspicion that this "evil sect" would gain a toehold in Japan if the Americans were tolerated. So, too, he warned, would other foreigners, since if the Americans succeeded where the Russians and Dutch had failed, then other foreign powers would be sure to seek similar concessions.

Mito was not a hard-core conservative. He recognized the recommendations of the most respected "Dutch scholars": that the Japanese should be permitted to learn from foreign nations. But he also acknowledged that 200 years of isolation had left the Japanese ill prepared for the culture shock. Mito was also worried about the political implications within Japan. The samurai class maintained peace on the assumption that they could prevent such embarrassments from occurring. Already, the townsfolk of Edo and the farmers of the shoreline could see that the rule of the shōgun was toothless. The nature of "barbarians" had changed significantly since the time of the Emishi.

When Perry returned in February 1854—sooner than promised, with twice the number of ships—the Japanese panicked. Out of fear that he would open fire without an actual answer, he was granted the Treaty of Kanagawa, which opened two ports to the Americans, promised to treat shipwrecked sailors kindly, and allowed for a consul onshore. One of the two ports was Shimoda, close to Edo but on the seaward side of the Izu peninsula, calculated to keep the Americans out of the bay. The other was Hakodate on the southern tip of Hokkaidō, as far from Edo as it was possible to get without blundering into Russian waters—presumably, like the access to Nagasaki in the south, this was an attempt to keep the intruders at arm's length.

The treaty also granted America "most-favored nation status," which meant that the United States would benefit from new terms added to any similar treaties signed with other countries. Similar deals were soon signed with French, Russians, and Dutch, with each of them piggybacking on concessions to the others. Meanwhile, the promised consul arrived in Shimoda in the form of Townsend Harris (1804–78), former trader and vice-consul in Ningbo, China, fresh from negotiating a Treaty of Amity and Commerce in Siam. Backed by the looming threat of further gunboat diplomacy, Harris was determined to hammer out further deals and statements of clear intent, and ruffled feathers immediately by refusing to deliver his communiqués to anyone except the shōgun himself—a waiting game of eighteen months, which he eventually won. In negotiations with the shōgun's officials, he eventually got the Japanese to agree to another Treaty of Amity and Commerce that promised diplomatic exchanges and some fluff about low tariffs on imports and exports, and yet more treaty ports to be opened in the next couple of years: Kanagawa (Yokohama) and Nagasaki, then Niigata and Hyōgo by 1863.

Harris's treaty also allowed for freedom of religious expression among American residents, which would inevitably lead to the construction of forbidden Christian churches on Japanese soil. He also inserted a clause guaranteeing "extraterritoriality"; that is to say, the right of Americans to be tried by their own courts.

The Harris treaty ensured that by 1863, foreigners in Japan were no longer a rare, exotic mystery in distant Nagasaki, shut off from the rest of the country. Instead, they had become an everyday sight in six Japanese harbors, along with their scandalously visible crucifixes—a symbol once punishable by death, now openly flaunted—and a swaggering sense of entitlement born from the knowledge that even if they committed a crime in Japanese eyes, they would only be tried by the forgiving courts of their own land. Or lands, since the "most favored nation" clause in everybody's documentation ensured that all concessions granted to United States would also be granted to the British, French, Russians, and Dutch.

"The foreigners arrived in numbers in Kanagawa and Yokohama," wrote the British diplomat Ernest Satow, "and affronted the feelings of the haughty *samurai* by their independent demeanour, so different from the cringing subservience to which the rules of Japanese etiquette condemned the native merchant."

The Japanese reacted to these impositions in a variety of ways. Almost all were in agreement that Western incursions were a dangerous development; what differed was the nature of the response. The educator Fukuzawa Yukichi (1835–1901), a former Confucian scholar and "Dutch studies" expert, returned from a fact-finding trip to Europe and the US convinced that it was in Japan's interest to modernize and effectively westernize as soon as possible rather than remaining mired in the traditions of the Confucian past. He would liken the coming social changes to a measles epidemic that Japan would have to live through in order to become stronger, but he referred pointedly to Westernization as "civilization" (*bunmei*); the implication was that there was a universally agreed standard of culture that the Japanese had yet to reach.

Selected *bakufu* students were sent abroad to learn about the West; they would return, sometimes years later, armed with ideas for reforms and improvements. Meanwhile, several of the larger and more devious domains also smuggled young representatives abroad without shōgunal approval in order to see for themselves and obtain prized foreign contacts and technology.

But all was not well. There was no way to put a healthy spin on the shōgun's surrender to these terms. He had failed in his duties. There were already bellicose samurai domains who thought they could do a better job—not only among the *tozama* outliers, but even among the branches of the Tokugawa clan such as nearby Mito domain, although its lord dared not say so in public. Some of their rank and file, however, would make their feelings plain. In August of 1859, barely six weeks after the first diplomats were installed, two Russian sailors were cut down in public. That November, somebody murdered a Chinese servant of the French vice-consul.

If there was any belief that these incidents were occasioned by misunderstandings—affronts, as Ernest Satow put it, to severe Japanese etiquette—there was soon more evidence to the contrary. In December 1860, the *Illustrated London News* bragged about the reception of the British envoy Rutherford Alcock (1809–97) at the shōgun's castle, noting the proud panache of Her Majesty's ambassador and remarking how different it was from the days when the Dutch had to crawl "on their hands and knees with their heads to the ground."

Within a month, Alcock's Japanese interpreter had been stabbed in the back at the legation entrance. Foreigners, and the Japanese who worked for them, were being targeted by *shishi* ("men of high purpose"). The culprits were rarely apprehended, but many of them seemed to hail from Satsuma and Chōshū, the two outlying domains with the greatest resentment for the shōgun. This, they seemed to be saying, was how you expelled the barbarians—if necessary, one at a time.

"But the plain truth is," wrote Alcock, "we hear of danger ever near and impending until, as day after day passes and no danger assails us, we grow hardened and indifferent." Nevertheless, there were catcalls in the streets and slights in the marketplace. Two Dutch merchants were killed in Yokohama; the French minister's servant was badly wounded, again in an attack at the gateway of his own legation. Not long after, the temple where the French minister was staying burned down under suspicious circumstances.

"We come here to ask for your hospitality, yet we are greeted with fire," the Frenchman observed.

In January 1861, Townsend Harris's Dutch interpreter was waylaid and fatally wounded by seven thugs on his way home from a dinner party. Alcock's assistants reported an ominous bustle of attempts by strangers to buy firearms in local shops—their sale was forbidden to the public, but such demand implied a number of interested parties. In October, an armed band of samurai broke into the British legation itself. There was a brief skirmish in the hallways with riding whips and revolvers against swords, until the legation's own Japanese guards belatedly retaliated with extreme force. They killed five assailants; the other nine got away. On one of the bodies Alcock found a document signed by the attackers, proclaiming that they did not have the "patience to stand by and let the sacred empire be defiled by the foreigners."

The men appeared to be *rōnin*—masterless samurai—from Mito domain. Alcock was not convinced, and even suspected that government officials had been aware of specific threats against him, but had neglected to pass on the full details. He later heard that a samurai lord from Tsushima, having been insulted by Russians in a far-off harbor, had ordered his men to pursue Alcock (all foreigners being the same) and bring him the Englishman's head in revenge.

Recently arrived in town after a long journey from Nagasaki, Alcock now saw the crowds that had lined his route in a different light. He had previously assumed they wanted to see *him*. He now suspected they had been waiting to see him *get murdered*.

The most famous incident occurred at Namamugi, near Yokohama, on September 14, 1862, when Charles Lennox Richardson, a British trader freshly arrived from China, was out riding with three companions. The party ran into a long procession of samurai—the lord of Satsuma was homeward bound from his time in Edo. It was a massive entourage: horsemen and outriders, bearers and litters, accompanied by porters and samurai on foot. Locals knew what was good for them and stayed out of their way. Richardson, by all accounts an impatient alpha male, was annoyed that the procession was blocking the road.

With the fateful last words: "I have been living in China for fourteen years. I know how to deal with these people," he pushed his horse onto the road, threateningly close to the bodyguards marching ahead of Lord Shimazu's litter. Somebody got shoved, harsh words were exchanged in two mutually unintelligible languages, and a fight broke out. In the brief clash of swords, Richardson was mortally wounded. Lord Shimazu gave his assent for his samurai to deliver the coup de grace. Later reports suggested that Richardson had suffered ten wounds, any one of which could have been fatal.

Ernest Satow was ready to give Richardson the benefit of the doubt, believing that he had been wheeling his horse to *comply* with the samurai demands at the time he was struck. The naval captain Henry St. John, drawing on local gossip not available to the authorities, claimed that the official story was off the mark, alluding to "an after-lunch expedition"—in other words, reading between the lines of his Victorian prose, the British men were drunk—and that the tragedy was caused by a "wilful lady"—suggesting, for some reason, that Richardson had been goaded into action to impress the only woman in the party, his friend's cousin Margaret Borradaille.

Whatever the reason, it was the worst possible test of all the treaties already signed. If Richardson had been Japanese, his behavior would have been regarded as a foolhardy assassination attempt, and nobody would have faulted the bodyguards' reaction. It did not help his case that another foreigner, Eugene Van Reed, had been earlier seen to dismount and bow, which had been the correct response in Japan since the time of the *Chronicle of Wei* over a thousand years earlier. Regardless, under the rules of extraterritoriality, this decision was not in the power of the Japanese to make. The *chargé d'affaires* demanded compensation of £100,000 from the shōgun, a ridiculously high sum equivalent to a third of the annual budget of the *bakufu*. The best defense the shōgun could hope for was for some carefully worded memorial from Emperor Kōmei (1831–67), "ordering" him to do what he had already done, and thereby ensuring that his acts were seen as loyal to a new consideration of the imperial will.

Back in landlocked, sleepy Kyōto, surrounded by a clique of ignorant advisers, few of whom had any appreciation of the shattering changes going on in the harbors, the emperor made his position inconveniently clear. He commanded the shōgun to do his job with the "Order to Expel Barbarians" of March 11, 1863. The shōgun was given eight weeks to comply.

This was simply not possible. Either the emperor was placing the shōgun in an intolerable situation in the hope he would resign, or the emperor really was terribly misinformed about the scale of the foreign threat and the impotency of any likely Japanese response. As ever in Japanese history, one must look behind the immediate players to their advisers. There were samurai who rather hoped that the emperor *would* sack the shōgun, so they could put themselves forward as his successor. Satsuma was undoubtedly one of the domains with the biggest grudge against the Tokugawa, which helps explain the shōgun's reluctance to take responsibility for any of their mistakes.

The samurai of the southern domain of Chōshū decided to show the shōgun how it was done, waiting until the deadline had expired and then opening fire on several Dutch, French, and American ships in the Shimonoseki Strait. Both the French and Americans sent retaliatory strikes against Chōshū's gun batteries, but without the ability to land a sizeable force of armed men, they were unable to shut down the Chōshū interference. The strait was effectively closed to foreign shipping.

In July, with the shōgun pleading his case to the emperor in Kyōto, his representatives came aboard a French warship to pay the British debt. Satsuma, however, still owed £25,000 itself, and Lord Shimazu was refusing to pay up on the grounds that this would not even be an issue if the shōgun had done his job and kept the barbarians out in the first place.

In August, a squadron of British ships left Yokohama to head down the coast to Satsuma. They arrived offshore at the city of Kagoshima on August 11, and presented a demand to comply within twenty-four hours. As the Japanese customarily dithered, the British went into action on August 12, seizing three foreign-built ships that were easily worth several times the indemnity owed. As they did so, however, Kagoshima shore batteries opened fire. The British ships fired back, eventually setting fire to 500 houses in the town and destroying several Ryūkyū vessels in the harbor. Leaving the city in flames, they steamed away again, considering their message delivered.

The samurai of Kagoshima were left standing waist-deep in the water, yelling after the departing ships that they were crewed by cowards; some of them maintained that since the British had not landed, the Satsuma samurai had won. The city had been evacuated before hostilities began, leading to remarkably few casualties among the Japanese—just five dead, whereas the British lost thirteen.

To say that Satsuma was suitably cowed would be a misrepresentation. The domain did pay the British their £25,000, but only by "borrowing" it from the shōgun (and never paying him back). Impressed, as only another bully can be, by the tactics of the Royal Navy, Satsuma soon sent envoys to Europe with orders for some ironclad ships of its own.

That still left Chōshū. On September 4, 1863, a force of English, French, and Dutch ships, with a tagalong vessel flying the Stars and

Stripes to make it clear that the US approved, opened fire from the sea. The Chōshū batteries retaliated only to suffer a series of daring and damaging raids by parties of British and French marines, who spiked many of their guns and chased the enemy into the forests. The following day, a larger Anglo-French party of marines seized strategic points among the batteries, while the Chōshū samurai sniped at them from the trees. Despite continued heavy small-arms fire, the landing party proceeded to demolish, dismantle, or remove all the Chōshū shore guns. "I have satisfied myself," wrote Admiral Kuper, a veteran of the bombardment of Kagoshima, "that no batteries remain in existence in the territory of Prince [Chōshū], and thus the passage of the straits may be considered clear of all obstructions."

As in Satsuma, the Chōshū samurai drew an entirely unexpected lesson from their defeat, deciding that the best course of action was to adopt the technology and tactics of their enemies as soon as swiftly as possible. The smoke had barely cleared before Chōshū agents arrived in Nagasaki at the home of Thomas Glover, a Scottish merchant, demanding that he help them buy some warships of their own. Within two years of what it called the "war in Japan," the *London Illustrated News* was reporting the presence of Japanese soldiers in "Western" garb, carrying rifles and drilling like European soldiers.

This required the assistance of European military advisers. Chōshū's new modern army was largely trained by the French; Satsuma's by the British. A smart shōgun might have pitted them against each other, but by 1866, diplomatic overtures from the domain of Tōsa had persuaded the upstart domains to join forces. Behind the scenes, foreign powers chose their own sides in what looked like a civil war in the making—the French offering tacit support to the fourteenth Tokugawa shōgun; the British secretly supplying arms to the would-be rebels. Some enterprising Japanese businessmen sold arms to both.

Although there had been several skirmishes and punitive expeditions, these were regarded as government policing actions. Open war broke out in January of 1868, with a cluster of rebel domains led by Satsuma and Chōshū seizing the imperial palace in Kyōto and proclaiming that the power of the teenage emperor Meiji had been "restored."

Many of the battles that followed were resolved with admirable lack of violence. Although the country was nominally split between the emperor's forces (i.e., the rebels, now with imperial "backing") and the shōgun's, all proclaimed themselves to be loyalists to the emperor. The fight was merely over how that loyalty might be interpreted. The emperor's forces marched with a banner of imperial authority, the sight of which unfurling on the frontline was often enough to persuade the shōgun's men to capitulate—after all, they could hardly charge upon the flag of the sovereign they claimed to serve. The shōgun himself, knowing that all was lost, ordered his men to offer no resistance. He did so in the knowledge that even after being downgraded to a mere daimyō, his family holdings would still leave him as one of the most powerful lords in the new order. However, ever since the Middle Ages, samurai had been apt to interpret their lords' orders in terms of what he *might* say, rather than what he actually had.

There were, consequently, pockets of armed resistance, particularly in north Japan. In a last-ditch effort to hang onto their pride and the old order, the shōgunal loyalists retreated to Hokkaidō, proclaiming the short-lived samurai Republic of Ezo, headquartered at the five-sided fortress of Goryōkaku in Hakodate. It fell in 1869, ending the war and marooning many of the most steadfast samurai in the far north. The south belonged to the supporters of the teenage emperor Meiji, who swiftly arranged a series of proclamations to dismantle the Tokugawa regime that had run Japan for two centuries. Modernization was now the keyword, starting with the moving of the capital from Kyōto to Edo, the city that had been the de facto center for 200 years. The emperor's new home, where he took up residence in the departed shōgun's castle, was soon given a new name, by which it is still known today: the East Capital, or Tōkyō.

By 1868, Meiji's government had issued a Five-Charter Oath—

a mission statement as vaguely worded, but also as influential, as Prince Shōtoku's Constitution had been a thousand years earlier.

> Deliberative assemblies shall be widely established and all matters decided by open discussion.
>
> All classes, high and low, shall be united in vigorously carrying out the administration of affairs of state.
>
> The common people, no less than the civil and military officials, shall all be allowed to pursue their own calling so that there may be no discontent.
>
> Evil customs of the past shall be broken off and everything based upon the just laws of Nature.
>
> Knowledge shall be sought throughout the world so as to strengthen the foundation of imperial rule.

Implicit in this mission statement was the desire, long held by the modernist domains, to assimilate the technology and ideas of the foreign invaders in order to place Japan on an equal footing with them. Then, it was believed, the Japanese would be in a better position to revoke the unequal treaties and all the indignities that had been imposed on Japan. After all, the rhetoric of the Europeans and Americans was that such things were only imposed upon "backward" nations for their own good, since they were unable to police their own unruly inhabitants or control their own harbors. This, at least, was the argument in the unstable, teetering country of China. Through restoring imperial authority and embarking upon an intensive program to catch up with the industrialized West, Japan hoped to avoid becoming the next China. Indeed, Japan instead hoped to become one of the imperialist powers then carving China up.

Although this chain of events is often termed the "Meiji Restoration," we might quibble about what was actually *restored*. Japan's 122nd emperor, Meiji, was now officially in charge, but a cynic might suggest that this was merely one more round of the centuries-long obfuscation. Would it not be more accurate to say that the Tokugawa family had lost its hold on power, to be replaced by a new faction of kingmakers drawn largely from the clans of Satsuma, Chōshū, and Tōsa?

The difference with the Meiji Restoration lay in its instigators' decision to kick away the ladder by which they had ascended. Even among the imperial faction there were those who still believed in "expelling the barbarians"; these old-school samurai were in for a rude shock, as the new Meiji government introduced a series of sweeping reforms. The samurai themselves would be effectively abolished within a decade, as the removal of the shōgun proved to be more than a shuffling of those in power—it was the opening act of an entire modernization process.

At first, the victory seemed to follow predictable lines. Possessions of the Tokugawa family, which included many cities and prefectures, were returned to imperial control, which, in days gone by, would have been the prelude to the division of spoils and the dispersal of new noble titles. However, a year later in 1869, even the emperor's supporters were ordered to return their lands to the throne. Eventually, every domain in Japan, whether it had been pro- or anti-restoration, was ordered to hand its powers back to the emperor. The entire system of feudal authority was dismantled and replaced with a system of prefectures with state-appointed governors.

This was not quite the great redistribution it might first appear—many of those governors were drawn from the old samurai families, and former lords gained the right to enjoy a tenth of their old income as a form of compensatory stipend. Most of the old daimyō and their fellow aristocrats were rebranded with a set of noble titles in 1884 in imitation of European nobility, creating an entire class of dukes and marquises, counts and barons: the *kazoku* or "glorious houses." Such titles were based on a set of deeply traditional criteria, including the highest rank held at court by one's ancestors and the highest revenue in *koku* that a lord had been receiving prior to the Meiji Restoration. More than a thousand years after their ancestors had first wriggled their way into court life, the leaders of the five branches of the Fujiwara family were hence rebranded as modern dukes. The rulers of outlying regions, such as the Hosokawa family that had once ruled Kumamoto, or the Shō family that had until recently been the kings of the Ryūkyū Islands, were now marquises. As an indicator of how things were likely to go from now on, the lords of Satsuma and Chōshū received a slight promotion from their likely rank, being made princes in recognition of their contribution to the Meiji Restoration. There would be similar promotions for other noble houses in the decades that followed, with even the ousted Tokugawa getting some upgrades by the early 1900s. They might have been on the losing side, but they were still close relatives of the imperial family.

The Five-Charter Oath might have appeared at first glance to push a notion of universal democracy—and, indeed, after 1945, the Japanese would decide that was exactly what it had been intended to do. However, at the time of the Meiji Restoration, the reforms still clung to many elements of the old order. Princes and dukes became instant members of the House of Peers, the upper chamber of Japan's parliament, while the lower nobility formed an electoral college that selected another 150 of their number to fill the rest of the places. Succession was by primogeniture, although there was a thriving trade in younger sons between houses, who jealously guarded their hereditary titles by adopting new heirs if childless.

As might be expected, the *kazoku* soon multiplied, particularly as the Japanese empire expanded overseas in the late nineteenth and early twentieth centuries. The initial 509 peers would climb to 954 by 1928, assimilating newly minted barons from the industrial sector as well as the royal families of conquered Korea and Manchuria as distaff members, and would reach 1,016 families by 1947, the year in which all peerages were abolished.

While many of the aristocracy came out unscathed, their loyal followers suffered far more. Samurai on the losing side in the Restoration lost their status, but even the winners were soon subject to a 50 percent pay cut. In 1871, a proclamation freed them from the requirement to wear swords, but this was regarded largely as a matter of fashion and personal preference. In fact, it was a harbinger of far more sweeping changes. From 1873, recruitment in the modern military became a matter of national conscription—soldiers were drawn from the entire population, although former samurai might stand a better chance of elbowing their way into the officer class. As the government scrabbled to fund its modernization ventures, it took out loans from British banks in the 1870s, and converted all samurai stipends to government bonds in 1876. The samurai felt cheated—the bonds notably scrimped on the value of their wages and accrued interest at contemptuously low levels.

In 1876, the proclamation on the wearing of swords was revised into an outright ban. Piece by piece, every element of samurai status had been undone. They had lost their purpose, their payments, and even the symbols of their authority. The smarter ones embraced modernization by joining the modern army or navy, or giving up altogether and fading into the general population. Others, however, had spent their entire lives as members of a medieval military aristocracy and were unwilling, or unsuited, or just plain unable to change with the times. Despite commands from their lords, some conservative samurai refused to accept the new order. Some, like the father of the educational reformer Fukuzawa Yukichi, sputtered in indignation at the introduction of such subjects as mathematics, derided for centuries as a *merchant's* creed. Others were far more active in their disapproval, continuing the assassinations and protests that had characterized the first decade of foreign incursions into Japan. For decades to come, Japanese politicians risked murder at the hands of irate conservatives who claimed to act out of loyalty to the unspoken true intent of the monarch and were determined to purge foreign influences.

In 1871, Emperor Meiji sent abroad his most important fact-finding junket, the Iwakura Mission, which comprised forty-eight envoys and an equally influential substratum of fifty-four students who were sure to form the bedrock of the next generation of diplomats, politicians, and industrialists. The Iwakura Mission spent two years abroad, and returned loaded with cherry-picked ideas for a modern nation: a French legal system, a British navy, a French army (no, wait… the French had just lost a war with Germany: a *German* army), and a Prussian education system—the uniforms of Japanese schoolchildren still feature crisp Prussian military jackets for the boys and Victorian sailor suits for the girls. Victorian Britain and the Kaiser's Germany were particularly influential, reflecting Meiji Japan's sense of itself as a constitutional monarchy with imperialist ambitions. Missionary societies began to affect the schools, particularly regarding classes for girls, as did American educational policies. Samuel Smiles's self-help regime found an enthusiastic readership in Japan, becoming one of dozens of foreign books to swiftly find their way into Japanese translation. Foreign advisers expanded outside the military realm into shipping, industry, and education; among them was the Greek-Irish author Lafcadio Hearn, who worked as a teacher in Kumamoto and Tōkyō, and whose love of things Japanese made him one of the most widely read commentators on Japan in the late nineteenth century. Hearn, who had a Japanese wife and children, famously sealed his love of Japan by taking Japanese citizenship, only to discover that this grand gesture disqualified him from a foreign expert's salary. Not long afterwards, he was fired from his position at a Japanese university and replaced by the author Natsume Sōseki, who was freshly returned from study abroad.

In another case, the American William S. Clark was invited to Japan in 1876 to oversee the development of the Sapporo Agricultural College, now Hokkaidō University. Clark's experience seems typical—as a "hired foreigner" (*oyatoi gaikokujin*), he was pumped for his ideas and lauded for his contribution, although he was swiftly packed off again after a short sojourn of eight months. The English-language wording of his contract referred to him as the president of the school, although the Japanese version only called him a deputy. When he left, his hasty and seemingly off-the-cuff remark to his students: "Boys, be ambitious!" became a catchphrase of the Japanese modernization effort, repeated everywhere from statues to proverbs to songs. However, it seems that he may have been misheard or misinterpreted—there are variant accounts that suggest his parting words were the far less welcome "Boys, be ambitious for Christ!" In today's Capitol building in Sapporo, the city he helped found, there is a lengthier version that seems more plausibly to be what he meant to say: "Boys, be ambitious! Be ambitious not for money or for selfish aggrandizement, not for that evanescent thing which men call fame. Be ambitious for that attainment of all that a man ought to be."

Ambition depends on one's point of view. Even in the heady days of Meiji enlightenment, there were those who cautioned against the wholesale adoption of Western culture merely for its own sake. The intellectual Kuga Katsunan warned that foreign ideas were only worth adopting if they contributed to the welfare of Japan. Eating beef (or "mountain whale" as polite society called it), or holding fancy-dress balls was all very well, but it was in Japan's interest to take the very best of foreign culture only where it suited it. In some cases, this was a technological issue—Japan benefited immensely from major advances in technology, since it was able to adopt the very latest in engines and machinery without having to invest in the intermediate stages of development. But in other areas, it seemed ludicrous. Consumption of dairy products, for example, was suddenly fashionable, particularly with the rise of cattle herds on the newly opened plains of Hokkaidō, but it was regarded as a fad. In fact, popular belief ascribed to it a rise in body odor—*batā-kusai*, the "stench of butter," which endures in Japanese insults as a term for unwelcome foreign influences.

Calls for moderation were one thing, but among the disaffected, any step was a step too far. Many in the outmoded samurai class refused to accept the idea that modern "ambition" required going into business like the merchants, losing their helmet-friendly *chonmage* hairstyle, and hanging their swords over the fireplace. The upper classes did their best to lead the way, with the court itself dropping its elaborate kimono in 1872, instead putting Emperor Meiji into a European-style military dress uniform. The following year, his wife appeared with him in public sporting her own eyebrows and white teeth. While modern slang gleefully embraced such concepts as Victorian high collars (*haikara*) and Savile Row suits (*sebiro*), there were those who refused to change. They were going to cause trouble.

The last gasp of the samurai came in 1877, when Saigō Takamori led the ill-fated Satsuma Rebellion. An instrumental brawler in some of the battles of the Meiji Restoration, Saigō was one of the samurai who expected the Meiji Restoration to end in the redistribution of the shōgun's wealth. An opponent of modernization, Saigō nevertheless became a key figure in the development of Japan's modern army, seemingly because he regarded it as the best way to resist further foreign influence. He was, however, left behind both literally and figuratively by the Iwakura Mission. Acting as caretaker of the Japanese government while the leading figures were away, he seems to have been entirely unprepared for them to return with such effusive praise for foreign systems and technology. After the coming of the Black Ships, the samurai class had been commanded to "Revere the emperor and expel the barbarians." Saigō argued that even his own domain had only accomplished the first part, and had entirely ignored the second, instead welcoming the barbarians in such numbers that the country was veritably flooded with them.

Saigō was up to something. He had set up several suspicious martial arts "schools" in his native Kagoshima, and was subject to investigations by government officials. They were jumpy because there had been other uprisings by disaffected samurai in other parts of Japan, and they were worried because the notion of expelling the foreigners and turning back the clock to a time when there were no clocks might sound ludicrous to modern ears, but was effectively what the Japanese had achieved once before during the Tokugawa era. The threat, however remote, of a samurai rebellion, particularly from within the ranks of the victorious rebels themselves, was a real and present danger to the Meiji authorities, who resolved to shut down Saigō's activities.

As had happened so often before in the wars of the samurai, the result was a conflict between two opposing concepts of duty—the imperial forces loyal to the modernizing emperor Meiji; and Saigō's rebels, loyal to the conservative commands of Meiji's late father, the emperor Kōmei. Saigō's plan was to march up the country from Kagoshima on Japan's southwestern tip, to "ask questions of the government" in Tōkyō. By doing so, it seems, he hoped to rally former samurai to his cause, and if his experience in Kumamoto—where his numbers were swelled by local recruits to an impressive 20,000—was any indication, he stood a fair chance of whipping up a dangerously powerful force by the time he reached the capital.

His rebellion, however, made it no further. Despite his growing support, Kumamoto Castle held out just long enough for imperial reinforcements to arrive. From that point on, Saigō's march on Tōkyō was a mere dream, turning instead into a far more hurried retreat back toward Satsuma.

Seizing Shiroyama, a hill outside Kagoshima, Saigō and his dwindling supporters dug in for a last stand. Saigō himself was badly injured, although popular legend attests that he was able to commit seppuku, going out in the approved samurai manner rather than meeting an ironic death in the modern fashion from a bullet wound. His few surviving men chose to die by drawing their swords and charging straight at enemy positions defended by soldiers with guns. The army Saigō faced was thoroughly modern inside and out, not merely in its armaments and uniforms, but also in its supplies; for food, it was heavily reliant on a newfangled innovation: canned goods.

The Satsuma Rebellion spelled the last gasp of the samurai, at least in their medieval form. Its supporters were discredited; their relatives disinherited—it's not for nothing that the titular subject of *Madame Butterfly* is sold into slavery after her father's disgrace in an unspecified rebellion. Having fallen on hard times, the Satsuma survivors, like many other samurai left by the wayside, sold off their family heirlooms, many of which made their way to Europe on ships returning to the West.

Western interest in Japanese art and culture had been growing for a generation. Rutherford Alcock, returning to London from his posting in 1862, mounted an exhibition of his collection, much of which had been obtained at knock-down prices from impoverished samurai. The same year, the first consignments of Japanese prints, textiles and objets d'art went on sale at La Porte Chinoise in Paris. An entire movement of European style and fashion, *japonisme*, created a swell of interest in this most distant kingdom, which had not only been closed to foreigners, but had also barred its own subjects from traveling abroad. Japan was hence doubly exotic, no less fascinating than the unknown Cipangu of Marco Polo's speculations.

Back home, Saigō's samurai were not the only Japanese unhappy with the changes; they were merely the ones whose romantic aims and end were the most likely to attract sympathetic attention. Many farmers, too, had been left behind by the reforms, stuck deep in hock to loan sharks and facing mounting interest payments. In 1884, the peasants of Chichibu near Tōkyō rose up with what were, for the government, worryingly rebellious slogans, demanding a more participatory democracy and the cancellation of their debts. Not every Western idea was equal in the eyes of the upper class, and the authorities found the echoes of the French Revolution worrying.

Proclaiming that 1884 was now Year One of Freedom and Self-Government, and that the Chichibu district office was the Headquarters of the Revolutionary Army, the rebels in Chichibu marched out against government troops, meeting with a predictable defeat. Thousands were arrested, hundreds convicted of felonies, and seven alleged ringleaders put to death. But despite being the largest uprising of the post-Meiji era, the Chichibu Incident remains largely unmentioned in the history books, which prefer to end chapters like this one with the Satsuma Rebellion. This, in part, reflects the convenient narrative of Saigō Takamori's revolt—he was behind the times, he was acting out of loyalty to an imperial order, and he notably failed. After, all, ever since the tragic end of Yoshitsune in the Middle Ages, the Japanese public have warmed to the underdog. The Satsuma Rebellion was a thing of the past, relying on connections and ideas that were outmoded, whereas the Chichibu Incident was arguably a worrying harbinger of the future. It relied upon concepts and ideologies that were still fomenting in Europe and unwelcome in imperial Japan, and foreshadowed many bugbears of the twentieth century—socialism, revolution, and even Communism. As a result, the authorities quashed the rebels not only on the battlefield and in the courts, but also in the historical record, writing them off not as politically motivated rebels but as angry hooligans and outlaws. Saigō Takamori is remembered as a misguided but good-hearted loyalist, commemorated with an oddly unflattering statue in Tōkyō that makes him look like a stocky tramp in a dressing gown leading a dog on a piece of string. Chichibu, however, faded from memory, except on the London stage, where Gilbert and Sullivan's 1885 comic operetta *The Mikado* chose for its location the fantasy town of "Titipu."

So much for those who resisted the changes in Japan. For others, it was a boom time. Those in the right place at the right moment, particularly among the more proactive of the merchant class who already had capital ready to invest, found that early trade opportunities paid immense dividends. The foreigners bought Japanese tea, silk, and lacquerware, seizing so much of it that there were local shortages and price hikes. In turn, they brought in shiploads of cotton and wool items, tons of iron, and rarities like sugar. It was the British who reaped the greatest and fastest rewards: they represented four-fifths of Japan's foreign trade for the next decade, thanks to a heavy maritime presence already in China and India that meant only a few hundred miles needed to be added to established routes in order to ensnare Japan within their trade patterns.

For those who were already embedded in the merchant class, or ready to exploit these new opportunities by joining it, there were fortunes to be made. The Sumitomo trading house swiftly capitalized on the availability of foreign technology to increase its copper-smelting and -smithing output. Reinvesting its dividends from the modernization boom, it set up ventures in lumber, machinery, warehousing, and banking. The presence of a Sumitomo bank encouraged preferential treatment for Sumitomo sister companies, creating an interlocking federation of corporations, many holding shares in one another and beating the competition by offering favorable prices to each other for raw materials, rentals, and loans. The result was a powerful bloc of companies known in Japanese as a zaibatsu, or financial clique.

Sumitomo was merely the first of these corporations. Another Edo-period company that reoriented after the Meiji Restoration was Mitsui, founding the Mitsui Bank in 1876 and similarly becoming the focus of a nest of related industries. Others capitalized on the new opportunities and gaps in the market. The Mitsubishi corporation began as a shipping firm in 1870, but soon reinvested its booming profits into coal mines (to reduce the price of fuel), shipyards (to reduce the price of repairs), and ultimately ironworks (to reduce the price of ships). Other, more diversified industries soon followed, creating a third zaibatsu of related companies. There were others, such as the Yasuda conglomerate that grew out of currency speculation and tax-farming in the post-Meiji world, as well as many smaller unions. But it was the largest of the zaibatsu that would come to dominate Japanese trade and industry in the post-Meiji world, particularly in their lobbying for better access to raw materials and their increasingly lucrative fulfillment of military contracts—in decades to come, the one would often aid the other, in a spiral of increasing militarization.

CHAPTER 8

THE EMPIRE STRIKES BACK: THE ROAD TO PEARL HARBOR

The fun part of their trip was all but over. Nicky still nursed the aftermath—a hangover from the previous night's rice wine binge and a throbbing pain in his right arm, where an elaborate dragon tattoo still smarted. The work of a master tattooist in distant Nagasaki, it had taken seven painful hours.

Nicky and Cousin George had met with eight Japanese naval officers in Nagasaki, each of whom had a Japanese wife. Nicky fancied the idea himself, although he blushed to record it in his diary. The Japanese people were so nice and welcoming; so many of them spoke passable Russian. Daytimes had seen a bunch of typically tedious functions, including a display of delicate ceramics, and a visit to some temple or other—in fact, the Suwa shrine.

Nicky and Cousin George had both read Pierre Loti's *Madame Chrysanthemum* on the long voyage, and were determined to get a little geisha action themselves. Some of their Japanese liaisons were quietly scandalized that these European aristocrats should have got the notion in their heads that Japan's famous female entertainers were little better than prostitutes, but it was a common misconception among white folk.

Nicky and George were tailed at all times by a flock of plainclothes policemen, who could have made their lives difficult. Instead, with customary Japanese indulgence, these authorities discreetly looked the other way when the two youths in their twenties "sneaked" off their shipboard accommodation for a party with their newfound officer friends. The officers brought real-life geisha, who sang songs and dragged the Russian boys into dances. Suitably well oiled, Nicky and George treated the baffled Japanese to some Russian songs. Later in the evening, they ended up at a European-style restaurant where someone had procured them a pair of the kind of Japanese girls they *really* wanted to meet in a private upstairs room.

Somewhat the worse for wear, and now even more impressed with Japanese women, the two boys staggered back aboard their ship shortly before dawn.

By the time Nicky made it to Kyōto, he was so in love with Japan that he refused the European-style chambers that had been prepared for him at the Tokiwa Hotel, demanding a room with a futon instead. That night, he surprised his handlers by demanding to be taken to see some Kyōto prostitutes do that dance thing again. He was duly taken to the Gion entertainment district, returning to his hotel, after indulgences unspecified, at two in the morning.

Crowds gathered to watch him watch Japan. His nocturnal pursuits forgotten, he charmed his hosts by asking repeatedly whether he should take off his shoes whenever he went into a new building. He watched a match of the old court keepy-uppy game *kemari* and applauded at an archery display. Nicky blew 10,000 yen on souvenirs, while his hosts beamed in pasted-on pride when he put a mere 200 in the poor box at the Honganji temple.

On a warm day in mid-May 1891, they took their entourage up into the mountains outside Kyōto for a day at the picturesque Lake Biwa. This required an entire convoy of rickshaws, not just for them, but for their assistants and flunkies, their assigned bodyguards, and local bigwigs. The town of Otsu anticipated their arrival with a newly built wooden arch festooned with Japanese and Russian flags, and even a Greek one in honor of Cousin George.

They poked around the lake, saw more exhibitions and local color, and flinched in surprise at a daytime explosion of fireworks.

But before long it was time to go. Nicky clambered into his rickshaw, the fifth in the long line, with George behind him and their Japanese liaison, Prince Takehito, in the one behind that.

If the Japanese authorities seemed a little jumpy, the boys did not notice. If Prince Takehito took occasional reports from frowning plainclothes officers, it did not trouble them. But as later events would show, the authorities already had some intimation that there was a security threat—perhaps it was just a rumor.

The rickshaw runners set off at a steady pace, turning off the main road and into a narrow street, kettling the rickshaws into single file.

It was then than the would-be assassin struck.

Nicky was too shocked to immediately register the sharp pain on the side of his head. He stumbled from the stationary rickshaw and saw a burly policeman, his curved Japanese sword clutched firmly in both hands, swinging at him for a second strike.

"What do you think you're doing?" he yelled, forgetting for a moment the unlikelihood that the man would even understand him.

The crowd was screaming and running in all directions. Nicky's hand went belatedly to the side of his face and came away wet with blood.

The sword-wielding policeman charged straight for him, and Nicky finally worked up the sense to turn and run. The policeman kept coming at him, darting through the scattering crowd in silent, deadly pursuit.

Ten paces down the street, Nicky hesitated at a street corner only to realize that the policeman was almost upon him. But as the officer raised his sword to strike the death blow, salvation arrived.

Cousin George had also given chase and caught up in the nick of time, smacking the policeman in the face with a bamboo riding crop. The would-be assassin reeled to the side only to be tackled by Nicky and George's own rickshaw runners, who piled on top of him in a flurry of fists, snatching his sword.

Only now appreciating what had happened, Nicky began to shake. He felt gratitude welling up inside him for the two semi-naked coolies who had saved his life. He leaned, trembling, on Cousin George, and only then began to wonder why nobody else in the crowd had come to his aid more quickly.

Nicky had changed his mind about Japan. These people were no better than baboons. And one day, when he was the tsar of Russia, he would make them pay.

It was no longer feasible to ignore the unclaimed wilderness of Hokkaidō—to do so invited Russian incursions. Even the shōgun had been aware of this, with Japanese expeditions to shoo away Russian explorers mounted as early as 1808. Now it was time to formally incorporate the island into the Japanese state. The new acquisition comprised a vast area—20 percent of the overall land mass of the home islands. This expansion officially incorporated the indigenous Ainu people into Japan, creating a new ethnic minority and a flood of breathless new noble-savage literature about the bear-worshipping native tribes of Japan's new frontier. Americans were prominent among the foreign experts drafted in to open up the plains of Hokkaidō, which only served to add to its wild-west aspect. Even today, Hokkaidō tourism favors homesteads and cattle ranches, cowboys and nineteenth-century architecture—at least until winter, when it's all about the snow.

The Ryūkyū Islands were similarly incorporated within Japanese territory, not as an outlying marchland, but as an official prefecture. This was accomplished with a series of wily diplomatic moves, beginning in 1871 when the crew of a shipwrecked Ryūkyū boat was massacred by Taiwanese aborigines. Japan demanded reparations from China; simply by entering negotiations, China was seen to be acknowledging that Japan represented the interests of the fishermen and therefore spoke for the Ryūkyū Islands, even though the archipelago had previously been regarded as a Chinese vassal. By 1879, the last king of the Ryūkyūs had abdicated and his realm would become a Japanese prefecture.

Such landgrabs were only the opening moves of imperialist Japan. As the Chinese had claimed not to be responsible for the eastern coast of Taiwan, where the murderous aborigines could be found, Japan launched an ill-fated punitive expedition against them in 1874. This was intended as the first step in the seizure of Taiwan, but it was beaten back by disease.

A newly outward-looking Japan took a substantially more active interest in the mainland. Qing-dynasty China was stumbling under the impact of foreign interests, while Korea, a "hermit kingdom" supposedly operating under a similar seclusion policy to Tokugawa Japan, was under pressure to open up in the same way. Coveting Korean resources, particularly coal and iron, and wary of Russian interference in the country, the Japanese took to heart the words of a Prussian military adviser who announced that Korea was a "dagger pointed at the heart of Japan." It was, after all, the location from which the infamous Mongols had launched their medieval attack. Whoever controlled Korea controlled the point from which Japan could be invaded.

A food shortage in 1882 led to a military mutiny in Seoul, from which Japanese diplomats had to flee on a British survey vessel. Japan responded by sending a naval task force to "protect Japanese interests"; China responded to this with a similar squadron.

Although matters were eventually settled diplomatically, Korea remained torn between pro-Chinese factions that emphasized the country's traditional role as a tributary state of China and reformists for whom "modernization" meant a strong role for the Japanese. An attempted reformist coup in 1884 led to a request from the Korean queen for a Chinese military response, in which forty Japanese residents were subsequently killed.

In 1886, China showed off its newly acquired modern warships, including the German-built giants the *Dingyuan* and the *Zhenyuan*, which put in at Nagasaki for a visit. The ships dwarfed anything that the Japanese had, and gave the false impression that China was modernizing at a similarly swift rate. Chinese sailors on shore leave got into a fight with the Nagasaki police, leading to eighty deaths and further escalating tensions between the countries. A second on-shore riot led to further deaths and Chinese protests that the Japanese police should not have been armed with swords. In recognition of the collateral damage, the Japanese authorities did disarm their constables, although behind the scenes, the climb-down concealed more enduring and useful works of espionage.

Spooked by the sheer size of the new Chinese warships, the Japanese increased their own budgets for European-made shipping. This was in spite of a report by Captain Tōgō Heihachirō, a naval officer who had not only met with the Chinese commanders in uniform but poked around the docksides at Kure while dressed in civilian clothes, and reported to his superiors that the Chinese sailors were slovenly and unkempt, their deck already scattered with junk; their guns used to string washing lines. A more enduring and useful spin-off from the unrest was the acquisition of a Chinese sailor's dictionary marked with odd numbers, which allowed the Japanese to crack the Chinese signaling codes.

By the time China and Japan went to war over Korea in 1894, the Japanese were able to read all their enemy's coded communications. Troop buildups in Korea by China and Japan did little to prevent an attempted coup by the conservative Donghak (Eastern learning) faction. Japanese troops put down the rebellion and then loitered in Korea long after it was supposedly suppressed. By July of that year, they had kidnapped the Korean king and forced him to annul all treaties with China; to proclaim a new, forward-thinking modernist regime; and to demand the withdrawal of Chinese troops.

In the war that ensued, the Japanese successfully pushed the Chinese back across the Yalu River and pursued them into Chinese territory. A last-minute naval action by the aforementioned Captain

Tōgō sped south to seize Taiwan in the last few days before a truce could be agreed. Although Japan was forced in later negotiations to hand back much of the land seized from China, it did retain its influence in Korea, as well as in Taiwan, which would remain a Japanese colony until 1945.

As far as the Japanese were concerned, the victory over China was a sign that Japan was truly modern—carving out slices of Chinese territory for its own exploitation in much the same manner as the British, French, Germans, and other foreign powers had. The British plainly agreed, signing the Anglo-Japanese Treaty of Commerce and Navigation in 1894. It stated that from July 17, 1899, extraterritoriality would be suspended—British subjects accused of a crime in Japan would henceforth be tried by a Japanese court. Similar arrangements followed with other countries to meet the same deadline, dismantling one of the pillars of the unequal treaties.

By 1900, Japan was an active participant in the suppression of the Boxer Rebellion in China, wherein a multinational task force marched on Beijing to come to the rescue of besieged foreign legations. However, Japan's landgrab and interference on the mainland would also put it on a collision course with Russia.

Some Japanese politicians argued that there was plenty of room for everybody in the ruins of China. Russia could have the rolling plains of Manchuria, for example, while the Japanese consolidated their interests elsewhere. But as might be expected with a foreign policy initiative that relied on conquest and seizure of another state's territory, it was difficult to call a halt to such expansion. Could the Russians be trusted not to push against the Japanese? Did not all evidence suggest that the only way to deal with foreign powers was through the obvious and clear flexing of military muscle?

Besides, why let the Russians have Manchuria? There was ample space for new farmland for crops—soybeans, sorghum, and millet. The edges of the region were thick with valuable forests, and there were massive coal deposits. Why let the Russians have what the Japanese themselves could surely take?

The hawks won out, although plainly the Russian tsar had worked out a similar plan for himself. Nicholas II had been merely the crown prince in 1890 when he had sailed out to Japan en route to Vladivostok for the inauguration of Russia's great Trans-Siberian railway. There had been hope that his arrival in Japan would initiate a great meeting of imperial minds, but it had turned into a diplomatic disaster when he was attacked by one of his own Japanese police escorts. The then-prince Nicholas left Japan with two enduring souvenirs—a tattoo he had picked up in Nagasaki and a scar on his forehead from the assassination attempt in Ōtsu. The Japanese authorities from Emperor Meiji on down were deeply embarrassed by the incident, and Nicholas received thousands of telegrams and well-wishes from the horrified Japanese public. The damage, however, was done, and Nicholas was heard ever after to regard the Japanese as an untrustworthy "bunch of monkeys." The date of the attack eventually found its way into the calendar officially used by the Russian navy, and the Trans-Siberian railway would find ever-escalating use in the transportation of troops and military equipment from Europe to the Far East.

In 1902, since Japan was now on an equal footing with foreign powers, it was able to sign more far-reaching treaties. The resultant Anglo-Japanese Alliance found each promising to come to the aid of the other if it found itself at war with more than one enemy. For the British, this allowed for the redeployment of ships from the China seas to increasingly tense European waters where Germany was growing in stature. For the Japanese, this guaranteed that if conflict broke out with Russia, no power would come to Russia's aid for fear of starting a war with Britain in Europe. In 1904, this led a confident Japan to attack Russian ships at Port Arthur on the Chinese coast. Back in Britain, where many of the Japanese naval officers had been trained, the decision by the newly promoted admiral Tōgō to strike before an official declaration of war was hailed by the London *Times* as "an act of daring." With his entire Pacific Fleet trapped in Port Arthur by Tōgō's surprise attack, the tsar was obliged to send a second-rate squadron from his Baltic Fleet on a long voyage to replace them. In a catalog of disasters, the Baltic Fleet limped around the world, denied anything more than a day's support from any harbor controlled by powers wary of the Anglo-Japanese Alliance. A journalist from the *Daily Telegraph* broke the news that the Baltic Fleet was illegally waiting in Cam Ranh Bay in French Indochina, thereby alerting Tōgō to its location and forcing the Russians to continue on their way without adequate supplies. Lacking the fuel to go the safer, longer way around Japan to Vladivostok, the Russians instead sailed straight through the Korea Strait, where Tōgō's fleet converged on them from both sides in the Battle of Tsushima, Japan's greatest naval victory.

The land war in Korea and northern China was not as clear-cut as Admiral Tōgō's clean sweep, but would see the Russians fought to a standstill in Manchuria. It had left both sides depleted by 1905, when the US president Theodore Roosevelt stepped in to broker a peace treaty. Once again, Japan was rewarded for its belligerence: its interests were secured in Korea, and it was now master of the former Russian possessions on China's Liaodong peninsula. The Japanese also gained the southern half of Sakhalin, a desolate island just to the north of Hokkaidō. There was, however, no war indemnity—fired up by wartime propaganda, the Japanese public had been expecting a payoff in additional to the territorial gains, but none was forthcoming. The news was met with such anger that an illegal protest in Hibiya Park escalated into two days of rioting in Tōkyō, with seventeen deaths and hundred of injuries.

Japan's quest for acceptance into the ranks of the imperialist powers was bearing fruit. The last Korean ruler was forced to abdicate, replaced by a Japanese governor. The Korean crown prince would study at the Japanese army college, marry a Japanese princess, and eventually became a lieutenant general in the Japanese military. Japan took over Korea completely in 1910—maps from the period show Japan and the Korean peninsula in the same color, as a single realm. Japan regained the right to set its own tariffs in 1911, canceling the last of the unequal treaties that had been forced upon it in the advent of Commodore Perry's Black Ships.

Emperor Meiji died in 1912, marking a symbolic end to Japan's incredible era of modernization. The mourning and ceremony that surrounded his passing overshadowed a more pressing issue—that he was merely the most prominent and recognizable of his generation. The reformers of the Meiji Restoration were similarly long in the tooth—indeed, the emperor's council of most trusted advisers was known as the *genrō*, or "old men"; they, too, were dying off, depriving Japan of their careful management of its growth. The elder statesmen who could remember just how far Japan had come were being replaced by a younger generation drunk on power and victory, dangerously enamored with the gunboat diplomacy of the other imperialist powers and determined to win further glory for Japan. In some cases, this manifested itself as a bullish but good-hearted sense of cultural burden—that Japan, as the first Asian power to shake off foreign domination, had a sacred duty to lead the rest of Asia into the modern world. Certainly, for many other developing nations in East Asia, Japan offered a fine opportunity for foreign study and investment. Others were already wary of the implications of a Japan that emulated predatory imperialist nations. "This has made me all the more apprehensive," wrote the Indian thinker Rabindranath Tagore, "of the change, which threatens Japanese civilization, as something like a menace to one's own person. For the...modern age, whose only common bond is usefulness, is nowhere so pitifully exposed against the dignity and power of reticent beauty, as in Japan."

Japan's next step on the ladder came with the outbreak of the First World War, when it wasted no time in declaring war on Germany in August 1914. Japan's prime minister, Ōkuma Shigenobu, promised to "take measures to remove the causes of all disturbance of peace in the Far East, and to safeguard general interests...to secure firm and enduring peace in Eastern Asia." Even at the time, this worried his British allies, who voiced their suspicions that he was planning a land-grab of German colonial possessions in the Pacific.

His foreign minister did not necessarily deny it, but offered the excuse that Japan's motivations were industrial rather than political. Japanese banks had invested vast sums of money in farms, mines, and factories on the mainland, and military action was necessary to protect those investments.

An overwhelmingly Japanese force, accompanied by a token British division, had besieged and overrun Germany's China port at Qingdao by the end of 1914, while the Japanese navy seized the Marianas, the Carolines, and the Marshall Islands.

However, Japan's main aim during the conflict was to gain as many concessions as possible on Chinese territory. In such perfidious schemes, Japan had learned from the best. Employing a variant of Britain's own Doctrine of Lapse, in which it appointed itself the savior of failing states, whether or not the governments of those states agreed, Japan presented China with the Twenty-One Demands in January 1914. Among other things, this called for recognition of its occupation of the former German possessions, Japanese control of what had previously been joint-venture mines and refineries, and Japanese control of the railways in Manchuria.

Effectively, China was being asked to offer concessions as if it were already invaded by Japan. Keen to preserve its neutrality, but also to win European support, China reluctantly agreed to the Demands in May 1915, but only a month later began negotiations to supply noncombatant laborers to the European front. It was the sinking of a ship carrying such men by a German U-boat in the Mediterranean in 1917 that drove China to officially declare war on Germany.

This placed the Chinese and Japanese in an odd position at the Paris Peace Conference at the war's end. Although they were both technically on the same side, China had been obliged to concede to the Twenty-One Demands in the expectation that they would annulled by the other powers. However, Japan also had expectations, particularly over the former German territories and concessions in Shandong, a peninsula easily the size of a European nation. The

Chinese wanted this territory back, but the Japanese expected to take over the German occupation, and had secured promises of support from Britain after providing several warships to protect Mediterranean shipping off the coast of Malta.

The Japanese delegation at the Peace Conference was itself divided between the opinions of two scions of the ancient Fujiwara family. Its leader, Saionji Kinmochi, was one of the last of the *genrō* elder statesman; he hoped to make Japan a peaceable player in the establishment of a diplomatic League of Nations. One of his deputies, however, was Konoe Fumimaro, an angry young aristocrat who regarded the entire conference as a farce to impose what he called an "Anglo-American Peace" on the world. The last thing Konoe wanted was an international body to arbitrate disputes, since it would represent the end of the previous century's race for territory, and Japan still had plans for conquest. In a forceful article in 1918, he wrote:

> Militarism is not the only force that violates justice and humanity. Economic imperialism, also, by enabling the most powerful to monopolize enormous amounts of capital and natural resources, prevents the free development of other nations and enriches the imperialists without requiring the use of force. Should the Peace Conference fail to suppress this rampant economic imperialism, the Anglo-American powers will become the masters of the world and, in the name of preserving the status quo, dominate it through the League of Nations and arms reduction, thus serving their own selfish interests...Should their policy prevail, Japan, which is small, resource-poor, and unable to consume all its own industrial products, would have no resort but to destroy the status quo for the sake of self-preservation, just like Germany.

Konoe represented a rising faction within the Japanese government: a hawkish group seasoned with a sense of inevitable economic pressure, already threatening that the same tensions that had led Germany to war in 1914 could force a comparably hard-pressed Japan to pursue a similar path.

Had the Paris Peace Conference proceeded differently, the likes of Konoe might have been appeased and impressed by the ability of the diplomats to win concessions with words at a lower cost than military action. Instead, the consolatory give and take of the conference left the Japanese feeling overlooked and dismissed. True enough, they managed to cling onto Shandong (which angered the Chinese so much that they refused to sign the Treaty of Versailles), but they failed to insert a clause forbidding racial prejudice into the charter of the League of Nations.

Konoe argued, as did many of his rivals, that for Japan to fully participate in a peaceful, international, diplomatic council like the newly founded League of Nations, it needed to be an *equal* participant. This meant not only the suspension of the unequal treaties and extraterritoriality, which Japan had already achieved, but also freedom of movement for Japanese migrants into California and Australia, where they were currently forbidden, and free trade for Japanese goods into other countries, where they were often subject to import restrictions. It was, as one Japanese aristocrat observed, ironic that the Japanese navy should have mobilized in the war to protect France even though Japanese merchant shipping was forbidden to trade freely with French Indochina.

During the intense negotiations, the Japanese even tried to quote from the American Declaration of Independence, with its famously self-evident truth that "all men are created equal," only for the British delegate, Arthur Balfour, to scoff that it was an eighteenth-century notion, applicable to all men in a particular state but not to the universal equality of all races.

It was a bad beginning for the League of Nations. Konoe's warnings seemed prescient. The Europeans and Americans were fearful of having the tables turned on them—the granting of free movement and trade to the Japanese risked opening the floodgates for a reversal of the old "most-favored nation" status. If the Japanese, why not the Indians? The Africans? The Chinese? The Americans and Australians were fearful of "Yellow Peril" immigration. The British had an empire that relied upon Africans and Asians knowing their place. A racial equality clause would simply not do.

Konoe called it the "end of idealism." It certainly made the Japanese merely halfhearted participants in the newly founded League of Nations. The Paris Peace Conference left Japan still believing strongly that only military power would achieve anything. And now it had Shandong, with a railway line into the heart of China, as well as a series of mandates to manage former German colonies in the Pacific, affording the Japanese navy refueling stations all the way to Taiwan and Palau and into blue waters.

The rise of Japan's military came hand in hand with other troubles. Japan's new colonies in Korea and Taiwan were undercutting local rice prices, pushing Japanese farmers out of business. The global recession of the 1920s did not spare Japan; the country also suffered a natural disaster in the form of the 1923 Kantō Earthquake, which leveled Yokohama and burned down half of Tōkyō.

The medieval concept of *gekokujō*, the low dominating the high, came back into public parlance. The last generation of the samurai had been co-opted into the army and the navy and trained up in modern warfare, and had inculcated its do-or-die attitude to younger officers with unprecedented access to military hardware. Many of these officers thought that Japan was not expanding fast *enough*, and were ready to fight other officers for the chance to push the boundaries even further. Although there were many reformers and modernists in the leadership, they were outnumbered by a vast class of former samurai who were determined to scramble their way to the top in the time-honored fashion of their ancestors. Meanwhile, for the first time in a thousand years since the frontier wars against the Emishi, the sphere of Japanese influence had an expanding border offering new lands to colonize. Instead of the relatively small-scale and insular conflicts over the reassignment of lands within the Japanese archipelago, Japan's new officer class had a whole continent of resources to fight over—an ever-expanding frontier that encroached upon China, Indonesia, and Manchuria. There were fortunes to be won and lost, not merely by the military but by its industrial colleagues—cotton mills and brothels, coal mines and railway lines—and entire national infrastructures to be built and maintained. Sometimes this was even expressed in terms that turned the condescension of the European powers on its head. Japan suggested that while China was a failed state, that country's ideal future lay in Pan-Asianism—a reclamation of Asia for the Asians; and who better to spearhead this reassertion of Asian values than the great empire of Japan?

The Japanese army and navy exerted an increasing influence on Japan throughout the 1920s, eventually propelling the country into a constant state of conflict that would lead the period from 1931 to 1945 to be remembered as the "Fifteen Years' War." While Japanese military conquests abroad fueled an ever-expanding and more vainglorious empire, the military at home became increasingly bold in its efforts to cram the government with its own agents. Where military sympathizers could not be appointed or elected, various factions began to pursue a policy of "government by assassination," carrying out targeted murders to steer lawmakers in their favor.

In 1931, a lieutenant colonel in the Japanese army attempted to mastermind a series of political assassinations and riots to set the stage for a military coup. In 1932, naval officers assassinated the Japanese prime minister. In 1934, cadets at a military academy were arrested in the final stages of plotting a military coup. On February 26, 1936, hundreds of soldiers mutinied in a Tōkyō-wide series of assassinations and attacks on strategically important institutions. Their aims, though not entirely clear, were parsed as a "Shōwa Restoration," implying that the emperor Shōwa, Meiji's grandson—later known as Hirohito—was somehow being ill-served by his administration. They presumably hoped to emulate the great reformers of the Meiji Restoration, but apparently this meant taking an even more belligerent stance. It is difficult to say for sure, because the emperor was having none of it. Incensed by their claims on his behalf, he took the controversial and drastic step of ordering the troops to stand down in a decree that characterized their actions not as a noble uprising, but as an unwelcome rebellion.

Emperor Shōwa's adviser Saionji Kinmochi, who had been one of the intended targets of the rebels, was appalled by the emperor's action. Yes, it had worked, but if the troops had refused a command from the incumbent Son of Heaven, it would have propelled Japan into a constitutional crisis. In an act of foolhardy brinkmanship, the emperor had come within a hair's breadth of bringing down his own regime.

On the mainland, his officers had already embarked on a prolonged experiment in the way that they felt Japan itself ought to be run. In northeast China, junior officers at first staged terrorist attacks, and then "responded" to them with extreme force, overthrowing the local despot and installing a puppet sovereign. Since northeast China comprised Manchuria, homeland of the former Manchu emperors of all China, the Japanese swiftly enlisted "Henry" Puyi, the deposed "last emperor," enthroning him as the ruler of what was now known as the state of Manchukuo. The League of Nations protested. Refusing to back down, the Japanese left the organization in 1933.

Manchukuo is an incredible dead end in Japanese history—a colonial experiment cloaked as a new state, sold to the Japanese public as a magnificent paradise with ready farmland and mining concessions. It attracted over a million Japanese colonists, particularly from among those elements who had been left behind by the reforms—the families of former shōgunal loyalists, for example, or farmers who had been bankrupted by the recession. For many in the military, it was an example of what could be achieved if the brakes on their activities were removed; many of its leading figures would return home after the war to become instrumental in Japan's economic recovery. For the Chinese, it was an arrogant and oppressive regime relying on slave labor and the illegal trade in opium.

Decades after its fall, Manchukuo remains a historical embarrassment. The terms "Manchukuo" and "Manchuria" are still taboo in Chinese; the region is now pointedly referred to as the Northeast, implicitly connecting it to a wholly Chinese center. Its monuments have been broken up; its cultural artifacts consigned to dusty archives. The residence of Henry Puyi still stands in Changchun, where it is called the Palace of the False Emperor; it sits next to a Museum of the Japanese Occupation of Northeast China that pulls no punches, even in its Japanese-language signage.

By 1936, the Japanese military had outmaneuvered all home opposition. Japan's left-wing activists, including would-be Marxists, socialists, and union agitators, were suppressed. Ministers for the army and navy sat in the Japanese cabinet, where they enjoyed increasing powers of veto over any dissenting civilian politicians. The illegal acts of junior officers—whether they were preemptive military actions abroad or political assassinations at home—received ever lighter censure under the growing assertion that they were acting in the interests of the emperor. Although Emperor Shōwa had admirably shut down the attempted revolt of 1936, neither he nor his ministers dared try a similar act when the army embarked upon its next grand scheme, the invasion of the rest of China. With Manchuria secure in 1937, Japanese troops on military maneuvers provoked an "attack" by the Chinese garrison at the Marco Polo Bridge on the outskirts of Beijing. Japanese forces also attacked Shanghai, beginning many years of hard-fought conflict in the Chinese hinterland. China's Nationalist government held out for foreign assistance, on the understanding that China was so vast and difficult to hold that Japan would have its work cut out for it. All too briefly, there was a degree of cooperation between the ruling Chinese Nationalists and the Communist insurgents to resist the Japanese invasion. For years to come, the Communists waged a guerrilla war in the hinterlands, the Nationalists retreated ever further away from the Japanese front line, and foreign powers offered what material aid they could to the temporary Chinese capital in Chongqing. In

Nanjing, the Japanese attempted a puppet state modeled on Manchukuo, with a quisling prime minister, Wang Jingwei. This operation, however, was nowhere near as successful in quelling local resistance as it had been in Manchuria.

The military's hold on the Japanese government became complete in 1938, with a National Mobilization Law that commandeered national industries and economic policy into a concerted war effort. Even political parties were suspended in 1940, on the understanding that the Japanese people were now all of one singular martial mind. Japan's prime minister was Konoe Fumimaro, who had predicted this very state of affairs two decades previously. He was also convinced that it was only a matter of time before Nazi Germany was the master of Europe. Accordingly, Konoe signed a Tripartite Pact with Italy and Germany in September 1940, scant weeks before the tide turned against Germany in the Battle of Britain, leaving the United Kingdom as a vital bastion for a counterattack.

The year 1940 saw celebrations throughout the Japanese empire to mark the 2,600th anniversary of the founding of the Japanese state. Despite the legendary status of the emperor Jinmu, his fairytale campaign along the Inland Sea was remembered by a nation that included such myths in the history curriculum laid down for its schools. Myth as history was made manifest and acknowledged in a mass act of reverence, coordinated by radio signal, in which the imperial subjects of the empire all turned to face Tōkyō and bowed in the direction of their sovereign. The implication remained that Japan was unstoppable, that it was divinely inspired, and that great conquests still awaited. There would, indeed, be some territorial gains in the following year, but they would be short-lived.

America had not entered the conflict, although by 1940 it had stopped supplying Japan with anything that might serve military aims. Japan was running low on iron, steel, and oil. American sanctions left Konoe's conquest-fueled state with few options—to keep feeding its military engine, it desperately needed new sources of raw materials. This led to the invasion of Southeast Asia in July 1941, at which point the United States shut down all trade with Japan and froze Japanese assets.

Japan had been on a collision course with America ever since its first postures of imperialism in the late nineteenth century; US diplomats had been warning their government of this fact since at least 1918. At some point, Japan would need to secure the Pacific by the same means it had secured neighboring countries. In this endeavor, its chief strategist was Yamamoto Isoroku (1884–1943), widely known as the "Reluctant Admiral." Yamamoto, who had seen American industrial capacity for himself, warned his superiors that Japan would stand little chance against the United States mobilized on a war footing. In order to protect Japan's flank while moving into Southeast Asia, Yamamoto outlined a plan to temporarily shut the US out of the Pacific. He planned a knockout blow on Hawaii, where the US Navy had its largest base, Pearl Harbor. In theory, such an action would buy Japan time to seize territory in the western Pacific, but as Yamamoto struggled to make clear, there would be an inevitable and devastating counterattack. He tried to explain this to a right-winger:

> Should hostilities once break out between Japan and the United States, it would not be enough that we take Guam and the Philippines, nor even Hawaii and San Francisco. To make victory certain, we would have to march into Washington and dictate the terms of peace in the White House. I wonder if our politicians (who speak so lightly of a Japanese–American war) have confidence as to the final outcome and are prepared to make the necessary sacrifices.

Yamamoto's warning was soon twisted by the simple expedient of leaving out the last sentence, turning it from a grim statement of impossible odds into a gung-ho exhortation for showing the Americans who was boss.

Nevertheless, he did his duty in leading Japan's attack on Pearl

Harbor on December 7, 1941. Supposedly, Yamamoto had expected his government to officially break off diplomatic relations beforehand, signaling that a state of war was likely. By accident or design, the message did not reach the US until after the attack, turning his assault into a replay of Admiral Tōgō's surprise attack on the Russians in 1904. This time, however, there was no praise from the English-speaking media. Instead, it was decried as a "date which will live in infamy."

Japan held the upper hand for roughly six months. While the US reeled from the shock of Pearl Harbor, Japanese soldiers made rapid gains in Asia. Hong Kong and Manila were in Japanese hands within a few weeks. Better-defended sites like Corregidor and Bataan held out a while longer. Singapore was taken by surprise with an attack from the supposedly impenetrable jungle.

But then the tables turned. A prospective Japanese advance on Australia was curtailed in New Guinea and at the Battle of the Coral Sea in May of 1942. The following month, America's counterattack reached the midpoint of the Pacific, the aptly named island of Midway, where the Japanese lost four aircraft carriers. Many in the home islands, an entire generation raised in a martial state, did not see the immediate implications of a series of battles fought ever closer to Japan itself until July 1944, when the fall of Saipan brought the Japanese mainland into bomber range.

Japan's wartime industry relied upon cottage workshops scattered throughout the cities. The American forces therefore pursued a strategy of carpet-bombing Japanese cities with incendiary devices, creating firestorms in residential areas and killing tens of thousands of Japanese civilians. In April 1945, US bombers also seeded the sea lanes with mines, shutting down most of Japan's shipping and severely reducing the food supply.

In the slow but sure advance, island-hopping across the Pacific, US forces had already encountered the Japanese resolve to fight to the death. The samurai ethic, rebranded in the modern age, manifested itself in suicide attacks. Although planes and resources were dwindling, a surfeit of eager pilots led to the inauguration of fearsome new suicide squadrons, the *shinpū*, who drove their exploding planes straight into the heart of Allied ships. It's thought to have been Japanese-American translators who spotted the classical allusion and gave the characters the alternative reading of "kamikaze," an evocation of the Divine Wind that had once saved Japan from the Mongol invaders.

Decrees from the emperor had exhorted the Japanese to fight to the last, to make Japan a "broken jewel" that the Allies would dare not attack. Even among those military leaders who might have realized that the war was lost, the new emphasis was on making resistance so fierce, so terrifying, that even the US would stop short of a full-scale invasion. Even if the Americans were so foolhardy as to attempt a landing on Kyūshū, Japan's generals were already planning Operation Ketsugō (Determinant), with provisions for 8,000 suicide planes, car bombs, rockets, and human fighters, which was intended to deliver such a terrible blow that it might, even then, force the Allies to rethink a physical invasion of the home islands.

In a sense, the policy worked. Plans for US landings in Japan, based on the 39,000 casualties sustained in the conquest of Okinawa, the largest of the Ryūkyū Islands, envisaged the loss of *millions* of troops, fighting for every inch of the home islands against soldiers determined to fight to the death, booby traps, false surrenders, and a local population ready to resist at every stage with sharpened bamboo stakes and suicidal knife attacks.

However, Operation Downfall, the US plan for the invasion of Japan, was never initiated. Operation Starvation, which dropped sea mines into Japanese shipping lanes, was already reaping deadly rewards among a population lacking food; most Japanese cities were in ruins. The Americans also had an ace up their sleeve, a secret weapon intended to shock even the hawks in the Japanese government into surrender.

CHAPTER 9

BROKEN JEWEL: OCCUPATION AND RECOVERY

There was a blinding light, like the flash from a giant camera, illuminating the entire countryside. The noise of the explosion rolled some seconds behind it. Several miles away in Nagatsuke, the windows were blown out on all the houses. Father John Siemes, a German priest, dusted the broken glass off his robes and forced his front door open through the debris, believing that a bomb had fallen near his institute, but there was no sign of any impact damage in the street, just a sea of broken glass from the shattered windows.

In the distance, where the city of Hiroshima used to be, a massive column of smoke was towering in the sky, topped by a rolling cloud that made it resemble a mushroom.

It was another half hour before baffling news began to drift in from the countryside. Anyone who had been outside at 08:14 on August 6, 1945 was reporting terrible burns, nausea and vomiting, blindness. Casualties were mounting, even though nobody could remember seeing more than a single plane in the sky.

By noon, Siemes's chapel and library had been converted into a makeshift hospital. He and his fellow monks rubbed lard on their patients' burns, but soon ran out of a commodity already reduced by wartime austerity. They were low on iodine, too, and bandages, but still the walking wounded kept coming.

Hiroshima, the new arrivals said, was on fire. A single huge explosion in the center of town had blown down almost every building. Only the very southernmost and easternmost edges of town had escaped total destruction, and these districts were now aflame, burning alive the survivors trapped beneath collapsed buildings.

There were people shambling through the streets like the undead, blinded by the light, dotted with shards of glass, their flash-burned skin sloughing from their bones. The river was littered with the dead and dying. There were screams from the burning buildings, and nobody had the strength to come to the rescue.

Late in the afternoon, news arrived that two of their fellow priests were in town, too badly injured to move. Siemes and his colleagues set out into town, past long lines of wounded Japanese and a limping column of soldiers.

There were garbled stories of a parachute. *A parachute? These white men were enemy paratroopers!*

No, Siemes explained, they were German priests on a mission of mercy.

I saw a parachute, said one woman. It was on its own. It came out of the plane this morning and came slowly down toward the city. It was still way, way up in the air when it exploded. That was the big flash of light.

Hiroshima had been relatively untouched by the war until this point. It had a series of air-raid precautions in place. There were safe places, food dumps, shelters...all had been wiped out at once. Siemes would later say that many of the deaths after the bombing could have been avoided but for the complete lack of services. There was no hospital to take the wounded to; no warehouse left standing with emergency provisions.

Night after night, the area was lit by hundreds of funeral pyres. Many of Siemes's own patients died. The fellow priests he had rescued from a nearby park showed signs of recovery, but suddenly weakened after a fortnight. Cuts on their bodies that should have healed after a few days remained open and bleeding.

There was something weird about the bomb that had been dropped on Hiroshima, as well as its companion, dropped soon after on Nagasaki. The emperor himself, in a radio address on August 15, referred obliquely to a "new type of bomb" in an oddly worded speech that turned out to be a proclamation of surrender.

The Japanese had been at war for fifteen years, and suddenly it was over.

But Siemes's patients kept dying.

American planes dropped leaflets in Japanese announcing that Hiroshima had been attacked by a *genshi bakudan*, an "atomic bomb" whose death toll was equal to that of a thousand B-29 bombers. They neglected to mention that the damage from the bomb included invisible gamma rays that were driven deep into the bones and even the genes of their victims, triggering tumors and cancers for decades to come.

The war was over, at least. But the Occupation was only just beginning.

Japan's military leaders had been ready to lose twenty million lives in the defense of the home islands. They were even ready to weather a couple more atomic bombs, on the understanding that the Allies could only have one or two. Emperor Shōwa had been pressing for surrender for some time; even when he got his way, he was fearful of a last-minute coup, and planned to tell the nation directly in order to ensure that no one would pursue the samurai custom of doubting what he might have meant. On the night before his address to the nation was broadcast, two guardsmen at his palace lost their lives protecting the recording from would-be conspirators.

The Japanese emperor had never before spoken to his people through the radio. For centuries, the rulers of Japan had issued written decrees and quiet audiences; Emperor Shōwa was not a man accustomed to public speaking. The Japanese he spoke was so rarefied and archaic, swirling with circumlocutions and euphemisms, that many of his subjects still required a translation. "The war situation," he observed, "has developed not necessarily to Japan's advantage, while the general trends of the world have all turned against her interest... We have resolved to pave the way for a grand peace for all the generations to come by enduring the unendurable and suffering what is unsufferable."

Shōwa consented to accept the demands of the Potsdam Declaration, an Allied policy statement from July 26, 1945, details of which had been kept from Japan's population—known only to a few daring individuals who had risked arrest by reading the leaflets dropped by Allied planes. The Declaration called not only for the surrender of Japan, but for the dismantlement of the state apparatuses that had dragged it into the dark valley of its imperial ambitions:

> There must be eliminated for all time the authority of those who have deceived and misled the people of Japan into embarking upon world conquest, for we insist that a new order of peace, security and justice will be impossible until irresponsible militarism is driven from the world.

Reading between the lines, we might see that the Allies' "new order of peace" referred to more than just the end of the current conflict. For many, the dropping of the second atomic bomb on Nagasaki on August 9 was the first shot fired in the Cold War, intended to hurry the Japanese along before the Soviet Union could take the northern islands while also warning the Soviets of America's nuclear capabilities.

Japan's new ruler was General Douglas MacArthur, the supreme commander of the Allied powers, there to oversee the complete retooling of Japan into a more acceptable form. Although thousands of non-American personnel were brought in to help dismantle Japan's war industries, the six-year Occupation period was largely a

US enterprise, flooding the country with American servicemen, policies, and ideals.

Wisely—and controversially—MacArthur intended to do his work without entirely overwriting the old order. This was in part because of the language barrier; he needed Japanese collaboration in administrating Japan, since even after the intensive hothousing of interpreters at wartime schools, the Allies still lacked a substantial number of Japanese speakers.

On the first day of 1946, Emperor Shōwa issued another proclamation, no less earth-shattering than his surrender had been. In it, he praised his grandfather Meiji's Five-Charter Oath, implying that the last few decades had been a misstep, and that the time was right to actually implement its calls for democracy, justice, and true modernity. The Oath had spoken of erasing "the evil customs of the past"—this now included militarism, and also the religious foundations of the wartime Japanese state:

> The ties between Us and Our people have always stood upon mutual trust and affection. They do not depend upon mere legends and myths. They are not predicated on the false conception that the emperor is divine, and that the Japanese people are superior to other races and fated to rule the world.

Emperor Shōwa was not a god. He was not descended from gods. He was a man whose name was Hirohito. This became known as his Declaration of Humanity (Ningen Sengen); arguments persist to this day among Japanese conservatives as to whether he meant it, and if he did, whether his renunciation applied to all emperors or just to himself.

Many, even among the Japanese, were surprised that he was still emperor at all. It had, after all, been common in the past for emperors in impossible positions to dodge trouble by abdicating. So much of the Fifteen Years' War had been waged in Hirohito's name, and presumably with his assent, that it seemed likely that he would be held accountable, not merely as the head of state, but as a war criminal complicit in uncountable atrocities, details of which were still only now coming to light. These included not only the deaths caused by the Rape of Nanjing and the Bataan Death March, but slave labor in the service of his empire, the drafting of "comfort women" (forced prostitution), and experiments in chemical and bacteriological warfare. He had, it was true, shut down the soldiers' revolt in 1936, but even his own advisers had regarded that event as being brinkmanship in the extreme. At what point in Japanese history had *any* emperor truly exerted anything but the subtlest of powers to truly command? Allied consultants chose to regard Hirohito's involvement in this light: While it was questionable whether he had helped start the war, it was undeniable that he had helped to end it. There was substantial complaint about this from other Allies, particularly the British, Australians, and New Zealanders, whose soldiers had been subjected to savage treatment as prisoners of war.

Besides, Hirohito's son and heir, Akihito, was only twelve years old, and his closest relatives and most likely replacements had been far more actively involved in the war effort as military men. Under advisement, General MacArthur chose to keep Hirohito in power, as a symbol of continuity and an effective means of commanding the Japanese to cooperate. Were Hirohito to be replaced by another figurehead, Japanese conservatives could use it as an excuse to fight back.

MacArthur's message to the Japanese people was that they, and their emperor, had been duped by a cynical military-industrial complex. In the Tōkyō war-crimes trials that would extend from 1946 to 1948 (and as late as 1956 in other parts of what had been the Japanese empire), lawyers pursued a new class of criminal—not merely the Class C offenders, who had not *prevented* war crimes, nor the Class B criminals who had *committed* them, but Class A criminals who had committed "crimes against peace" by leading Japan itself into war. This controversial designation, contested even by some Allies, was a weapon to take down the politicians, industrialists, and military men who had initiated Japan's wars of conquest, and to parade them before the public not as heroes and idols, but as "plain, ordinary murderers." If, MacArthur argued, the Japanese were seeking those responsible for the fire-bombing of Tōkyō, for the starvation in the countryside, for the loss of loved ones and the annihilation of Hiroshima and Nagasaki, it was these men, not the Allies, who were to blame.

If the Allies hoped for unanimity of purpose, they didn't get it. Although news of it was suppressed for years, one of the judges in the trial refused to play along. India's Radha Binod Pal (1886–1967) issued a 1,235-page dissenting statement decrying "victor's justice" and questioning the validity of the Class A accusations. If war were a crime, then surely everyone was guilty? If the Japanese had been compelled to seize Southeast Asia by American sanctions, did this not make the American state indirectly responsible? If the American people did not stop the indiscriminate fire-bombing of Japanese cities, did this not also make them guilty?

Judge Pal's document had elements within it of Konoe Fumimaro's complaints in 1918 about an Anglo-American Peace. It suggested that the root causes of war lay not in beliefs of invincibility and manifest destiny, but in the deprivations caused by capitalism and colonialism, in which the Americans and Europeans had led the way. Pal was no apologist for the Japanese—he found their actual war crimes "devilish and fiendish," but neither was he prepared to take part in what he saw as the lynching of an entire sector of society simply because they had been on the losing side of a trial by combat. He ended by quoting Jefferson Davis, the ill-starred leader of the Confederate States of America: "When time shall have softened passion and prejudice, when Reason shall have stripped the mask from misrepresentation, then Justice, holding evenly her scales, will require much of past censure and praise to change places."

Japan was in ruins. For many in the home islands, the true hardship came not in the war years but in the years that followed, with insufficient housing and nationwide malnutrition, the crisis augmented by the sudden return of almost seven million soldiers and colonists from the lost territories of the Japanese empire. There were rumors that the Japanese military had secretly hoarded tons of food and other supplies, and that such men formed a shadowy underworld cartel, the *kuromaku*, now supplying the black market economy. With many Japanese only receiving 70 percent of their already meager rations, such unofficial suppliers became integral to many people's survival, a fact made clear when a Japanese judge who had nobly refused to spend any money on black-market food starved to death.

By 1947, US food aid had been increased, largely out of fear that any further decrease in food supplies would cause civil unrest and only feed left-wing agitation. The arrival of grain ships from the US, Canada, and Australia was heavily publicized by the Occupation-controlled media, although such coverage masked the fact that this was not charity, but a sale of foodstuffs that the Japanese government would eventually have to pay for. It also conveniently dumped US grain surpluses on Japan, a country that had to swiftly retool its dietary expectations to rely on wheat rather than rice. It is hence in the postwar period that we see the true rise of what is now known as Japan's national dish—ramen. The Chinese-style dish had long been known in Japan, but it took on its modern form in the postwar era: wheat noodles in a lard-laced soup with scraps of black-market meat, intended originally as a hearty filler for hungry industrial workers.

The year 1947 also saw the activation of Japan's new constitution, which was knocked up in a hurry in 1946 by a committee of American lawyers, albeit with Japanese advice. Heavily influenced by the United States' own principles, to the extent of repeating verbatim an assertion of "life, liberty, and the pursuit of happiness," the new constitution abolished the old peerage and other undemocratic institutions. It established the emperor as a figurehead without political power, and decreed not only freedom of religious worship, but the exclusion of the state from religious involvement—thus ending the grip of the "myths and legends" of state-sponsored Shintō on the population and opening the floodgates for new religions and cults. Universal suffrage now extended to women, who were no longer bound to obey their husbands in the home. The new Japanese constitution attempted to impose liberal democracy, overnight, on a nation that had spent an entire generation under what amounted to martial law, and which less than a century before had been an authoritarian state under the rule of a military despot. In an attempt to convey what this meant in practice, a delegation of seventy Japanese opinion-formers was brought to Washington, Berlin, and London in 1947, in an echo of the Meiji-era Iwakura Mission, but specifically to learn the workings of a state in which rule was by the people, for the people. Pointedly, the delegates arrived with gifts for their hosts—crucifixes made with wood from an olive tree close to ground zero at Hiroshima.

The new constitution's most radical imposition was Article 9, which proclaimed that "the Japanese people forever renounce war as a sovereign right of the nation and the threat or use of force as a means of settling international disputes." Article 9 has been a point of contention ever since its establishment, not least because even the Occupation authorities swiftly came to regret it. A Japan without a military was a Japan that relied upon the US to defend it—a handy excuse for bases on Japanese soil, but an easy target for isolationist campaigners in Washington. Meanwhile, the proclamation of the People's Republic of China in 1949, and the outbreak of the Korean War in 1950, turned Japan from a supposedly pacifist nation into America's "unsinkable aircraft carrier" in the Pacific. The Occupation forces had originally arrived with the intention of demilitarizing and possibly even deindustrializing Japan in order to remove the forces that had motivated its imperial expansion. It was hence a matter of luck for the Japanese that the concerns of the Cold War caused their American masters to reconsider and retrench partway through the Occupation. The encouragement of Japan's left wing was no longer regarded as a welcome element of democracy, but as a socialist agitation that needed to be contained. The breakup of the zaibatsu was curtailed or suspended, and factories slated for decommissioning were instead retooled for new purposes. As for the renunciation of war, while the Occupation was still rolling, the authorities found enough of a loophole to inaugurate a 75,000-man-strong "National Police Reserve" that would eventually grow into a Self-Defense Force—which, to outside observers, looks suspiciously like an army, navy, and air force. Its existence was justified by the claim that it was intended *solely* for self-defense—jets, for example, lacked the long-range fuel tanks required for attacking foreign countries—and hence did not contravene Article 9's renunciation of military aggression. In decades to come, Article 9 would invite new complaints from abroad—that Japan was enjoying the fruits of other nations' military protection without providing substantial contribution of its own. This would become particularly notable in the 1990s, when resource-poor Japan was accused of being a prime beneficiary of the Gulf War despite fielding no troops in it.

Much is still left to be written about the men and women of the Occupation regime, some of whom formed the first postwar generation of Japanese scholars: people like Donald Keenc, who arrived as a military interpreter and eventually became a Japanese citizen and an acknowledged expert, even among the Japanese themselves, in Japanese literature. William Edwards Deming, a management specialist brought in by MacArthur to oversee rice statistics and the national census, gave lectures on the value of quality control in saving money and increasing market share; his name later became synonymous with Japan's "miracle" management system, and he was awarded the status of Japanese Sacred Treasure. Others are not as well known, like David Conde at the Civil Information and Education Division, who fostered the development of Japanese labor unions, inadvertently creating new headaches for the authorities by letting the genie of socialism out of the bottle once more, even as the US itself commenced its Cold War witch hunts. Few Japanese recognize the name of Beate Sirota Gordon (Order of the Sacred Treasure), although she was the American lawyer who wrote the clauses on women's rights into the Japanese constitution. And whatever happened to Charles Egbert Tuttle (another Order of the Sacred Treasure), who spent two years in the Occupation fostering the rebuilding of Japan's newspaper industry, and who had been encouraged to fill a niche in the educational market by first importing books for Occupation personnel and ultimately translating them for the Japanese? Tuttle set up his own company to specialize in East–West publications; it also spun off into the Tuttle-Mori agency, which brokers many international deals bringing Japanese books to the West and vice versa.

The Occupation authorities, however, relied on Japanese assistance, and that often meant employing people who had undeniable associations with the wartime administration. One of the war-era bureaucrats dragged back into service under the Occupation and long afterwards was Kishi Nobusuke (1896–1987), an economic planner who had been inspired by a 1929 visit to Soviet Russia under the sway of Stalin's first Five-Year Plan. Kishi had formerly served as Manchukuo's deputy minister for industrial development; in a country where the full ministers were merely local figureheads, this made him the business tsar for the entire state. He masterminded Manchukuo's decade as a powerhouse of industrial development founded on slave labor, low wages, and a black market in opium, which he funnelled abroad through connections to organized crime. A committed fascist and expert money launderer in his younger days, Kishi had been determined to turn Manchukuo into a military-focused state that could support a Japanese war. In 1940 he returned to Japan as a government minister, becoming one of the signatories of the tardily delivered declaration of war against the United States in 1941. Throughout the war, he put his Manchurian experience to use conscripting Chinese and Korean slave labor, but resigned and formed his own political party in 1944, funded largely by business associates from his Manchukuo days.

Imprisoned and awaiting trial as a Class A war criminal, Kishi was sprung by the Americans in 1948 and injected back into public life as an antidote to the rising left. He would be instrumental in another failed political party, the Japan Reconstruction Federation, in 1952. He finally fought his way back into government in 1953 as a member of Japan's Liberal Party, from which he led a 200-member breakaway faction to join the Democratic Party in 1954, ultimately forming the Liberal Democratic Party (LDP).

The LDP came to power in 1955, and there it remains to this day but for only a handful of years out of office in the last seven decades (1993–96 and 2009–11). Although Kishi did briefly serve as prime minister from 1957 to 1960, he largely ruled from behind the scenes, sitting on a war chest of vital campaign funds from suspicious sources. For this, he was attacked by a rival in his own party, who noted: "No matter how tightly you seal a bucket of shit, you still can't put it on the family altar." Kishi, however, remained confident that his party would still come to him for the much-needed campaign money, dirty or not; he replied: "There are plenty of buckets of shit to go around."

Kishi's Manchukuo contacts, now home after the breakup of the empire, helped him forge strong links with the captains of postwar Japanese industry, many of whom were snidely referred to as the Kishi Savings Bank (*Kishi no chokinbako*). Rumors persist that there was in fact some truth to the legends of the *kuromaku*—that the Japanese military had indeed hoarded secret treasure, but that this had fallen into Allied hands, and was now administered as a secret Cold War resource, the M-Fund, earmarked for holding off Communism. Kishi, it is said, managed to persuade the US vice president Richard Nixon to sign over control of the M-Fund to him in 1957, and poured its riches into his own pockets as well as Japan's postwar reindustrialization. In a triumph of political cunning, he also threw himself into negotiating war reparations (and later aid packages) with Southeast Asian nations, agreeing to pay damages "in the form of capital and consumer goods produced by the Japanese industries and services of the Japanese people," which allowed him to funnel lucrative contracts back to his industrial allies.

Kishi's model for the collusion of government and industry, with his former home at the Ministry of Munitions repurposed as an interventionist Ministry of Trade and Industry (MITI), has come to be known as the 1955 System, named for the year in which his party first gained power. It allowed Japan to maintain the heady momentum it had picked up during the Korean War, and was a significant contribution to the economic growth in the 1960s that would come to be called the "Japanese miracle." While Kishi faded from the spotlight, his brother Satō Eisaku (Kishi had been adopted as a child, hence the differing surnames) would be prime minister of Japan from 1964 to 1972. Kishi's grandson, Abe Shinzō, was elected to the same post in 2006 and 2012.

Although the Occupation officially ended in April 1952, America's hold on Japan would continue in many forms, not only through continued imports and trade agreements, but also through a controversial and unpopular Treaty of Mutual Cooperation and Security that allowed for a continued US military presence on Japanese soil; riots over the inauguration of the latter in 1960 were a contribution to Kishi's resignation as prime minister.

It was also not until the Occupation forces had left that there was any widespread discussion of issues that they had suppressed, such as the nature of collateral damage from atomic weapons. This became a cause celebre in 1954, when a Japanese fishing boat, the *Daigo Fukuryū-maru* (Lucky Dragon V), was caught in the fallout from one of the US atomic bomb tests at Bikini Atoll in the Marshall Islands.

It was not lost on Japanese conservatives that the Americans were using the hulks of Japan's once-great navy, and the islands that had once been Japanese mandates, to test their doomsday weapons. When the radio operator of the *Daigo Fukuryū-maru* died as a result of complications from radiation sickness, he did so uttering, "I pray that I am the last victim of an atomic or hydrogen bomb."

He was not. Unlike conventional weapons, atomic devices could affect their victims years or even decades later; their damage might not even become evident until the birth of a new generation that was not even alive at the time of the original conflict. Details of such side effects had been censored by the Occupation forces, and only later came to public light, particularly when the US Food and Drug Administration declared that tuna from the test area was unfit for human consumption. When the US paid compensation to the fisherman's widow, even though it was careful to specify that it had nothing to do with radiation damage, the act opened the door for further discussion of Japan's *hibakusha*—the "victims of the Bomb"—and would ultimately lead to a 1957 law providing for their medical care.

Famously, the incident also inspired one of the box-office blockbusters of 1954, director Honda Ishirō's *Gojira* (*Godzilla*), which reimagined the threat of nuclear destruction as a giant monster marching on Japan's slowly recovering cities, unleashing a new menace.

Godzilla, however, was not the face that the Japanese cinema wished to present to the world in 1954. That came in the form of Kurosawa Akira's *Seven Samurai*, an acknowledged masterpiece that formed part of the rehabilitation of the samurai class as the defenders of the poor folk, rather than their swindlers. Neither film, however, won Japan's Academy Award that year. In an indicator of how different Japanese critical reception can be from either the popular vote or the foreign view, the award-winning film was Kinoshita Keisuke's *24 Eyes*, a sentimental weepy about a schoolteacher on Japan's Inland Sea who watches as her class grows up and is ultimately dragged into the Fifteen Years' War.

Just as American grain was dumped on the Japanese diet, American movies had initially filled the gap in entertainment. As cinemas rebuilt, Japan's movie industry struggled to get back up to speed. Early Occupation policies exposed the Japanese to previously unseen scandals such as the sight of two actors kissing, but shielded them from dangerously evocative elements such as swordplay, even in the Japanese release of *The Mask of Zorro*. Disney cartoons swamped the children's market until the release of Japan's first feature-length animated color cartoon in 1958.

In popular culture, the Occupation period also fostered many long-term changes. Kabuki theater, once renowned for ripping its stories from the headlines, swiftly reoriented itself under the Occupation as an entirely traditional, old-fashioned art form, clinging solely to its "classical" repertoire. It has remained so ever since, overwriting the era when Kabuki actors would reenact the day's news in skits and adaptations written overnight, obscuring its former relevance and significance and rendering it as hidebound and outmoded as the Noh theater it once supplanted.

Japanese publishing in the postwar years was hampered by a paucity of resources, both among publishers and their readers. Rental book libraries allowed entire communities to share a smaller print run in turn. Most notable in the period was the rise of comics—at first for all children, but then with a bifurcation into boys' and girls' markets. The aging of the readership and an awareness of new markets would eventually lead to truly adult comics for both men and women. The most enduring figure in the world of what has become known as "manga" is Tezuka Osamu (1928–89), a prolific artist remembered fondly by the Japanese as the initiator of a cinematic sense in comics and the introducer of increasingly adult storylines. Tezuka, however, was merely one of an entire generation of artists whose work would form the bedrock of much postwar popular culture. Although his status as the "god of manga" is deserved, he is also the beneficiary of a literary estate that has brilliantly managed his profile since his death, keeping the spotlight on his achievements and confining his less publicity-savvy rivals to the shadows—Yokoyama Mitsuteru (1934–2004), for example, who died in a house fire that presumably also destroyed the bulk of his archives.

Other manga artists, despite their relative lack of fame abroad, initiated entire sectors of what is now regarded as Japanese "tradition." Of particular note here are Mizuki Shigeru (1922–2015), who not only retold many Japanese ghost stories but also interpolated some of his own making, and Shirato Sanpei (1932–), who exploited the anti-samurai tone of early postwar culture to retell historical stories with new underclass heroes, the fictional shadow warriors, or ninja.

The postwar period saw a brief boom in the preexisting tradition of *kami-shibai* or "paper theater," in which traveling storytellers presented street shows using rented picture boards held in place by a frame on the back of a bicycle. Anyone could watch for free, but only the children who bought candies from the storyteller could sit at the front. The *kami-shibai* stories were often rented from a central company, which supplied the adventures of Cold War spies, fugitive princes from Atlantis, and young boys catapulted into space, sometimes in serial form. *Kami-shibai*, however, was soon a dying art form, pushed out of the public eye after 1953 by the rising interest in television.

Here, too, America enjoyed an unexpected primacy, since it was sitting on an archive of several years of product that could be repurposed for foreign audiences. Throughout the 1950s it was cowboy stories, hospital dramas, and Superman that dominated the Japanese airwaves. Exotic new shows retained the untranslatable foreign name, with a brief explanation to summarize the general theme. This policy is still common in Japanese broadcasting, leading not only to unwieldy titles such as *Zany Theater ABBOTT & COSTELLO, ADDAMS Family of Ghosts*, and *LARAMIE Ranch*, but local imitations such as *Space Adventure COBRA* and the World Masterpiece Theater cartoon *Girl of the Alps HEIDI*.

The first Japanese TV broadcasts reached only a small audience of wealthy early adopters in Tōkyō. But soon the sets spread to bars and public places; then, as prices fell, into middle- and working-class homes, spurred by such landmark events as the marriage of Prince Akihito in 1959 and the Tōkyō Olympics in 1964. By the time the people of Japan settled down in front of their new *color* television sets to watch the opening ceremony of the Tōkyō Olympics, one of the most-watched broadcasts in Japanese TV history, they were living in a country a world removed from the burnt-out ruins of only a generation before. Japan had entirely transformed. Again.

CHAPTER 10

THE NEW BREED: THE JAPANESE MIRACLE

The Self-Defense Force commandant at Ishigaya barracks was a little jumpy around Mishima Yukio. This was, after all, one of Japan's most famous novelists, but also something of a loon, given in recent years to parading around mountainsides with his "Shield Society," a group of handsome young men in snappy military uniforms.

Nevertheless, General Mashita Kanetoshi humored the visiting celebrity and his four young "cadets," complimenting them on their bearing and manners. Warily, he asked Mishima if the police really let him walk around with his sword.

Mishima laughed and reached out for his weapon, explaining that it was a samurai blade made by a famous smith. That really didn't answer the question, but Mashita had little chance to protest, because Mishima was asking his assistant for a handkerchief. He was going to give the blade a little wipe, and show it to the general so that he could examine the artistry of its manufacture for himself.

No. He wasn't.

The call for the handkerchief was a signal. The young men of the Shield Society grabbed the general, bound and gagged him, then jammed his office door shut with a pile of furniture. Politely and apologetically, Mishima then issued his demand: that the general should order his soldiers to assemble outside beneath the balcony so that Mishima could address them on an important matter. If he refused, Mishima would kill himself.

True to samurai custom, the soldiers ignored their general's orders, mounting two rescue attempts before they obeyed, and only assembling beneath the office after some pushing and shoving at the barricade.

Mishima stepped out onto the balcony at noon, half an hour later than planned, wearing a headband emblazoned with the motto of a Japanese hero, "Seven Lives for the Fatherland," and faced the assembled ranks of the soldiers. He began his carefully prepared speech about the state of modern Japan—a Japan that was drunk on prosperity and falling into moral emptiness. Where, he wondered, was the real spirit of the samurai? Recalling the soldiers of the 1930s who were committed to purifying Japan, he argued that it surely lay in the Self-Defense Force, that vestige of Japan's once-proud warrior tradition, denied even the name of an army but still containing coiled military might, a sense of justice, the power to seize control and drag Japan back onto a course of righteousness, if only the soldiers below him had the will. It was, he argued, incumbent on the Self-Defense Force to be the agent of constitutional change, because at the moment, "all of you are unconstitutional."

Or, at least, it was something like that. Nobody could really hear Mishima properly because the soldiers were calling him an idiot. His hostage demands had called for them to be assembled, but they did not seem to have got the message about not "interfering" with his speech. And so they jeered at him, laughing at his attempts to be a tinpot hero with pretty-boy minions, calling for him to let their commandant go.

Nobody could really hear the soldiers, either, because there were three helicopters overhead. Mishima had a thirty-minute speech prepared, but he was not too far into it before he was frowning and looking at his watch. After seven minutes, he gestured that his time was up.

"Isn't there anyone among you fellows who will follow me?" he asked.

He bellowed something at the troops below about the spirit of the samurai, and how it was time to rise up and die, and then he was joined on the rooftop by his deputy (and, it was said, lover), Morita.

Together they gave the *banzai* salute, wishing ten thousand years to the emperor, and then they went inside.

"I don't think they even heard me," he muttered to his men, unbuttoning his jacket.

He knelt on the floor, Morita standing over him with the sword.

Then he stabbed himself in the stomach, dragging his dagger cross his abdomen from left to right. His reached, floundering, for the brush by his side, hoping to carry out his plan to write a final message in his own blood, but seppuku was designed to be agonizing.

He slumped forward, and his men hissed at Morita to deliver the death blow.

Morita had had plenty of practice…with bamboo sticks and imaginary opponents. He had never cut off someone's head before, and his first attempt missed completely, striking Mishima's shoulder. His second struck Mishima's neck, but did not drive anywhere deep enough, leaving the head hanging half off.

He slashed again twice more, but Mishima was still inconveniently alive. Morita pleaded with Furu-Koga, a better swordsman, to take over, and Furu-Koga snatched the sword from away, severing Mishima's head with a single blow.

Morita knelt in the spreading pool of Mishima's blood and unbuttoned his own jacket. Now it was his turn.

The spectacular suicide of Mishima Yukio (1925–70) was a shock and embarrassment to the Japanese media. Only two years earlier, Mishima had been seriously considered as a candidate for the Nobel Prize for Literature, losing out to his colleague Kawabata Yasunari—only, it was rumored, because as a younger man, he was liable to have another shot at it later. Mishima had enjoyed a fantastically varied career, not only as the author of intense, histrionic prize-winning novels, but also of bill-paying pot-boilers. Only the former have been published in English, demonstrating his estate's careful management of his profile abroad. He wrote plays about Madame de Sade and Adolf Hitler, and even starred in a gangster movie. Famously employing Japanese characters who were arcane or difficult to read, his novels were often caught up in a self-regarding poetry of their own construction—in an embittered moment, his translator John Nathan once ridiculed them as "an exhibition of the world's most ornate picture frames." But they also dealt strongly with the matter of postwar Japan as viewed by the generation reared during the Fifteen Years' War, assured firstly of imperial victory, but then exhorted to die gloriously in the defense of the emperor…then suddenly told that it at all been a lie, and that the samurai mindset was an aberration.

Mishima's last great work, the four-volume *Sea of Fertility*, took as its theme the decline of the Japanese spirit, as the great men and virtuous women of the Meiji era were supplanted by feckless, irresolute weaklings tainted by unwelcome foreign influences. Mishima's other works often spoke of the postwar period as if it were an alternate universe in which Japan (and himself within it) had been turned aside from its true fate of a glorious death in war and repurposed into a pale shadow.

Although his comments hid personal issues that ran significantly deeper—not least his own obsession with the decline of his physical body—Mishima's identification of the postwar generation was not entirely off the mark. People born since 1945, which by 1977 would be fully half the population of Japan, were mainly too young to remember starvation or the Occupation. They had, however, been fed a diet with increased amounts of wheat, dairy, and meat; the boys grew on average 17 centimeters (7 inches) taller than their fathers, but were often not as fit, having spent much more sedentary lives. They even thought and spoke differently, having been raised on books and television translated from English, and hence lacking many of the registers of politeness and respect ingrained into traditional Japanese. They were "motorized" by access to private transport, and "computerized" by their long-term affinity for high technology. And they were sick of hearing about the martial mistakes of their parents' generation. As the hippie trend filtered into Japan, this new generation observed the Vietnam War with a degree of teenage smugness, looking down on both their colonialist parents and Watergate-era America. They were, as a pop song of the early 1970s proclaimed, "children who did not remember the war."

Another term arose for them in the Japanese media: the New Breed (*shinjinrui*), implying that they were practically a different species, coming of age during a boom-time period after the Tōkyō Olympics in which Japan had enjoyed year-on-year growth of 11 percent, divorced from the concerns of the elder generation to the extent that a Meiji-era figure would have found them almost unrecognizable as Japanese.

The Tōkyō Olympics were a landmark event for Japan, beginning with the symbolic value of Japan's acceptance back into the global community—the sporting event had originally been slated for Tōkyō in 1940, but was postponed due to the war. It also functioned as a red-letter day for urban planning and government initiatives, which included a monorail into town from Tōkyō's Haneda airport, several new expressways, and the inauguration of new high-speed trains. Referred to in Japanese as the *shinkansen* (new trunk lines), they are known abroad as "bullet" trains, and became an international symbol of Japan's high-tech development.

The Tōkyō Olympics saw the first large influx of foreign visitors since the wartime Occupation forces and the ever-present US servicemen, instilling in the Japanese a newfound interest in the power of tourism. This created a momentum all of its own when the sports fans went home, not just in the continued promotion of Japan as a vacation destination for foreigners, but in the fostering of a vibrant domestic tourist industry. After all, why create all that infrastructure only to move workers and freight around when it could also move customers?

Local authorities tried to find ways to make their own town more interesting than the next one. Japan enjoyed a boom in odd local museums, art-installation boondoggles, landscaping, supposedly original local delicacies…and castles. The mid-1960s saw the sudden sprouting of castles all over Japan, restoring not only originals destroyed in the war, but also sites that had been burned down in the Meiji Restoration or even decommissioned by the Tokugawa shōgunate in the seventeenth century. Under the Tokugawa, castles in Japan had been famously restricted to a single one per province; now, in some places, it was almost possible to see the battlements of one from the battlements of another. What town *wouldn't* want to restore a samurai-era fortification if there was even a whisper of one in an old chronicle? It would function as a town hall and museum, it would look good on the postcards, and it would add to the chances that a coachload of corporate workers on a management retreat would stop there for lunch.

But who were these corporate travelers? They were a new army for Japan's postwar world who would become known as the *sararīman* (salaryman).

MacArthur's reforms had initially included the breakup of the zaibatsu corporations. By 1950, Japan had become a convenient manufacturing zone to supply the US military, with the Korean War supplying 27 percent of Japan's export revenue in the period, and the disparate companies that had once formed part of the zaibatsu began to drift back together. This was not a conspiracy as such; merely the inevitable outcome of having companies with similar names, often beholden to the same bank, with workers whose personal associations extended across the divide. These new federations of related companies were not quite the financial cliques of old, but would become known as *keiretsu*—"integrated systems."

The railway companies soon discovered, for example, the immense value of real estate at the terminus. The transformation of Japanese workers into a commuter population guaranteed that every evening would see a mass of workers disgorged from their skyscrapers and heading off to catch the train home. But since they were sure to miss dinner on the average two-hour commute, and there was liable to be little to do except sleep in a dormitory suburb or a soulless one-room "mansion" apartment (which comprised 25 percent of new Japanese housing by 1983), why not try to catch their attentions before they got on the train?

Vast shopping districts and dedicated malls sprang up around the major junction stations and terminuses of the Japanese railway, jammed with department stores and hotels, theaters and cinemas, food courts and boutique restaurants. In many cases, preferential floor space was offered to companies within the same *keiretsu*.

Japan's export economy continued to rise throughout the 1970s, despite the damage done to manufacturing by an international rise in oil prices. Early successes included cheap transistor radios and cameras that undercut foreign market leaders. By 1975, the car manufacturer Nissan (Datsun) had replaced Volkswagen as the leading exporter of automobiles to the US, the largest market for cars in the world. By 1980, Japan had outstripped the US as the world's largest producer of cars—a fact that emerged in the same year as the layoffs of 200,000 American autoworkers, leading to accusations that Japan was exporting unemployment along with its automobiles.

But the customer was always right, and many American customers favored the smaller, fuel-efficient Japanese compact, which was less likely to break down. A US government report from 1982 disagreed, noting that there was little that could be said to be "superior" about the technology of Japanese cars, merely about the management system that listened to the customer and inspired loyalty and commitment in its workforce. Political advertisements in the US raised the specter of imperialist Japan, and asked consumers if they really wanted to drive with their family to the Hirohito Memorial Shopping Mall. If so, warned the commercial: "Go on, keep buying Japanese cars."

A change in the valuation of the American dollar in 1985 suddenly increased the value of the yen. This *endaka* (high yen) phenomenon could have spelled disaster for Japanese exports, but was shrewdly met by offshore investment. It was, for example, useful for car manufacturers like Honda to relocate their assembly lines to the United States, which both made better use of the high yen and stopped American protests about loss of jobs in the US auto industry. The high yen was used to snap up not only foreign subsidiaries and factories, but other investments like retirement homes and hotels. The effect was felt particularly strongly on Australia's Gold Coast, where up to 70 percent of prime real estate land was in Japanese hands by 1988. In Europe, however, suspicions were raised about the nature of the factories, with accusations that the Japanese were merely bolting together parts shipped from Japan. In the case of one photocopier assembly line, up to 98 percent of the parts were Japanese, turning the supposed factory into little more than a "screwdriver plant" that put the finishing touches on a production line still largely based in Japan, merely in order to get around import restrictions.

Collaboration between ventures with similar goals led to the industrialization of many unusual processes, including entertainment. Although there had been forerunners a decade earlier, it was only in the 1970s that Japanese entertainment began take the policies that had worked so well for *keiretsu* in manufacturing and reapply them to the media. With new awareness of the potential for spinoffs and cross-promotional advertising, the latest properties would be initiated by a consortium of interested parties, a production committee or *seisaku iinkai*. The committee would include not only the studio that made the property, the publisher that released the tie-in novel or comic, and the manufacturers that made the merchandise, but also the talent agency that provided the actors and the record company that supplied the theme song. Such a unity of purpose commodified every aspect of the production process, creating prepackaged hits that were foregone conclusions, not the least because the magazines that reported them as such were also in on the deal. That's not to say that some of Japan's great media success stories were not reasonable reflections of public taste—part of the production committee's job was to respond to consumer interest, after all. But it also created some intriguing templates for commercial success, many of which have been stamped out again and again in the decades since—toy-friendly superheroes fighting alien foes...no, a *team* of superheroes...no, a team of superheroes who *combine* to make a super-toy—but now you have collect the entire set.

Toys were one of Japan's first successful exports in the postwar period, a fact recognized in 1965 with the zoning of Omocha no Machi, the "town of toys," a business district where forty-four companies pooled their warehousing and manufacturing resources in order to create an entire district dedicated to a single industry. The toy industry also offers a glimpse of Japanese industry's ability to roll with the punches—facing competition from cheap labor in Hong Kong, the Japanese toy industry was able to pivot yet again, emphasizing functionality and miniaturization. By the 1970s, Japanese toys had become smaller and more compact, which meant that even though more action figures could fit into a single transport container, those figures had a greater functionality. Some, like the ubiquitous "Transformers," were two toys in one.

Japan achieved similar successes in the electronics market, where ministry directives shielded Japanese companies from foreign competition. Often, Japanese manufacturers exploited innovations made abroad, acquiring some 30,000 patents from American electronics firms. Early developments in radios led to other efforts in miniaturization—most famously the Sony Walkman, which turned listening to music in public places into (at least theoretically) a purely personal experience. Sony's Betamax videocassette format was, however, beaten out of the global market by the arguably inferior VHS format favored by Matsushita, in part at least because Matsushita dealers were receiving a kickback from the manufacturer that allowed them to offer a discount to American consumers. Matsushita played a long game, betting on the returns from dominating the market in hardware, which would create a larger market share for the software (VHS tapes), and in turn encourage consumers to choose the option with the most tapes available. When videotapes themselves became obsolete, Japan was ahead of the field with the digital replacement; Sony, Toshiba and Panasonic (Matsushita) were collaborating with foreign colleagues on the creation of the new Digital Versatile Disc in 1995.

Not every initiative achieved its desired aim, but that in itself shows the resilience of Japanese industries. A decade-long program to create artificial intelligence was called off in 1992, but spun off several new innovations in other areas of computing, including increased chip function and parallel processing. Fuji became the world leader in film only to successfully and almost entirely reorient itself as a digital company when it foresaw the end of analog formats. So, too, did Canon and Nikon, both now market leaders in digital photography.

When the Japanese postwar economy was at its peak, the Western publishing world was overrun with books attempting to explain the Japanese "miracle." Supposed secrets of Japanese management were often rooted in American ideas—it was Henry Ford, after all, who had hit upon the idea of double-dipping his workers' salaries by renting them the houses they lived in and selling them their lunches from his own commissary. Japanese pundits speak wistfully of the value of the Deming Circle, but Deming was American, just as ready to advise Ford Motors as Matsushita Electrics—in the wake of his fame in Japan, Ford eventually got around to hiring Deming in the 1980s.

The Japanese miracle owed far more to a handful of unique factors—the postwar acquisition of the most up-to-date plants and machinery, the industrial boom brought on by the Korean War, and the willingness of the generation of Japanese raised in wartime austerity to put their all into working for a better tomorrow. It certainly helped that, as a state "without an army," Japan was did not find itself bogged down in foreign misadventures like Vietnam. It also benefited to a great degree from the collusion of the Japanese government, most particularly the economic powerhouse of its Ministry of International Trade and Industry, which masterminded long-term industrial policies: offering grants and loans for developing new specialties, zoning entire areas for related industries to encourage an economy of scale, and even steering government tariffs and export policies to nurture new industries. It was often said that Japan's postwar growth had been managed by an "iron triangle" of interests ever since the days of Kishi Nobusuke, comprising the corporations, the bureaucracy, and the ministries that offered support. Such support, unsurprisingly, also went both ways: at the end of a career in a ministry, a successful government bureaucrat could usually expect to leave his post and walk into a management or advisory position at one of the companies his ministry had helped. This practice came to be known as *amakudari* (descending from heaven), a term formerly used to describe the "retirement" of emperors that would enable them to rule from behind the throne.

At least part of the Japan's twentieth-century miracle can be attributed to such "companyism" or "frontier capitalism"—a retooling of the former wartime zaibatsu mindset into similarly influential corporate juggernauts. The narrative of corporate Japan offered a form of paternalism—the company would offer lifetime employment, promotion by seniority, a hopefully non-adversarial union consultation, and perks with affiliated companies. The company was also a center for workers' social lives, not only in after-hours drinks and entertainment, but in group trips and even spousal matchmaking.

Some modern scholars deride the stereotype of the salaryman as racist—reducing the Japanese to a mob of identikit businessmen in shirtsleeves. But the salaryman was an entirely recognizable symbol of the Japanese economy in the late twentieth century. In 1950, they comprised 30 percent of the workforce; by the peak of the phenomenon in 1995, an astounding 70 percent.

All, however, was not as it seemed. Much as the distinctively attired medieval samurai was unable to retreat, the salaryman in an open-plan office needed to keep conspicuously busy. Japanese workers logged significantly higher overtime hours than their Western counterparts, sometimes actually working, but often simply putting on the *performance* of working hard by staying late in order to be seen to be at their desks. Corporate entertainment became a lucrative source of money in the food and drink markets, but also a millstone around the neck of a salaryman who might have preferred to be home by midnight. As for office perks, these, too, were often in the service of the company rather than the individual, such as the handing out of packets of prepaid tickets for a sister corporation's new movie. The value of these "bonuses" was only redeemable if the worker could somehow shift them onto his friends—most of whom were colleagues who were also liable to be stuck with ten seats for a film nobody wanted to see. In a not-unrelated phenomenon, some Japanese box-office blockbusters in the late twentieth century were discovered to be playing to empty theaters, the seats "sold," but not in a fashion that Hollywood moguls would appreciate.

Lifetime employment was an easy promise to make to a fresh graduate, but it rather ignored the fact that he might not want to work in the same job for his entire career. There might be some opportunity for transferral between sister companies, but even so, a lifetime was a tall order. Nor did such guarantees recognize the demographic reality: that if a corporation took on a year's class of, say, 400 new graduates, only one of them probably stood a chance of being company chairman. Promotion by seniority was hence also something of a lie. By the 1970s, the implications of "lifetime employment" also started to become clear—the picture showed not happy retirees skipping out the company gates bearing a golden carriage clock, but embittered senior staffers, shunted aside from the promotional ladder into constructive dismissal—the former marketing manager assigned to the security detail on the gate, or the office drudge moved to a drafty office and given pointless tasks to do. Such individuals became known as the *madogiwa-zoku* (window tribe), but they did not resign, because that would most likely reduce them even further to *sodai gomi* (oversized garbage), the cruel housewives' term for a husband underfoot around the house. Others took the initiative by becoming *datsu-sara* (ex-salarymen) and going into business for themselves, sometimes in startups partly funded by their former employer, as a liability shield to try out new technologies or strategies.

The emphasis, too, on "salary*men*" ignored the conditions of the 48 percent of the Japanese workforce that was female. Women were regarded as a second-class sector of the workforce, divided into "office ladies" under twenty-five who performed secretarial functions and would eventually leave on marriage; and a less visible labor force of older women working part-time in factory assembly, food preparation, and other unglamorous jobs, or in the "pink collar" sector of nursing and childcare. Women's salaries were low in comparison to their male counterparts; childcare for working mothers was rare, and the entire structure of the workforce worked on the assumption that motherhood was the responsibility and vocation of every woman.

There were some unexpected payoffs, not least in the understanding that wives held the domestic purse strings; the husband might earn the money, but the wife controlled the spending. A woman who was happy to leave the workforce for marriage—assuming that her marriage was stable and her husband a remunerative worker—could expect to have packed her kids off to high school by her late thirties, at which point she would become the center of a whole new leisure sector. In 1979, the sociologist Abe Yōko observed that women from thirty-five to forty-five represented an entirely unforeseen consumption bloc, exploiting the empty nest while their husband was still at work, throwing themselves into a variety of hobbies and pastimes. Their archetypal spouse, meanwhile, stumbled home from after-work drinking just before midnight, handing over his pay packet and remaining none the wiser as to where the money was going.

During the 1980s, a second female consumption bloc became even more influential, with the realization that many of the "office ladies" of the urban workforce were banking on marriage and retirement before age twenty-five, but were still living rent-free with their parents and sitting on a disposable income for the four or five years that they were in the workforce. Such "parasite singles" became the target market for cosmetics and fashion, branded goods and foreign vacations, and were a major impetus for the widespread adoption of "cute" goods that extended their younger days into adult life. A case in point was Sanrio's Hello Kitty, a brand created initially to adorn pencil cases and lunchboxes for schoolgirls in 1974, which achieved newfound popularity as an icon of Japanese womanhood in the 1980s.

Some Japanese women resisted tradition in an altogether new way by refusing to play along with the semi-arranged marriages that had once been the default means of matchmaking eligible singletons. In 1945, 69 percent of all Japanese marriages had been arranged by *omiai* (the meet-and-greet), whereby a professional marriage broker would set up a series of formal dinners between families whose eligible children seemed to meet suitable criteria of wealth, class, and status. That figure, however, has steadily fallen ever since, as more proactive, Western-influenced Japanese favor dating and personal choice. Today, only 6.2 percent of Japanese marriages are set up through *omiai*, although traditionalists wryly observe that marriage brokers' ability to prescreen and investigate potential spouses makes *omiai* arrangements much more reliable than random romance.

Other Japanese simply refused to get married at all, or did so significantly later, with more than half waiting until their thirties. Meiji-era girls tended to marry at sixteen; by the 1950s, this had risen to twenty-three, and today the average age for a woman's marriage is 29.3. This, in turn, reduced the number of likely childbearing years, contributing to the rise of smaller nuclear families. An increase in the number of only children (and hence in daughters bearing the weight of family expectations), as well as a greater general awareness of women's rights, encouraged some women to resist the pressure to regard themselves as walking wives-to-be and to make better, more long-term choices regarding their education and career. The self-fulfilling prophecy that a woman with a diploma in home economics wasn't going to get promoted past the typing pool anyway began to crumble.

Other elements of Japanese "success" merely shoved failure to where it could not be seen. There was much talk in the 1980s of the genius of Japanese corporations' "just-in-time" system, which reduced warehousing costs by ensuring that new materials were only ordered and delivered when they were needed. While that did indeed achieve its stated purpose, it did so only by relying on a diverse supply chain of small businesses, which were invariably the first to be sacrificed in the event of any slump in demand.

There was, however, a particular flaw in the Japanese miracle that brought it to an end. All this investment was ultimately based on bank loans secured against collateral. However it was held—whether in company stocks or shares—in the end most of the collateral came down to real estate, which had become preposterously overvalued. Tracing the book value of certain Japanese companies back to the source would reveal loans upon loans, taken out from a bank in which the company was itself a shareholder, secured on land that was worth only a fraction of its supposed value. Japan's miraculous economy was a bubble, and it was about to pop.

CHAPTER 11

COOL JAPAN: THE LOST DECADES

David had remained calm when the tremors began. The Japanese teachers briskly, urgently instructed their pupils to stand up and file out: *Quickly now, but don't run.* Books juddered from the shelves in the classrooms. Chairs jerked into new positions across the floor. One girl, disobeying orders to leave everything, grabbed a scrapbook bearing the signatures and doodles of her classmates—tomorrow was the last day of school, after all.

There were earthquakes every day in Japan, but most were barely noticeable. *Did I just lose my balance, or did the ground move beneath me? Did a passing car just make the bridge wobble, or was it the ground underneath it?* A day earlier, there had been a larger one, notable for actually feeling like an earthquake, that had made the school shake. And now this one, enduring far longer than usual.

Everybody knew the drill. The school gymnasium was a designated safety zone for the whole area—reinforced against quake damage and sited on higher ground, sufficiently far from the sea to guarantee protection from tidal waves. Somehow it didn't feel right for David to enter the gymnasium when his pupils were still lagging behind, so he lurked at the doors as the kids filed in. With them were a couple of early-bird parents who had arrived to pick up their children from school, and a busload of pensioners from the old people's home, some of them in wheelchairs.

Finally, the shaking ceased. David flicked the light switches experimentally, but there was no power. Through the high windows of the gymnasium, he saw a darkening sky that threatened rain.

The children giggled and squealed. Some clutched at their parents.

Through the wide glass doors of the gymnasium, David saw a man in a hard hat rushing toward him, clad in an overall that marked him out as a municipal employee—a janitor perhaps, or a security guard. He was gesticulating wildly, shouting something over and over again.

"A tsunami is coming!"

Really?

It was an oddly panicked reaction for the normally pragmatic Japanese. The gymnasium was two whole miles from the shoreline. And besides, if there really were a tidal wave rushing toward the town, then surely the sirens would have sounded…?

Unless the sirens had lost their power along with the lights.

The rushing official reached the doors.

"A tsunami is coming!" he yelled. "Get upstairs! Upstairs!"

The crowd began to move with some reluctance. There was no elevator for the old people, and the kids knew for a fact that there weren't enough chairs to go around on the second floor balustrade. Couldn't they just stay put on the ground floor? Or maybe the stage? Surely that was high enough?

There was a noise like a train passing by. A low rumble, getting ever closer, thick with clicks and clanks and cracks.

Outside the door, David saw the cars jostling in the car park, shunted by some unseen force, then suddenly tossed like dice. A surge of black water rushed between the gym entrance and the nearby school building and continued to rise. In fits and starts, it splashed against the glass doors, seeping under the gap at their base.

David took an involuntary step backwards as the puddle reached out to him. Black water was now knee-high against the doors, pushing them inward, creating a new gush of water as they swung open.

Now the flood outside was already waist-high, jammed with trash cans and bicycles, cardboard boxes and tree branches.

David turned to run as a car slammed sideways into the glass door, propelled through them by the force of the torrent, the noise it made drowned out by the sudden screams in the hall. The flood rushed in, turning the rows of seating into a spiked mace of protruding chair-legs, tripping the fleeing townsfolk underfoot.

The stage itself began to lift from the ground, floating unsteadily on the rising waters, turning from a safe refuge into a collection of tipping blocks.

David found himself clinging to the curtains at the side of the stage, hanging desperately onto the arm of a man who was himself clutching at a screaming woman caught in the maelstrom.

The water was cold, cold enough that it was hard to grip.

David met the man's eyes in a desperate moment, and the man's hand slipped; the couple was immediately engulfed in the vortex of black sea. Instead, David reached out, his hand straining to add extra inches, to grab a floating desk occupied by a fellow teacher and four petrified children.

Suddenly he found his grip, hanging onto the desk for just long enough for the marooned pupils to clamber along his arms and onto the balcony.

Wait. The balcony?

The waters were ten feet deep now; he was floating within reach of the upper level. David hauled himself over the ledge and onto the second floor, panting with the effort, his wet clothes stingingly cold, his hands numb.

The noise began to die down, the screams turning to sobs, the rushing waters losing their roar and lapping mockingly at the walls.

David shivered. There would be no school tomorrow.

The earthquake and ensuing tsunami that precipitated the March 11, 2011 Fukushima disaster were a dramatic cap to the long, slow stagnation experienced by Japan in the early twenty-first century. Shrinking populations and persistent economic decline have left the very existence of some communities in Japan in doubt.

Yūbari, in Hokkaidō, was a mining town of 120,000 people in 1960. It has shed 90 percent of its population over the last fifty years, as the mines were shut down and families went elsewhere in search of jobs. In 2007, with a population of only 10,000, the city filed for bankruptcy. In 2016, the last karaoke bar shut down. By 2020, when the median age of the population rises to sixty-five, Yūbari will hit another tipping point: the majority of the population will be aging retirees with rising medical needs and a declining tax contribution.

Although parts of the city are indeed abandoned, others have been successfully rewilded. A demolition scheme in the 1970s and 1980s removed street after street of tenement housing for mine workers; today, the mountainsides are thick with trees again. Mountain deer frequently wander into the streets as the "green archipelago" turns even greener again. The infrastructure remains in place, and the locals try enthusiastic attempts at encouraging visitors, like a fantasy film festival or a local mascot with a melon for a head...but Yūbari is bypassed by the new expressway, and frankly, the most interesting thing to see here is a glimpse of how many other parts of Japan might look by the year 2060. It takes a birth rate of 2.1 to replace a population. Japan's birth rate is currently 1.4—which, warns the National Institute of Population and Social Security Research, means that the population is fated to fall by a third to 87 million by 2060. The net gain established in the times of legend by Izanami and Izanagi is now being reversed.

Japan's rewilding is one of the amazing stories of modern times. We should look behind the statistics and concede that many of today's ghost towns are in Tōhoku, which has yet to recover from the apocalypse of the 2011 earthquake, tsunami, and nuclear disaster. Even in the prosperous south, the dormitory suburbs can be effectively deserted during the day, even if they are occupied at night—I have often been the only person walking the sun-baked streets. In an oddly symbolic gesture in 2016, rewilding of a sort even impinged upon Ginza, the upmarket Tōkyō district that is the most expensive square on a Japanese Monopoly board, when the Sony corporation announced it would be demolishing its landmark headquarters and replacing it with a small city park for the 2020 Olympics.

Japan reached its economic peak at the end of the 1990s, with Japanese names dominating the world's largest banks and the global rich list, but also making conspicuous foreign purchases—not merely expensive works of art like van Gogh's "Sunflowers," but also New York's iconic Rockefeller Center. In 1989, Sony made a stab at securing a vital part of the software for its business by acquiring the US movie maker Columbia Pictures; Matsushita retaliated a year later by buying MCA (Universal). But as the Japanese economist Shimada Haruo warned, Japan's prosperity was based on "investment alchemy using fictitious values"—it ultimately all relied on land prices that, if they had been real, amounted to the real estate of Japan being worth a hundred times as much as the entire United States. This plainly was not true: it was a fiction based on the state capitalism that had been fostered in one form or another for the last century, as Japan's government aided its workforce in catching up with foreign nations. But that aim was now demonstrably achieved, and had taken Japan out of isolation into an exposed position where it was integrated into a truly global economy and subject to the fluctuations in fortune of global finance. Whereas Western companies were often financed by shareholders with an interest in due diligence, Japanese companies were more likely to be financed by banks that could look the other way in the event of irregularity.

When the Bubble burst in 1991, real estate in Tōkyō lost 40 percent of its value in three years. Numerous institutions deemed "too big to fail" were bolstered by friendly loans from sister corporations, creating "zombie companies" that had to be fueled by constant cash injections or supply chains that went for months without payment.

Sheer bad luck subjected Japan to a series of further blows. The Kobe earthquake in 1995 wiped billions from Japan's economy. Only a few months later, the Aum Shinrikyō death cult unleashed a terrorist attack on the Tōkyō subway. In 2001, al-Qaeda's terrorist attack on New York's World Trade Center plunged much of the

Western world into a war in the Middle East, and led Japan's then-prime minister Koizumi Junichirō to urge Japanese tourists to spend their money at home. The September 11th attacks also led to increased pressure on Japan's government to wriggle around the impositions of Article 9 of the Constitution, and to provide physical rather than merely financial aid to a war effort designed to secure vital oil.

The bursting Bubble ushered in a period known at first as the Lost Decade (*ushinawareta jūnen*), subsequently pluralized into the Lost Decades when Japan couldn't seem to catch a break. Banks stumbled and merged, and the population struggled under the introduction of a new consumption tax that pushed up the price of everything and continued to increase the percentage it leeched. Many Bubble-era mortgages on expensive houses, some of which would have taken more than a generation to pay off, now cost more than the house and land they purchased, leading to a spike in defaults and non-payments.

At least part of the Lost Decades' reputation was unfounded, since in real terms, Japan continued to enjoy smaller but still positive growth. The economy stagnated rather than truly slumping, and if any dividend was truly dropping, it was the demographic one, as the postwar generation that had deferred its profits and worked all those overtime hours faced retirement and downsizing. Emperor Hirohito died in 1989, and the postwar generation over which he had presided began retiring in the 1990s, shrinking the labor pool and leading to many difficult decisions about the transfer of ownership at corporations that had previously run on handshakes and personal connections.

The slowing of the Japanese economy refocused attention on its supposedly world-beating workforce. The Japanese education system had, it was previously presumed, somehow contributed, although a cynic might argue that it achieved very little besides grinding any originality of thought out of its participants. Japanese schoolchildren continued to outperform most other nations in staged tests, but the education system arguably valued *only* the tests, stamping out class after class of pupils whose performance was largely assessed based on box-ticking and multiple-choice examinations rather than any creativity. One infamous Japanese literature exam, for example, merely asked pupils to correctly identify the sources of a number of opening lines, thereby making it possible to pass by reading only the first words of Kawabata Yasunari's novel *Snow Country*, which are, somewhat obviously: "The train came out of the tunnel into the snow country."

University might be expected to provide some actual abilities—as indeed they do for some Japanese students—but for many, tertiary education was a vacation from the tortures of the "exam hell" required to get a scholar there in the first place. Meanwhile, personal and *keiretsu* connections between industry and educational establishment led to vertical integration even in recruitment, with certain universities known as prime hiring zones for particular sectors of the economy. Would-be lawyers knew precisely which Tōkyō alma mater would gain them a pre-graduation internship at a prominent law firm; would-be engineers knew just where they had to apply in Chiba; would-be travel agents knew a little college in Kyōto where all the best companies looked first for their new hirings. Although this streamlined the process efficiently for employers, it was a new form of hell for the students themselves, who would often face the prospect of delaying their application for one or two (or more) years in order to ace the right exam for the right college. Such students—chiefly boys because, of course, boys were the ones who could expect actual careers—became known by the term for masterless samurai—*rōnin*.

Even *rōnin* needed to blow off steam, and the combination of arrested development among both young men and women, as well as an understanding of the material limitations of Japanese life (personal space, privacy, time) led to the cultivation of a new demographic. In 2005, the Nomura Research Institute published an investigation into the world of "*otaku* marketing," outlining a new business model for appealing to small but wealthy niches within consumer society. The term *otaku* (nerd) originated in the world of animated cartoons, but was swiftly applied elsewhere, in everything from tourism to cameras, muscle cars to manga. The main sector was young singletons with a disposable income, but Nomura also recognized the existence of older weekend hobbyists with more responsibilities. Either way, such *otaku* consumers could be expected to be willing collaborators in the ransacking of their own wallets for as long as they could be guaranteed customizable products; an event-led, participatory fandom that gave them bespoke, unpiratable, or uncopiable experiences; and a "gamified" consumer experience that rewarded them for acquiring all variants. This was summarized as the "three C's: Collection, Creativity and Community." We see the outward manifestation of *otaku* culture today in anime conventions and gaming swap meets, and in the phenomenal dressing-up boom known as cosplay, as well as in the swappable lenses of Canon or Nikon cameras and vacation bookings that allow for customizable tours. But we also see it reflected in an ongoing diversification and narrowcasting within the Japanese media.

Some Japanese industries continued to weather the storm, particularly in the entertainment sector, where Japanese games remained world leaders. Arcade games in the 1970s, miniaturized and repurposed as home consoles in the 1980s and beyond, turned Sega, Nintendo, and Sony into household names, along with their mascot characters, leading to a newfound appreciation of the market value of *kontentsu* (content). As Japan reoriented from a manufacturing economy to a postmodern service economy, its government recogized the value of popular culture for advertising the country as a tourist destination. In 2005, the same year as Nomura's report, the trade minister Nakagawa Shōichi wrote: "Japan aims to establish intellectual property and the content industry as key factors in economic revitalization. In particular, digital media and proactive international initiatives are likely to cause rapid market expansion, contributing to related industries such as tourism and manufacture." In other words, now that the miracle-era corporations have sold all the hardware to foreign consumers, Japan can continue to profit by excelling at the software: computer games, animated movies, and high-tech toys. Nakagawa was a minister in the government of Asō Tarō, a politician who trumpeted his love of manga to court the youth market, and whose initiatives to push "Cool Japan," including overseas comics competitions and grants for domestic animation companies, have long outlasted his administration.

Not everybody is a cheerleader for Cool Japan. In 2013, the academic Ōyama Shinji, then at London University's Birkbeck College, derided it as a smokescreen of spiky-haired pretty boys and dancing schoolgirls, designed to hide a corporatized and uninspired Japanese entertainment industry. Yokoyama noted that the spokesmodels for Cool Japan were frankly unemployable in the gray-suited companies they represented—foreign *otaku* who saw Japan as a place of punk dreams and high-tech toys were being sold a lie. The artist Murakami Takashi, whose "Super Flat" style has become one of the icons of Cool Japan, was similarly damning, claiming that Cool Japan was merely a buzzword that "was intentionally created to satisfy the pride of the Japanese, and is nothing more than ad copy to allow public funds to go to advertising companies."

Such cynicism is writ large on Japan's youth, who find themselves completing exam hell and an expensive college education without the former guarantees of a salaryman lifestyle. A new archetype in the Japanese media lifted a foreign acronym—NEETs, standing for Not in Education, Employment or Training (interchangeable with the term "freeter," from "freelance" and the German *arbeiter*, meaning part-timer)—to describe those who rejected the core values of the Bubble era, preferring instead to participate in the consumer economy at the barest subsistence level, working only at menial jobs to pay the most minimal bills.

A postindustrial economy still requires industry; it still needs raw materials and energy. Consumers need someone to make the items they consume. Japan's industrial leaders search increasingly further afield in a globalized economy, and their political colleagues obliged in 2013 with a $32 billion aid package to Africa, where Japan and its biggest Asian rival, China, now duke it out over influence and connections.

Japan's new era of enforced austerity has led to a rise in secondhand goods. Thrift shops specializing in rigorously screened high-quality items have flourished. No broken toys or buttonless jackets here; the secondhand shops of Japan rely on the crumbs that fall from the table of the Bubble generation, many of whom seem to have an endless supply of unopened high-end branded goods sitting at the back of their closets—unwanted or forgotten gifts, or unused impulse purchases. I found one handbag in a Kyōto "thrift" store with an asking price of $1500. Even aged or scuffed items have a certain value, as they imply that the owner has had access to expensive goods for longer than they really have. This, it seems, is the underlying rationale of Japan's twenty-first century *boro* (run-down) aesthetic—scruffy is the new neat. Meanwhile, modern Japan's obsession with integration assures that nobody loses out. For example, several of Japan's biggest publishers are investors in Book-Off, a chain selling used books, allowing them—but not their authors—to derive a small sum from secondhand sales of their product.

Ironically, one of the most iconic symbols of Japanese austerity dates from the height of its 1980s growth—a brand that isn't a brand. Muji, or more properly Mujirushi Ryōhin (no-brand quality goods) was launched in 1980 as a spinoff from the chain of Seibu department stores, promising consumers no-nonsense generic goods, cheaper because they had been stripped of all extraneous packaging and marketing—this was hence better value, but also better for the environment. In fact, Muji's recycled brown-paper packaging and laconic labels had a Zen aesthetic all their own, while the company's concentration on bin-ends and leftovers proved so successful that it soon ran out of them. In the case of its bestselling packages of broken mushrooms (why insist on them whole when they will be broken up for cooking anyway?), the company was reduced to buying whole mushrooms and then breaking them up and repackaging them to keep the orders filled. The stores in Japan became, to some extent, victims of their own success, doing so well that it became impossible to sustain the "small-is-beautiful" aesthetic and supplies across an entire chain of stores. Meanwhile, despite the meaning of the name, foreigners came to regard Muji as another brand.

For some, mere austerity was not enough. Some societal dropouts took things even further, with Japanese journalists and psychologists outlining the rise of the *hikikomori* phenomenon—hundreds of thousands of Japanese, primarily from the generation that reached its teens as the Bubble burst, became almost entirely isolated from society, shutting themselves away or disappearing into virtual existences on the internet. Buried within the rhetoric of Cool Japan is the possibility that much of the *otaku*-focused economy rests on the interests and concerns of some 1.5 million young Japanese who are borderline *hikikomori* cases. Others are shut in by more prosaic concerns, forced to care for their aging parents (or, more likely, in-laws). For much of the twentieth century, Japanese law and political rhetoric regarded a family unit, or *ie*, as a three-generational household comprising grandparents, parents, and kids. This was a rural anachronism, disrupted by the Miracle era of growth in which workers left their ancestral homes to flock to the cities; they formed nuclear families more recognizable to modern Westerners, cutting off both a source of ready child-minding and the cheapest form of care for the elderly. Japanese pension provisions and childcare pricing continued to limp far behind the times, assuming the existence of a tri-generational ie rather than the urban reality.

The defining event for Japan in the early twenty-first century was a disaster beginning on March 11, 2011, with an undersea earthquake about 70 kilometers (43.5 miles) off the northern coast. It was the most powerful Japanese earthquake ever recorded, measuring 9.0 on the Moment magnitude scale; it shifted the entire island of Honshū 2 meters (6.5 feet) to the east and jolted 180 kilometers (112 miles) of seabed upward, causing a sudden rise of between 6 and 8 meters (19.5 and 26 feet). It caused severe damage in the

Tōhoku region in northern Japan, for which reason it is often referred to as the Tōhoku Earthquake.

But the earthquake was only the beginning. The seismic shift generated a monstrous flood—a *tsunami* that looked nothing like Hokusai's "Great Wave," the default image of a tidal wave. Instead, it was a surge, a seemingly unstopping onrush of the tide that powered on across sea walls and deep inland, gathering up a dangerous grist of cars, telegraph poles, and broken houses, creating a wet wall of concrete and lumber.

News coverage favors the damage. We know that more than 15,000 people were killed by the combined earthquake and tsunami, mostly by drowning, the bulk of them being old people who were unwilling or unable to outrun the wave. Families were split apart—the tsunami occurred during the school day. The effects were felt as far away as Antarctica, where rough waves broke an ice shelf, and California, where a man trying to photograph the abnormally high tide was washed out to sea. But the news rarely reports things that *didn't* happen. It didn't report the buildings that did not collapse in the earthquake because of heightened safety regulations. The earthquake was powerful enough to liquefy the soil in the car park of Tōkyō Disneyland, and yet the capital was largely undamaged, shielded from the tsunami by the Chiba peninsula and preemptive sea walls, and by decades of rigorous anti-earthquake architecture. The news rarely notes the thousands of people who made it to safety because of a state-of-the-art early warning system. Reporters had other things on their mind, like the Fukushima nuclear reactors.

The tsunami took a number of power stations offline, drastically dropping the capacity of Japan's power grid and depriving millions of homes of electricity. In the weeks that followed, observers got a history lesson in the days of Japan's modernization, when it turned out that power could not be diverted from southern Japan to the north because the two halves of the country operated on different frequencies, having been installed by engineers from rival countries in the 1890s.

Safety measures were in place to take the Fukushima reactors offline in the event of an earthquake, and for diesel-powered backup generators to pump coolant. These, however, were themselves shut down when the tsunami overwhelmed the reactor's 10-meter (33 feet) sea wall. It was, ironically, precisely the situation that had been predicted in a 2007 safety report that had been dismissed by managers as unrealistic. The meltdowns, venting of radioactive steam, discharge of contaminated water, and other measures led to evacuations of the surrounding area and continued questions about the likely long-term effects. One paper estimates that in decades to come, higher incidences of cancer among affected people are liable to increase the eventual death toll from the combined earthquake-tsunami-meltdown by another 10,000. And that is before one considers the likely dangers from policing the damage that has been "contained" behind steel and concrete walls, and from efforts to create artificial permafrost to seal in the groundwater. In 2015, high waves from Typhoon Etau washed away sacks filled with contaminated soil from the site, taking with them tons of contaminated water. Simply by continuing to exist, the Fukushima site has created several Level 3 "serious incidents" in addition to the original Level 7 "major accident" that started it all.

The aftermath of the Tōhoku disaster, arriving after twenty years of stagnation, left Japan in an impossible situation. It certainly crippled the incumbent government, a short-lived showing by the opposition, which was forced to introduce further austerity measures and lost power, once again, to the Liberal Democratic Party. It shut down a proposed initiative to bring jobs to the north by moving certain industries out of the southern plains. It increased consumption taxes even further, and plunged the Japanese into an unwinnable debate about energy sources—should they back oil, which would drag them into global politics, or nuclear power, which would risk decimating another swathe of Japan?

The new prime minister, Kishi Nobusuke's grandson Abe Shinzō, won the 2020 Olympics for Tōkyō, at least giving him some hope of investment and tourism, but his main hopes were pinned upon his "three arrows" of fiscal stimulus, monetary easing, and structural reforms. These buzzwords seem intended more to justify the "three arrows" part—a reference to a samurai parable in which a single arrow might be broken in two, but three grasped together are far stronger. In fact, Abenomics, as it was soon called, was a lifeboat made of patches and bailouts, in which the yen was devalued but Japanese workers continued to pay consumption tax for anything they bought with their dwindling salaries. Meanwhile, Abe's government drifted inexorably to the right, saber-rattling over tiny strategic islands in the South China Sea and infringing on press freedoms.

Japan's trade deficit continued to rise—not least because the shutdown of the nuclear power stations returned the country to its economically dangerous reliance on imported fossil fuels. As with many other aspects of modern Japanese politics, initiatives seemed to ignore the root causes of any problems, and instead made futile attempts to address their outward manifestations.

But the biggest problem Japan currently faces is demographic. As in many other postindustrial countries, the generation born in the 1960s is retiring, creating a "graying population" of pensioners supported by a declining workforce of taxpayers. Japanese policymakers speak hopefully of the infrastructure projects and reforms that were introduced as the Tōkyō Olympics approach in 2020, but also with mounting concern about the "2030 Problem," when the retirement of the following generation will place an even heavier burden on the only children, the underpaid, the unemployed, and the unemployable of the next.

As noted in a business report by the Keidanren business conclave, Japan already relies heavily and invisibly on immigrant or offshore labor. In an ironic reversal of the seventeenth-century *sakoku* edicts that banished from Japan anyone with three foreign grandparents, incentives were offered to any South American with a single Japanese grandparent. Such quarter-Japanese, it was implied, were better than the entirely non-Japanese equivalent. Out of sight, working in overseas subsidiaries, was out of mind; although, as with other modern societies, a manufacturing sector once lost to cheaper overseas labor was impossible to recover. Even in digital media such as Japan's world-famous *anime* business, many aspects are outsourced overseas; desktop publishing and the internet allow colorists, layout artists, and in-betweeners to work in China or South Korea, reducing the value of such labor for Japanese nationals below the level where it is possible to earn a living at it.

Such factors have been physically repeated in other industries, where corporations met the souring of the Japanese miracle by offshoring their manufacture, keeping the corporation lean but jettisoning thousands of Japanese workers. A trend in modern Japan has been the establishment of factory ghettos of foreign labor, recruited as far afield as Vietnam for tours of duty in Japanese sweatshops. Their output counts as domestic product, although their wages and conditions are below that which would be expected by Japanese workers.

With immigration such an unpopular fix, Abe's administration hit on the idea of mining and repurposing Japan's own population, encouraging women to return to the labor force with a new buzzword of *womenomics*. Japanese women currently occupy a meager 3.1 percent of boardroom seats in corporate Japan; compare this with 19.2 percent in the United States. Abe hoped to increase the ratio of Japanese women in the boardroom to 30 percent by the year 2020, a steep ascent that even his own advisers cautioned was unlikely.

But instead of offering palpable, quantifiable incentives to the female workforce, Abe's schemes seem to offer too little, too late. Women were promised "better access" to childcare, although little was done to help them pay for it. They still were not guaranteed pay parity, and a promise of three years' maternity leave was liable to make women seem *less* employable to corporate personnel managers. That merely left a quota stipulation, seemingly intended to browbeat companies into putting more women in the boardroom. It's not clear where Abe expected these new women to come from, and grumbles soon issued from the boardrooms of Japan that it would amount to little more than tokenism. Moreover, it's not all that clear that Japanese women want to be thrust into the management culture of golf and whisky and late-night karaoke that so preoccupied their fathers.

Abe's womenomics scheme ignored many ingrained aspects of Japanese society. One business survey reported a percentage of salarymen who simply announced they could not abide the prospect of obeying a female boss, which is not all that surprising when one considers the example set by the Imperial House. Despite several reigning empresses in Japanese history, the current rules of the succession specify the necessity of a male heir. This led to an ideological scuffle in the early twenty-first century, as lawmakers attempted to reform protocols in order to allow Crown Prince Naruhito's only daughter, Princess Aiko, to be recognized as the next in line to the throne. The issue was not merely one of women's equality; it was of the likelihood that a female child of an emperor would "leave" the Imperial House to marry, but still become empress, thereby effectively starting a new dynasty and breaking a line supposedly unbroken since the time of legends. It also raised the specter of the Occupation, not merely because the 1947 Imperial Household Act that set these rules was the last decree of the old imperial government, but because that same act disinherited entire branches of the nobility. Those branches might be reinstated to bring in male heirs to continue the line, but doing so would undermine part of the Occupation reforms. Another possibility, offered only half in jest by a member of the Imperial Household, was to permit princes to take multiple concubines in order to increase the odds of a male heir.

For a while, it seemed like the law was indeed about to change, until the birth of a boy to Emperor Akihito's younger son in 2006 postponed the debate for another generation. The prospect that all of Japan might be obliged to bow to a "woman boss" was curtailed.

From the outside, womenomics seemed like a smart solution, although it has enjoyed remarkably little support in Japan. That is hardly surprising, since Japan's social-security and taxation systems implicitly support a deeply conservative concept of the division of labor within a nuclear family. One can hardly show up for the annual general meeting if one is also an unpaid nursemaid to one's bedridden mother-in-law.

Despite advances in women's liberation since the 1970s, it seems that many in Japan still secretly favor the notion that women are expected to beautify the office for a while before marrying one of their coworkers and leaving to have babies and/or care for their aging in-laws. Although Japan in 2017 has 38 million women in employment, many of them are still clustered in the lower echelons of the workforce, as disposable work-gangers packing convenience-store salads, or as "semi-skilled" carers.

Womenomics was not a magic wand that could dispel the ingrained attitudes and traditions of the Japanese workforce. Abe himself got a taste of his own medicine when he tried to set the tone by cramming his cabinet with five new female appointees, two of whom soon resigned over unrelated spending scandals.

An aging, shrinking population is a matter of some concern to many modern societies, but in Japan it is magnified by the linguistic and racial isolation of the people. It took the Sumō Wrestling Association decades to recognize the validity of foreign champions, claiming for a while that Samoan, Hawaiian, or Mongolian wrestlers lacked *hinkaku*—an unquantifiable Japanese sense of class or virtue that eluded outsiders. Such arguments, which have formed part of Japanese politics since the nineteenth century, are known as *nihonjinron*—a "thesis of Japanese uniqueness" often cited as an excuse for trade restrictions or immigration blocks. One cannot simply hand out passports to immigrants in order to make new Japanese people—the language is hard to learn; the culture makes it easy to visit but difficult to stay. In its projections for the 2020s, the Keidanren business organization warned Japanese policymakers that immigration was destined to become a vital factor in sustaining the Japanese economy and population. Japan's future hence relies upon a great rethinking of attitudes toward foreigners, toward women, and toward families. Straightforward realities in demographics may prove to be as revolutionary and transformative as the Occupation, the Meiji Restoration, or the coming of the Black Ships. Japan's history is not over, but a new chapter is just about to begin.

Notes on Names

The official genealogy of the emperors of Japan stretches back as far as 660 BCE, all the way to Jinmu, descendant of the Sun Goddess. In order to simplify matters, I have not bothered to give reign periods for those early emperors that even the imperial house regards as legendary and difficult to pin down. The first half-dozen centuries of this list are widely regarded as imaginary, but even the more recent portions are subject to grade inflation. Japanese sovereigns in the Dark Ages probably referred to themselves as some variant of "great king"; they did not first use the term "Son of Heaven" until the seventh century, and even then, their decision to do so shocked and insulted the rulers of China. The official names and numbering of the Japanese emperors are barely a century old, but to simplify matters, I have used the term "emperor" for all Japanese rulers, even before this point. I run the risk of scandalizing anyone from Tang-dynasty China when I do so, but these are the hazards an author must face.

The reader should also be aware that most emperors are referred to not by their given name, but posthumously by their era title. Hirohito, for example, was never known by that name among his respectful subjects—during his reign, he was simply "the emperor"; after his death, he was the Shōwa emperor. Shōwa is hence not his name but his title. Throughout this book, I often use the emperors' reign titles as if they are names. I think you would rather hear about Emperor Keikō than have me repeatedly refer to him by his given name, which was Ōtarashi-hiko-oshirowake no Sumera-mikoto. Similarly, as the Japanese themselves do, I refer to certain figures by their given names: Tokugawa Ieyasu is referred to as Ieyasu in order to distinguish him from all the other Tokugawa clansmen I mention, not to imply that he and I are on friendly terms. A similar policy, dumping surnames in favor of a more recognizable appellation, is usually followed with artists, so Katsushika Hokusai is referred to not as Mr. Katsushika, but by the name with which he signed his paintings, Hokusai.

Japanese nomenclature is incredibly fiddly. It's bad enough in the medieval period, when women's names are rarely recorded at all out of a Confucian sense of decorum, while clansmen are apt to show their connections with confusingly similar personal names: I only need to mention Yoshitsune, son of Yoshitomo, brother of Yoritomo, and eyes start glazing over. In more ancient times there is also the issue of descriptive titles, where we must decide whether to transcribe the name itself, such as Amaterasu; or to translate its actual meaning: Heaven Shines. When dealing with matters of legend, I often do both. Unfortunately, some archaic names are so ridiculously long that the author is left with an impossible task—either to refer to tongue twisters like *Oho nushi no kami* or translate them as oddities like Deity Master of the Great Land. As with all my other books, I have tried to walk a line that allows for the most memorable and impactful uses of names, largely on a need-to-know basis.

If you can read Japanese, the words on a page often appear as multilevel concepts, both as names and as the classical roots that impart meaning. In many cases, the meaning of a name in Japanese is more obvious on the page than the meanings of our own—nobody would seriously refer to me as The-Lord-Gave Merciful, but the ancient languages that clash in the construction of my own name are long hidden from modern English. In Japanese, they are often manifest and apparent. But when you see a Japanese girl called Genitals-Bellows-Panicky-Princess-Lady, you feel obliged to keep it in Japanese—until you realize that then you have to talk about someone called Hoto-tatara-isusuki-hime-no-mikoto. Gustav Heldt, in his translation of the *Kojiki* (*An Account of Ancient Matters*), takes things to deliberate extremes to emphasize the blunt, surprisingly mundane quality of so many seemingly mysterious Japanese names.

Here is his account of the family of Emperor Kinmei (509–71):

> Brave Man Land's Grand Shield dwelt in the mighty halls of Spread Isles…and took to wife one Lady Stone…who dwelt at Cypress Corner. She bore him the mighty prince Many Paddies, then the mighty one Jade Storehouse Grand Jewels Spread, and then the mighty princess of Canopy Stitchers.

I have also deliberately clung to some anachronistic terms in order to simplify matters of geography. I refer to the southwesternmost main island as Kyūshū (nine states) throughout this book, even though it only gained that name when medieval reforms recognized the presence of nine provinces there; and indeed, today it retains the name despite only having seven prefectures. Similarly, the northernmost main island only gained its name of Hokkaidō (north-sea way) when it was incorporated within the Japanese empire in the nineteenth century, seemingly to head off the approach of land-grabbing Russian explorers and traders. Previously, it had been known variously as Watarishima or Ezo. At many points in the text I have used similar shorthand, to save me having to tell you things like this again instead of getting on with more pressing matters, like the brief history of Japan.

Further Reading

The opening vignettes in each chapter are sourced from or inspired by particular books in the bibliography, beginning with the introduction, which relies upon Delgado's account of the Mongol armada. Chapter one refers to Pearson's book on ancient Ryūkyū Island archaeology; chapter two, Heldt's translation of the *Kojiki* and Aston's of the *Nihongi*; chapter three, Wang's accounts of Chinese court ceremonies chapter four; McCullough's translation of *The Tale of the Heike*; chapter five, Whitehouse and Yanagisawa's translation of Lady Nijō's diary; chapter six, Keene's translation of Chikamatsu's *Love Suicides at Sonezaki*; chapter seven, Feifer's account of the arrival of the Black Ships; chapter eight, Keene's biography of Emperor Meiji; chapter nine, Siemes's diary of the bombing of Hiroshima; chapter ten, the biographies of Mishima Yukio by Nathan and Inose. The opening of chapter eleven draws on Birmingham and McNeill's *Strong in the Rain*, particularly the experience of David Chumreonlert, a Texan of Thai descent who was working as an English exchange teacher at Nobiru Elementary School on March 11, 2011.

As per the other books in this Tuttle series, this work is intended for the general reader, and omits detailed specialist discussions or foreign-language citations. I am, however, permitted a small amount of space to push the sources from the complete bibliography that may prove most useful to the reader who wishes to investigate further. For a glimpse of the best achievements by modern scholars, the reader is advised to start with Karl Friday's collection *Japan Emerging: Premodern History to 1850.* The late Mikiso Hane's *Premodern Japan* has recently been updated in a new edition with materials from Louis Perez. Reflecting modern trends, I have deliberately brought ecological issues to the fore, particularly with regard to the deforestation and reforestation of Japan, for which I draw on Conrad Totman's *The Green Archipelago*.

My chapters on early Japan draw on recent research and discoveries summarized in Junko Habu's *Ancient Jōmon of Japan*. J. Edward Kidder's *Himiko and Japan's Elusive Chiefdom of Yamatai* goes into far greater depth than I can here, not only on matters of archaeology, but also of historiography—the story of writings on Yamatai, including the decades-long argument about where it might have been. Joan Piggott's *The Emergence of Japanese Kingship* takes the story out of the mists of Himiko and into more verifiable rulers.

Richard Pearson's *Ancient Ryukyu* offers unprecedented detail on the remote island chain, where the earliest "Japanese" archaeological remains are to be found. Massimo Soumaré's *Japan in Five Ancient Chinese Chronicles* includes bilingual texts and extensive explanatory notes.

As reflected in my choice of chapter title for the Middle Ages, there's little to top Ivan Morris's account of court life in ancient Japan, *The World of the Shining Prince*, although modern readers have multiple versions of *The Tale of Genji* to choose from.

The battles of the samurai era have received perhaps the most coverage by armchair historians; the best place to start is William Wayne Farris's *Heavenly Warriors*. Charles Boxer's classic *The Christian Century in Japan* focuses on the meteoric rise and apocalyptic fall of the missionaries between the sixteenth and seventeenth centuries.

For the often comical shenanigans behind the scenes on Perry's Black Ships, including breakdowns, crashes, and wily Japanese small print in the treaties, Robert Erwin Johnson's *Far China Station* offers plenty of gossip on the US Navy in Japanese waters. Bennett's *Japan and the London Illustrated News* reprints decades of articles from that journal, and is an absorbing chronology not only of events, but of what was regarded as newsworthy by journalists of the day.

Peter Duus's *The Abacus and the Sword* and Louise Young's *Japan's Total Empire* are the best gateway into Japan's amazing, short-lived continental experiments in Korea and Manchuria. The works of Brett Walker, particularly *The Conquest of Ainu Lands*, does the same for the Japanese march into Hokkaidō.

For Japan in truly modern times—less history than reportage—there is a surfeit of material by modern authors to choose from. Among the dozens of foreigners who have written about their travels in the archipelago, Alex Kerr and Alan Booth are the two who seem to have derived the most from the experience, although this occasionally runs to umbrage and dismay. For an understanding of the bigger picture, Taggart Murphy's *Japan and the Shackles of the Past* is a good place to start.

Bibliography

The editorial policy of the Tuttle *Brief History* series avoids references and citations, although I have been unable to resist naming particular books and authors in my text where I think it necessary—the eerily prophetic "Song of the Black Ships," for example, is mentioned in dozens of books about Commodore Perry, but hardly any of them bother to cite its origins in Nitobe's *The Intercourse Between the United States of North America and Japan.*

This bibliography is also necessarily brief, but includes every book I have actually quoted from or leaned on to any great degree in my main text.

Adolphson, Mikael. *The Teeth and Claws of the Buddha: Monastic Warriors and Sohei in Japanese History*. Honolulu: University of Hawaii Press, 2007.

Alcock, John Rutherford. *The Capital of the Tycoon: A Narrative of a Three Years' Residence in Japan*. Two volumes. New York: Harper & Brothers, 1863.

Aston, William George (trans). *Nihongi: Chronicles of Japan from the Earliest Times to A.D. 697*. Rutland, VT: Tuttle, 1972.

Batten, Bruce. *Climate Change in Japanese History and Prehistory: A Comparative Overview*. Cambridge, MA: Harvard University, Edwin O. Reischauer Institute Occasional Papers in Japanese Studies, 2009.

Bennett, Terry. *Japan and the Illustrated London News—Complete Record of Reported Events 1853–1899*. Folkestone: Global Oriental, 2006.

Best, Jonathan. *A History of the Early Korean Kingdom of Paekche together with an Annotated Translation of the Paekche Annals of the Samguk Sagi*. Cambridge, MA; Harvard University Press, 2006.

Birmingham, Lucy and David McNeill. *Strong in the Rain: Surviving Japan's Earthquake, Tsunami, and Fukushima Nuclear Disaster*. New York: St Martin's Press, 2012.

Booth, Alan. *The Roads to Sata: A 2,000-Mile Walk Through Japan*. New York: Kōdansha America, 1997.

Boxer, Charles. *The Christian Century in Japan 1549–1650*. Manchester: Carcanet, 1951.

Brienza, Casey. *Manga in America: Transnational Book Publishing and the Domestication of Japanese Comics*. London: Bloomsbury Academic, 2015.

Chen Cheng et al. (trans.) *The Classic of Mountains and Seas*. Changsha: Hunan People's Publishing House, 2010.

Conlan, Thomas. *In Little Need of Divine Intervention: Takesaki Suenaga's Scrolls of the Mongol Invasion of Japan*. Ithaca: East Asia Program, Cornell University, 2001.

Cooper, Michael (ed.). *They Came to Japan: An Anthology of European Reports on Japan, 1543–1640*. Ann Arbor: University of Michigan, 1965.

Deal, William. *Handbook to Life in Medieval and Early Modern Japan*. New York: Oxford University Press, 2006.

Delgado, James. *Khubilai Khan's Lost Fleet: History's Greatest Naval Disaster*. London: Bodley Head, 2009.

Duus, Peter. *The Abacus and the Sword: The Japanese Penetration into Korea 1895–1910*. Berkeley: University of California Press, 1998.

Farris, William Wayne. *Heavenly Warriors: The Evolution of Japan's Military 500–1300*. Cambridge, MA: Harvard University Press, 1992.

Feifer, George. *Breaking Open Japan: Commodore Perry, Lord Abe, and American Imperialism in 1853*. New York: Smithsonian Books, 2006.

Friday, Karl. *Japan Emerging: Premodern History to 1850*. Boulder: Westview Press, 2012.

Habu Junko. *Ancient Jomon of Japan*. Cambridge: Cambridge University Press, 2014.

Heldt, Gustav (trans). *The Kojiki: An Account of Ancient Matters*. New York: Columbia University Press, 2014.

Hendy, Richard. "Yubari, Japan: a city learns how to die," *The Guardian*, August 15, 2014. http://www.theguardian.com/cities/2014/aug/15/yubari-japan-city-learns-die-lost-population-detroit

Hesselink, Reinier. *The Dream of Christian Nagasaki: World Trade and the Clash of Cultures, 1560–1640*. Jefferson, NC: McFarland & Co., 2016.

Inose Naoki with Hiroaki Sato. *Persona: A Biography of Yukio Mishima*. Berkeley: Stone Bridge Press, 2012.

Johnson, Robert Erwin. *Far China Station: The U.S. Navy in Asian Waters 1800–1898*. Annapolis: Naval Institute Press, 1979.

Keene, Donald. *Major Plays of Chikamatsu*. New York: Columbia University Press, 1961.

_____. *Emperor of Japan: Meiji and His World 1852–1912*. New York: Columbia University Press, 2002.

Kerr, Alex. *Dogs & Demons: The Fall of Modern Japan*. Harmondsworth: Penguin, 2002.

Kidder, J. Edward. *Himiko and Japan's Elusive Chiefdom of Yamatai: Archaeology, History and Mythology*. Honolulu: University of Hawaii Press, 2007.

Landor, Arnold Henry Savage. Alone *with the Hairy Ainu: Or 3,800 Miles on a Pack Saddle in Yezo and a Cruise to the Kurile Islands*. London: John Murray, 1893.

Leggett, Trevor. *Shōgi: Japan's Game of Strategy*. Rutland, VT: Tuttle, 1966.

Leiter, Samuel. *New Kabuki Encyclopedia: A Revised Adaptation of Kabuki Jiten*. Westport: Greenwood Press, 1997.

Maki, John. *A Yankee in Hokkaidō: The Life of William Smith Clark*. Lanham: Lexington Books, 2002.

McNicol, Tony. "Japanese Royal Tomb Opened to Scholars for the First Time," *National Geographic*, April 28, 2008. http://news.na-

tionalgeographic.com/news/2008/04/080428-ancient-tomb.html
Minohara, Tosh et al. (eds) *The Decade of the Great War: Japan and the Wider World in the 1910s*. Leiden: Brill, 2014.
Morris, Ivan. *The World of the Shining Prince: Court Life in Ancient Japan*. Harmondsworth: Peregrine, 1979.
Morton, W. Scott and J. Kenneth Olenik. *Japan: Its History and Culture*. Fourth Edition. New York: McGraw-Hill, 2005.
Murphy, R. Taggart. *Japan and the Shackles of the Past*. New York: Oxford University Press, 2015.
Nathan, John. *Mishima: A Biography*. Rutland, VT: Tuttle, 1974.
Nichiren. *Writings of Nichiren Shōnin*. Translated by Kyōtsu Hori. Honolulu: Nichiren Shū Overseas Propagation Promotion Association, 2002.
Nitobe Inazō. *The Intercourse Between the United States of North America and Japan—An Historical Sketch*. Baltimore: Johns Hopkins Press, 1891.
Oka Yoshitake. *Prince Konoe Fumimaro: A Political Biography*. Lanham: Madison Books, 1992.
Ooms, Herman. *Imperial Politics and Symbolics in Ancient Japan—The Tenmu Dynasty 650–800*. Honolulu: University of Hawaii Press, 2009.
Pearson, Richard. *Ancient Ryūkyū: An Archaeological Study of Island Communities*. Honolulu: University of Hawaii Press, 2013.
[People's Court Daily]. *Trials of Justice: Commemoration of the 70th Anniversary of the Victory of the Chinese People's War of Resistance Against Japanese Aggression*. Beijing: People's Court Press, 2016.
Piggott, Joan. *The Emergence of Japanese Kingship*. Stanford: Stanford University Press, 1997.
Polo, Marco. *The Travels*. Trans. by Ronald Latham. London: Penguin, 1958.
Rafferty, Kevin. "Why Abe's womenomics program isn't working," *Japan Times*, December 31, 2015. http://www.japantimes.co.jp/opinion/2015/12/31/commentary/japan-commentary/abes-womenomics-program-isnt-working/#.VwY_8UfD8bx

Ruoff, Kenneth J. *Imperial Japan at Its Zenith: The Wartime Celebration of the Empire's 2,600th Anniversary*. Ithaca: Cornell University Press, 2010.

Samuels, Richard J. "Kishi and Corruption: An Anatomy of the 1955 system." Japan Policy Research Institute Working Paper No. 83, December 2001.

Satow, Ernest. *A Diplomat in Japan*. Berkeley: Stone Bridge Press, 2006.

St. John, Henry Craven. *Notes and Sketches from the Wild Coasts of Nipon* [sic]. Edinburgh: David Douglas, 1880.

Schuessler, Axel. *ABC Etymological Dictionary of Old Chinese*. Honolulu: University of Hawaii Press, 2007.

Shigematsu Setsu. *Scream from the Shadows: The Women's Liberation Movement in Japan*. Minneapolis: University of Minnesota Press, 2012.

Siemes, John. "The Atomic Bombings of Hiroshima and Nagasaki, Chapter 25: Eyewitness Account," at http://avalon.law.yale.edu/20th_century/mp25.asp.

Smart, Richard. "Tōkyō's 50-Year Itch: Why is Sony Knocking Down its Flagship Building?" *The Guardian*, June 28, 2016. https://www.theguardian.com/cities/2016/jun/28/Tōkyō-sony-flagship-building-olympics-park

So Kwan-wai. *Japanese Piracy in Ming China During the 16th Century*. East Lansing: Michigan State University Press, 1975.

Solt, George. *The Untold History of Ramen: How Political Crisis in Japan Spawned a Global Food Culture*. Berkeley: University of California Press, 2014.

Soumaré, Massimo. *Japan in Five Ancient Chinese Chronicles: Wo, the Land of Yamatai, and Queen Himiko*. Fukuoka: Kurodahan Press, 2009.

Tagore, Rabindranath. *The Spirit of Japan: A Lecture*. Tōkyō: Indo-Japanese Association, 1916.

Tames, Richard. *A Traveller's History of Japan*. Fourth Edition. Moreton in Marsh: Chastleton Travel, 2008.

Teeuwen, Mark and Kate Wildman Nakai (eds) *Lust, Commerce, and Corruption: An Account of What I Have Seen and Heard, by an Edo Samurai*. New York: Columbia University Press, 2014.

Totman, Conrad. *The Green Archipelago: Forestry in Preindustrial Japan*. Berkeley: University of California Press, 1989.

Tsang, Carol Richmond. *War and Faith: Ikkō Ikki in Late Muromachi Japan*. Cambridge, MA: Harvard University Press, 2007.

Vlastos, Stephen. *Mirror of Modernity: Invented Traditions of Modern Japan*. Berkeley: University of California Press, 1998.

Walker, Brett. *The Conquest of Ainu Lands: Ecology and Culture in Japanese Expansion, 1590–1800*. Berkeley: University of California Press, 2006.

Wang Zhenping. *Ambassadors from the Isles of the Immortals: China-Japan Relations in the Han-Tang Period*. Honolulu: University of Hawaii, 2005.

Whitehouse, Wilfrid and Yanagisawa Eizo. *Lady Nijo's Own Story: The Candid Diary of a Thirteenth-Century Japanese Imperial Concubine*. Rutland, VT: Tuttle, 1974.

Young, Louise. *Japan's Total Empire: Manchuria and the Cult of Wartime Imperialism*. Berkeley: University of California Press, 1999.

Index